Texas and the Texans
by Henry Stuart Foote

Address:
HardPress
8345 NW 66TH ST #2561
MIAMI FL 33166-2626
USA
Email: info@hardpress.net

George Bancroft's.

1841.

(Foote
ITR

Stephen.

TEXAS

AND *Geo. Bancroft's*

THE TEXANS;

OR, *from the author.*

ADVANCE OF THE ANGLO-AMERICANS

TO THE SOUTH-WEST;

INCLUDING A HISTORY OF

LEADING EVENTS IN MEXICO, FROM THE CONQUEST BY
FERNANDO CORTES TO THE TERMINATION
OF THE TEXAN REVOLUTION.

"MAGNA EST VERITAS, ET PREVALEBIT."

Heaven is free
From clouds, but of *all colours* seems to be
Melted to one vast Iris of the *West*,
Where the *Day* joins the great *Eternity;*
While, on the other hand, meek Dian's crest
Floats through the azure air, a region of the blest!
A single star is *at her side*, and reigns
With her o'er half the lovely heaven.

BY HENRY STUART FOOTE.

IN TWO VOLUMES:
VOL. I.

PHILADELPHIA:
THOMAS, COWPERTHWAIT & CO.

....

1841.

J. FAGAN, STEREOTYPER.

T. K. AND P. G. COLLINS, PRINTERS.

(2)

ADVERTISEMENT.

To the Reader of these unworthy volumes, the Author feels himself bound to address a word or two, by way of apology, for the many imperfections which the eye of criticism will not fail to detect. I am at least no intruder upon the attention of the literary world. Eighteen months since, I chanced to visit the Republic of Texas, upon a jaunt of recreation and curiosity; and was invited, whilst there, to undertake a History of the War of Texan Independence, by more than twenty of the most conspicuous actors in that war. The communication which I received on the occasion, together with my reply, has been long before the public, in leading newspapers on either side of the Sabine. However unfit I may have considered myself for the task proposed, I did not feel at liberty to decline it: and now it is for others to determine whether I deserve censure or approbation for the manner in which that task has been executed.

Perhaps I might justly lay claim to some slight allowance on the ground of having, as many know, been almost constantly occupied in professional labours during the preparation of this work for the press.

Those who choose to attribute a portion of the deficiencies discernible in " Texas and the Texans," to the necessary enlistment of the Author in the fierce political strife of the past summer, and his having had repeatedly to encounter such sturdy opponents as S. S. Prentiss, Baylie Peyton, and George S. Yerger, Esquires, besides an uncountable host of small-fry agitators, may be certain of doing nothing more than strict justice in the premises.

A third volume of " Texas and the Texans" will be issued some time during the coming autumn, in which the history of the country will be continued up to the present period ; accompanied with a large mass of valuable statistical information, now in a course of accumulation. To these will be added a correct Map of Texas, compiled from the latest official surveys.

H. STUART FOOTE.

Raymond, Miss., January 5, 1841.

CONTENTS.

CHAPTER I.

Page

Introductory remarks. Condition of Europe, and of Spain in particular, at the period of the Mexican conquest 13

CHAPTER II.

View of the Mexican Empire at the period of its invasion by the Spaniards, with some observations upon the moral condition of the Mexicans as a people 28

CHAPTER III.

View of the Conquest of Mexico by Fernando Cortes, with some notice of the leading historic facts connected therewith 50

CHAPTER IV.

Comparative view of various instances of National Conquest; with special observations on the General Moral Effect of the Conquest of Mexico upon the Aboriginal or Native population . 71

CHAPTER V.

Examination of the Spanish Colonial Policy, and its effects, in a moral point of view, upon the general colonial population. Rapid citation of leading historical particulars connected with the Revolution in Mexico, resulting in the establishment of the Federal Constitution of 1824 82

1 *   5

CHAPTER VI.

Page

View of the Reformation in England, from its original introduction to the Revolution in 1688. Its influence upon the character and history of the British colonists in America, both before the year last-named and after. Causes which concurred to give ascendancy to the principles of the Reformation in that part of North America settled from Great Britain, and which must yet give them a still wider diffusion 103

CHAPTER VII.

View of the relations between Spain and the United States at the close of the American Revolution. Unfriendly feeling between the two countries. Progress of that unfriendly feeling, with some explanation of the causes of the same. The Miranda expedition. Burr's project; *What was it?* 122

CHAPTER VIII.

View of Aaron Burr's project for opening all Spanish America to the Anglo-Americans and their institutions; with some remarks upon his conduct and character, not elsewhere to be found 149

CHAPTER IX.

Return of Colonel Burr to the United States in 1812. Expedition of Magee into Texas during that year. Magee takes Nacogdoches and Goliad. His small force is besieged in Goliad for a whole winter. They turn out in the spring and defeat General Salcedo. Death of Magee. Capture of the town of San Antonio by the Patriot forces. Dreadful massacre there. Defeat of Toledo. Kemper, Ross, Perry, and other valiant Anglo-Americans introduced to the reader. La Fitte, the Pirate of the Gulf 181

CHAPTER X.

Long's early history. Appointed by the citizens of Natchez to head an expedition into Texas. Arrives at Nacogdoches and takes possession of the place. Establishes civil government. Declares the country an Independent Republic. Offers Head-

Page

rights and Bounty lands. Disposition of his military forces. Journey of Mrs. Long to Nacogdoches. Long leaves for Galveston Island. Advance of the enemy. Flight of the people from the country. Long and his lady at Natchitoches. She goes to Alexandria. He returns to Texas. Meets his followers at Bolivar Point. Learns the disasters of his expedition. Leaves for New Orleans. Returns to Texas. Captures Goliad. Is assassinated in Mexico 197

CHAPTER XI.

HISTORY OF THE FREDONIAN WAR.

Major Benjamin W. Edwards. Grant of lands by the Mexican government to Moses Austin : his death : confirmation of the grant to his son, Gen. Stephen F. Austin, who established his Colony on the Brassos and Colorado rivers in Texas. Progress of Austin's Colony. Grant of lands about Nacogdoches to Haden Edwards. Texas visited by Major Benjamin W. Edwards in 1825. His interview with General Austin at San Felipe de Austin. He calls on his brother at Nacogdoches; finds him involved in serious difficulties. Proceedings of various kinds, resulting in the adoption of preliminary arrangements for the prosecution of a War against the Mexican Government; of which arrangements a more particular account is reserved for a succeeding chapter 218

CHAPTER XII.

Attempt of Fields the Cherokee Chief to obtain a grant of lands from the Mexican government. Dishonest conduct of that government towards him. Some account of John Dunn Hunter. League offensive and defensive formed between the Fredonians and twenty-three Indian tribes. Fredonian Declaration of Independence. Various exertions to maintain the war about to be commenced against the Mexican government. Fredonians seize upon Nacogdoches ; defeat an attack made upon them by Norris the Alcalde. Circular addressed to the settlers in Austin's Colony, to the neighbourhood of Pecon Point, and to the citizens of the United States. Conduct of Col. Austin at this period : motives for it. The Fredonians threatened with an immediate attack by the Mexican government, which is postponed by causes not known... 239

viiii

iiiii

CONTENTS.

CHAPTER XIII.

Page

Major Edwards declared Commander-in-Chief of the Fredonians. Pursuit of Norris, the Alcalde. Approach of the Mexican army. Alarm and confusion of the Colonists. Death of Hunter. Abandonment of Nacogdoches by the Fredonians, and termination of the war. Correspondence between Major Edwards and the Mexican commander. Character of Major Edwards .. 276

CHAPTER XIV.

Prosperous condition of Austin's Colony after the suppression of the Fredonian insurrection. Conduct of Colonel Austin as Empressario. His difficulties and trials. Letter to Major Edwards. View of Mexico in 1824, and for some years afterwards. Political conflicts there: Presidency of Victoria; that of Guerero; downfall of Guerero and elevation of Bustamente; prostration of Bustamente in consequence of his attempt to crush the State authorities and to establish a consolidated system of government. Elevation of Santa Anna, who proves unfaithful to his declared principles: his conflict with, and triumph over Congress and most of the State governments. Massacre of Zacatecas 292

TEXAS AND THE TEXANS.

CHAPTER I.

Introductory remarks. Condition of Europe, and of Spain in particular, at the period of the Mexican conquest.

THE attention of the civilized world has been attracted in an extraordinary manner, for several years past, to the contest which was understood to be in progress between *Texas* and *Mexico*. It is quite manifest that this contest has awakened a livelier and more diffused sympathy, and has called into exercise a greater and more earnest curiosity in regard to its probable result, than would seem, at first view, to be warranted either by the magnitude of the interests involved in it, or the amount of physical energy which it was likely to bring into action. It is only by taking a more deliberate and scrutinizing survey of this imposing struggle of arms, that we are able clearly to descry the grand *moral* bearings which appertain to it; from which alone it has derived that peculiar dignity which enrobes it, and that remarkable capability it has displayed of enkindling a deep, and fervid, and sustained interest, in the bosoms of enlightened men everywhere, however distant from the actual scene of commotion. It is certainly not the successful battles which have been fought in Texas for National Independence;—it is not the effusion of heroic blood which, streaming along her virgin plains, has endued them with a deathless immortality;—it is not the tide of indiscriminate havoc which lately breaking over her confines,

like a volcanic flood, was seen to mark its dreadful course
with the dispeoplement of her infant towns and villages,
and the spoliation of her fair plantations and pasture-
grounds ; it is not *these*, separately or collectively—nor yet
the barbaric gold so profusely lavished by the hands of a
murderous and unprincipled despot, in maintaining the
grisly ranks of his mercenary armies ;—but it is that
sublime collision of moral influences, for the first time,
now met in dread encounter, which has gathered, as it were,
the generous-minded of all nations, around the outspread
arena of conflict, as anxious spectators of the solemn exhibition going on within it, and which has, to some extent,
bound up the fate of countless generations yet unborn, of
all people, and tongues, and countries, in the grand *catastrophe*.   It is with these views, that an attempt is made in
the present work, to go somewhat beyond the accustomed
limits of historic narrative ; and, not content with delineat-
ing the current of *physical* events along its whole *visible*
course, to ascend that current likewise, and trace it out, as
far as practicable, up even to those remote fountains now
overshadowed by the umbrage of ages, in which its primeval flowings originated.

The Discovery of America, by Christopher Columbus,
marks the year 1492 as one of the most striking eras in
the history of the world which has yet arisen.   It has been
already productive of consequences betokening a modification almost *radical* in the moral condition of mankind ; and
the causes, under the influence of which this modification began its progress, have not yet lost any portion of their potency, but are continually operating with a steadily accele-
rated force, promising, in coming time, to eventuate in a
thorough revolution in *society* and *manners*.   Circumstances,
chiefly of an accidental character, having little, if any connexion with intrinsic *merit* of any kind, placed within reach

of the Spanish Government and people a disproportionate share of those advantages, whether solid and permanent, or superficial and transitory, which seemed likely to emerge from the successful enterprise of the illustrious Genoese Navigator. Whether these advantages were judiciously husbanded, and generously diffused, and by being subjected to the principles of an enlightened and liberal policy, were made promotive of the true happiness and abiding honour of the Spanish people, as well as nobly auxiliary to the general improvement of the world, is, unfortunately, a question no longer subject to dispute.

It is proper here, briefly to look into *the condition of Europe* at the period of this momentous discovery of a new continent in the Western hemisphere,—with a view of ascertaining, as far as may be practicable, *how* it has happened, that in one portion of the vast territory opened by the genius of Columbus to the enterprise of civilized colonists of the Old World, a secure abode has been provided for *Science* and the *Arts*, where, beneath the majestic banner of civil and religious freedom, the mind of man, disburdened of the shackles of prejudice, and redeemed from the paralyzing sway of bigotry, dares to assert its own *absolute independence*, acknowledging no authority save that of cultivated *reason*, and yielding no obedience save to the lessons of *truth ;* whilst, in another portion of the same continent, more ample in extent of territorial surface, and greatly more favoured by the bounty of Providence, the dignity of man, as a moral agent, has been utterly prostrated, and the true ends of human exertion almost wholly disregarded ; whilst *ignorance* and *vice,* and anarchical despotism have been permitted to wield the sceptre of a vile and debasing dominion over the most sacred rights and most precious privileges of humanity. The causes which have co-operated in the development of this remarkable *contrast* are a little difficult of descrial, by reason of their remote location both in point of time and physical space ; and the intrinsic complexity of the subject has been not a little enhanced by the mystifying sophistry of several writers of note, who have chanced to be *directly interested* in the dissemination of *error.*

When the huge and cumbrous fabric of Roman greatness had been effectually overthrown by the co-operating energies of a host of enemies, who, without concert or conspiracy of any kind, had ruthlessly embattled for its destruction,——when

> " The Goth, the Christian, time, war, flood, and fire,
> Had dealt upon the seven-hilled city's pride ;"——

when the time-honoured mistress of the world——the imperial Commandress of nations, had been fated,

> " To see her glories star by star expire,
> And up the steep barbarian monarchs ride,
> Where her car climbed the Capitol,"

and *She* stood forth, clad in the habiliments of mourning and desolation, as " the Niobe of nations,——a ruined urn within her withered hands, speechless and crownless in her voiceless woe," it cannot be denied, that then the most gloomy and portentous season was seen to open upon the *moral hopes* of man, of which authentic history has preserved the memorial. It was not the subversion of that colossal dominion which Rome had wielded in the days of her meridian glory ; nor the simple cessation of an *ill-balanced* system of civil government into which the most incongruous and antagonizing elements had found entrance, and maintained unceasing discord ; it was not the limitation and ultimate destruction of an authority once held to be of boundless extent and of irresistible majesty, nor the apportionment of her wide-spread territories amongst the numerous rival potentates whose rude thrones were established upon her melancholy ruins; it was not all these, nor indeed any of these, which have furnished occasion for the permanent regret of succeeding generations, or of which mankind in the present age have substantial reason to complain. But it was the obscuration of that high *moral grandeur* which appertained to Rome as the genial mother and bounteous conservatress of *Science and the Arts,* which in her fall suffered an eclipse that it is to be feared will not even yet pass away for centuries; it was the subsequent erection of *artificial barriers* to the resuscitation of intellectual light, which yet possess in a large portion of the civilized world a solidity and baleful vigour absolutely appalling to the eye of philosophy; it was the establishment of a system of worse than barbarous ethics, under the influence of which, *Knowledge* should be recognized as *crime,* the mind of man should not dare to seek, or audibly to hope, its own enlargement, and his soul be doomed to an emasculation which should rob it of all its divinest energies:—it was *these,* and *it is still these,* which seem almost to justify the apprehension that Earth will ne'er again behold

" That brightness in her eye
She saw when Rome was free."

That the *Christian Priesthood* held in their custody all the learning which survived the flood of barbaric violence, is a fact so universally acknowledged as to render all discussion of the point unnecessary in this place. How it happened that Learning thus survived, and what *manner* of existence was allowed to it by its sacred custodiants, may reward a moment's examination. A French author,* of high rank in the literary world, has recently explored this subject with an ability seldom equalled, and I gratefully avail myself of the lights furnished by him, in elucidation

* Guizot.

2 *

of the topic under review.   At the close of the fourth century and beginning of the fifth, Christianity was not, as in
the days of the Apostles, a *simple belief :* its teachers were
no longer possessed of a power exclusively *spiritual :*
Christianity had become an institution, whose frame-work
was of most solid construction, and bore, in every part of
it, tokens of contrivance and skill.   It gradually formed
itself into a solid body : it had its *government*—a body of
priests ; a settled ecclesiastical polity for the regulation of
their different functions ; revenues ; *independent means of
influence.*   It had the rallying points suited to a great society, in the provincial, national, and general councils, in
which were wont to be discussed, in common, the affairs
of the society.   In a word, the Christian religion, at this
epoch, was no longer a religion ; it was a *church*, and as
such, was able to fortify itself against exterior violence.
Nor was this all : for it is evident that the ecclesiastics of
the Christian Church, by means of the *corporate* authority
with which they stood invested, had it in their power, likewise, to afford a shield to that portion of the learning of
the ancients which happened to be in possession of its
functionaries.   Whatever hostility may have been cherished for classic erudition, among the earlier ecclesiastics, on
account of its Pagan origin, and its inseparable connexion
with a religious system, which they felt it to be a sacred
duty to abhor ; yet fatuity itself could be hardly expected
to prove entirely insensible to the obvious *temporal* advantages resulting from its possession, at a time when negotiations affecting the most vital interests of the church, as a
society, were necessary to be continually carried on, with
unlettered chieftains, to whose usurping violence all physical obstacles had proved ineffectual, and from whom no
favour could be gained except by superior subtlety and
address.

It is quite remarkable, that the early policy of the Christian *establishment* was, in one material respect, entirely opposed to that which it has in general striven to enforce. It was indispensable to its own safety, amidst a multitude of armed barbarians altogether hostile to its interests, that the line of *separation* between *Church* and *State*, between *spiritual* and *temporal* dominion, should be distinctly drawn, and sacredly observed ; at least until the *pious arts of conciliation* so well known to Ecclesiastics of all ages, should be effectually tried, and the diffusive leaven of Christianity should be poured into the hearts of the new rulers. Accordingly, we find the Christian Ecclesiastics of those days to have been strenuous champions of an exclusive and independent spiritual dominion. But when the Church found herself no longer in danger—when barbarian monarchs, either persuaded by reasons of state, or influenced by genuine conviction, had become thoroughly enlisted in her cause, and the wielders of Ecclesiastical power had become ambitious of a more extended *temporal* sway, we find the utmost zeal and ingenuity put in exercise, in order to bring about a thorough *consolidation of Church and State :* thus rearing up a fabric of authority, which, though deriving its elements in part from earth, yet cemented by influences deduced from heaven itself, would be able to bid absolute defiance to all power that could not lay claim to an origin equally exalted.

The dominion of the Church, it is true, was a *moral* dominion, and yet was it most evident that this moral dominion might secure to itself great additional efficiency by the rigorous and skilful employment of *physical* means. *The Church, therefore, leagued itself with temporal rulers, in order to establish* its own supremacy over the human mind.

This *Union of Church and State* which has been noticed, continued to exist in Europe for several centuries ; nor can it be doubted, that whilst the Church lost much dignity by the association, and suffered serious moral depravation, yet that its *refining* influence was sensibly felt in the administration of civil affairs.   I regret to acknowledge, though, that the Church, during this whole period, did nothing to bring about a revival of the Arts and Sciences ; its policy, indeed, was directly the reverse, and extraordinary assiduity was used by the Christian priesthood everywhere to secure to the members of their own order the perpetual enjoyment of that disgraceful *monopoly of learning* which then existed.   Not only were no facilities supplied by the Church, as such, for the general diffusion of knowledge ; but all the management of a subtle priesthood was put in requisition for the purpose of devising new obstructions to a convenient and profitable interchange of thought amongst the laity, and renewed exertion was constantly made with a view to immersing the whole popular mass in a brutish ignorance, which should entirely disqualify them for the task of detecting the arts of knavish imposition by which they were held in subjection.

Ecclesiastical power had reached its meridian height in Europe about the period when the famous Crusades to the Holy land were undertaken.   At this time the intellectual gloom, which had been long engendering, seems to have deepened into the darkness of midnight.   One of the first beneficial effects which arose from the Crusades, was the generation of something like a diffusive *public sentiment* throughout Europe.   All Europe was now, for the first time, united in a common cause ; all classes of the population, in all countries where Christianity bore sway, evinced a hearty excitement in that cause.   The torpor of ages was at once shaken off, and the energies of the human mind, no longer held captive, were now seen to soar rejoicingly aloft upon the wings of a new-found freedom.   The artificial barriers which had heretofore withheld persons of the same communities or neighbourhood, from a familiar personal intercourse, were either extinguished or suspended by the overwhelming enthusiasm of the period ; and men were found jostling against each other in the ranks of the Crusaders who, until then, had never even heard each other's names. An active and profitable intercourse of ideas sprung up among all the co-labourers in this grand project ; and the minds of the crusading multitude became suddenly enlarged and strengthened by the observation of foreign manners and customs, and by an influx of notions, both practical and theoretical, till then undreamed of. It is unquestionably true, as has been asserted by another, that *the seeds of the Reformation were sown by the hands of the Crusaders.*

But, unhappily for man, the attempt to re-ascend to the heights of moral dignity once occupied, and meanly relinquished, is much more difficult than even the slow and painful progress from a state of unmixed barbarity and ignorance. *Error, in all countries, must be first effectually dethroned before the reign of Truth can be firmly established :* and all the vicious and enervating social habitudes, engendered by artificial arrangements, repugnant to nature, are ever found to make obstinate resistance either to the sober lessons of reason, the persuasive voice of eloquence, or even the sturdy monitions of experience. Accordingly, the Crusades did not immediately usher in the Reformation ; but a season soon intervened of greatly increased mental activity in several parts of Europe, which chiefly evaporated in the dark and profitless disputations of *scholastic philosophy,* or in the still vainer effusions of a wild and untutored fancy. It was not until the year 1520 that we find Luther assuming the attitude of open and invincible hostility to ecclesiastical tyranny, and lanching those thunderbolts of argument and denunciatory eloquence which were soon to throw the world into commotion.

It was in the year just named, that he publicly burnt at Wittemberg the Bull of the Pope of Rome, which contained his own condemnation.   Thus was the standard of *intellectual liberty* and *independence*, for the first time, boldly unfurled in Europe—a standard, whose peculiar honour it is, never to have been since signally depressed in presence of its foes ; but, whether fluttering in joyous exultation above the heads of emancipated millions, or waving, in mournful dignity, along the grim fields of disaster and carnage—whether flaming, as a talisman of hope, amidst the fierce horrors of a fiery martyrdom, or nerving the hearts of its defenders on the bloody battle-fields of Freedom with increased courage and confidence, in moments of greatest uncertainty and peril, has been ever borne forward and aloft, " over the land and over the sea," until now, in more than one country, planted firmly upon the lofty watch-towers of *constitutional liberty*, it blazes, with a radiance almost celestial, in view of an admiring world—a trophy of victories already achieved, and a symbol of prophetic glory for the time to come.   But, anterior to this grand movement on the part of Luther and his compeers, several events had occurred which rendered the scheme of *moral regeneration* then projected, far more easy of execution, than it must otherwise have proved.   The overthrow of Constantinople by the Turks, in the   fifteenth   century, had cast upon the shores of Italy a large number of Greeks who had been former inhabitants of that city ; who brought with them a higher intellectual culture, and a more elevated social refinement, than anywhere then existed within the pale of Catholic dominion.   Some of the ancient manuscripts, too, had been already redeemed by antiquarian diligence, from beneath the huge heaps of Ecclesiastical rubbish which had for ages concealed them from the view of men, and others had been newly introduced from various parts of the Greek Empire, then in ruins.——These manuscripts, in which lay embosomed the choicest treasures of heathen lore, were numerously copied and extensively circulated. The seasonable invention of *paper, painting in oil*, and *engraving on copper*, had supplied facilities not until then enjoyed, for scattering through Europe the illustrious masterpieces of Grecian and Roman art. About this time, too, the *mariner's compass* was imparting a new and potent stimulus to commercial enterprise, which already avowed the generous ambition of bringing the whole terraqueous planet under the inspection of civilized men, and of rendering every part of it tributary to the advancement of *knowledge* and *social happiness*. The art of Printing, a short time before invented, and just beginning to attract attention, was quietly rearing that fulcrum upon which has been since established a moral lever which may be said already to move and control the world ; by means of which, the lessons of universal truth shall ultimately obtain a duration as abiding as time, and an influence as extended as the habitations of men.

Religious reformation having begun its course under circumstances altogether so auspicious, a success truly astonishing has waited on its progress ; for, in a little more than three centuries, the slender streamlet, which, at the bidding of Luther, gushed forth from the hard rock of Catholicism, has deepened and widened into the vast ocean which we now behold. But the Reformation was far from spreading with equal celerity in all the various States of Europe ; and in *Spain* and *Italy*, its regenerative spirit was entirely precluded from entrance, as well by the civil institutions there subsisting, as by others which the ever-toiling sagacity of the Priesthood subsequently projected. It is not, therefore, by any means surprising, that in Spain, the human mind remained for centuries perfectly *stationary*

—during that whole period making no valuable contribution to any department of knowledge. The restlessness, under political and religious tyranny, elsewhere exhibited in Europe, was not at all visible in Spain ; a dark and listless apathy pervaded the whole popular mass there. No desire of improvement in the form of government — no wholesome curiosity for practical knowledge—no steady and sober contention for true moral glory, was anywhere to be perceived. Not a ray of light stole upon the thick darkness which enshrouded the benighted people of Spain, save, here and there, some meteoric effusion merely, whose dazzling and deceptious brightness for a moment flashed along the horizon, and was instantly lost again in circumambient gloom. The cumbrous weight of sacerdotal chains, rendered free and vigorous intellectual action of any kind, absolutely impracticable. *Superstition* sat like an incubus upon the soul of man, and held all its noblest faculties in a state of hopeless enthralment.

Throughout Europe, from the termination of the dark ages up to the breaking out of the Reformation, the whole progress of society and government, had been decidedly *theological.* The Ecclesiastical impress was to be seen upon every thing whatsoever, of artificial formation.—Even the mathematical and physical sciences were constrained to pay reverential homage to Church authority. Ethics existed nowhere save in the notions of the Priesthood ; Ecclesiastical dogmas prescribed the whole code of moral conduct. But in Spain, the dominancy of the Church over all other things whatever, was more complete than anywhere besides. In no other country was the union between *Church* and *State* so firmly cemented ; in no other country, have the evil effects of that union been so clearly manifested. All the institutions of Spain bear striking marks of Ecclesiastical policy ; the genius of the Priesthood predominated even in the system of Jurisprudence. Government in Spain, from the days of the Visigoths, was indeed little more than a pure Theocracy. It was at most a monarchy under Ecclesiastical control and supervision ; and the laws which emanated from the Council of Toledo, and which, after the lapse of many centuries, yet have respect in Spain, exhibit intrinsic evidence, that the Bishops of the church, who were known to have borne sway in that body, were not inactive in the work of providing by legislation, for the perpetuity of Ecclesiastical power. Many of these laws are considered as indicating their sacerdotal origin by a know-ledge of classic lore which the laity there have never pos-sessed ; and they are thought to abound in *general views* and *theories* wholly incompatible with Barbarian manners.

Under Ferdinand and Isabella the two states of Castile and Arragon were consolidated into one nation. These sovereigns, during their joint reign, greatly extended the ter-ritorial possessions of Spain, and acquired much renown by splendid achievements in war ; especially by overthrowing the magnificent kingdom of the Moors. They have both been much eulogised by historians ; and the character of Isabella, in particular, has been tricked out in all the gor-geous embellishments of tinselled rhetoric. I shall not di-rectly dispute the justice of encomiums lavished by writers of established reputation ; nor do I feel authorised seriously to complain of the injury unavoidably done to mankind, in thus challenging their admiration for personages, however successful they may have proved themselves in the works of devastation and bloodshed, whose whole course on earth, with one or two exceptions alone, was deeply deleterious to the cause of virtue, obstructive of the march of reason, and extinguishing to the spirit of freedom.—But *truth* demands the suggestion, that it would be found a task of exceeding difficulty, even for such as have been most acute in discerning the glory of monarchs, to specify a single measure of government, projected by Ferdinand and Isabella, which was marked with a liberal and enlightened regard for the natural rights and solid happiness of their own subjects, or which denoted a generous desire to promote the true welfare of mankind in general. The establishment of the modern Inquisition in Spain, which was introduced under the auspices of these sovereigns, and in a form more replete with horrors than the juggling malignity of a demoniac priesthood had ever before succeeded in devising, has affixed a brand of infamy to their characters, which the enlightened judgment of successive generations will continue to deepen and prolong to the end of time.

Without entering here into the *organic frame* of the Inquisition, as it was, at this time, put in exercise in Spain, or exploring all the melancholy details of oppression and suffering with which its operation stands associated upon the pages of authentic history;—it may be confidently pronounced to have proved the most efficient engine which has ever been employed for beating down freedom of opinion, for debasing the minds and enervating the souls of a whole people, and plunging them into the lowest depths of degradation and woe—a degradation not of a transient and fleeting character, and a woe almost beyond the reach of remedy. For it was not for a short season only that the people of Spain were doomed to endure the iniquitous and grinding tyranny of the *Holy Office*. From century to century of sorrow and debasement, were they compelled to cower beneath its relentless sway; until, at length, grown callous under continual suffering, and losing all sense of the native dignity of man's nature, under the multipled contempts to which they were subjected, they were seen absolutely to hug the chains which bound them in captivity, and to exult over the tokens of moral defilement by which they stood surrounded.

The *modern* Inquisition (as it was called, to distinguish it from the tribunal of that name erected in France at the termination of the Crusades) having been ushered into authority by Ferdinand and Isabella, under the nefarious sanction of Pope Sixtus IV. of Rome, and employed with unsparing severity in wringing from the unoffending Jews, who inhabited the commercial cities of Spain, the treasures which they had earned by honest industry, grew and flourished abundantly under the imperial patronage of their grandson Charles V.; until during the reign of the cruel and bigoted Philip II., who succeeded Charles upon the throne, it attained such a fierce, and bloody, and uncontrolled ascendancy, that it was henceforward recognised as sitting enthroned among the sceptred powers of earth, dealing out *infamy*, and *confiscation*, and *death*, through all the regions encompassed by its sway. Nor was it until the volcanic commotions which occurred in France, towards the close of the last century, and which almost shook the earth to its centre, that the authority of the Holy Office was at all questioned in Spain; nor can it be even yet truly said that its power is wholly eradicated. The *moral effects* of the system will not disappear for ages ; for the wounds inflicted by Bigotry and Fanaticism combined, yield not easily and at once to any moral medicaments yet ascertained ; they ever evince a *scrofulous* tendency, and require the free application of *caustic* remedies before healing balsams of any kind can be advantageously resorted to.

It was in the year 1519, a single year anterior to the grand era of religious reformation, that a body of lawless adventurers from Spain, under the command of the celebrated Fernando Cortes, landed upon the coast of Mexico, and attempted, by a course of bloody and rapacious violence, to seize upon the whole country then under the dominion of Montezuma, the Mexican Emperor. The view which has already been presented of the *moral influences* at that time prevailing in Spain, and which continued to prevail, with increased force, so long as the tide of emigration from that country to Mexico was supplying this portion of North America with a population of European origin, will serve to account for many things which would seem otherwise strange and unnatural both in the *peculiar policy* adopted by the Spanish Government for the regulation of its colonial interests in Mexico, and in the subsequent history of this unfortunate people under Spanish rule.

CHAPTER II.

View of the Mexican Empire at the period of its invasion by the Spaniards, with some observations upon the moral condition of the Mexicans as a people.

NOTHING has at any time occurred in the history of the human race more remarkable in several respects, than the sudden conquest achieved by the daring genius of Fernando Cortez, over that extensive and populous region in North America, whose inhabitants, in the beginning of the sixteenth century, bowed in solemn homage, and with almost idolatrous adoration, before the august and seemingly stable throne of the imperial Montezuma,—the wise, the warlike, the patriotic, but unfortunate and martyred monarch of heathen Mexico. The striking numerical disproportion apparent, between the diminutive band of fierce but disciplined warriors who encircled the enterprising banner of the conqueror, and who, at his command, impetuously rushed through blood, and fire, and devastation, to wealth, and dominion, and renown,—and the almost innumerous multitude of another race and complexion who entered the strife of arms in defence of their own native land, their ancestral institutions, their honoured altars and cherished firesides, against the relentless violence of usurping strangers, might well awaken a feeling of surprise, if not of incredulity, in minds not accustomed to estimate the force of circumstances such as are shown to have accompanied the hideous work of subduction. Some of these circumstances will now be cursorily presented and remarked upon, as they will serve to throw considerable light upon transactions hereafter to be detailed, and perhaps furnish grounds for something like a plausible conjecture as to the ultimate destiny of a country relative to which much cloudy and conflicting surmise is at present indulged. "The *beginning*," says one,* "holds in it the *end*, and all that leads thereto; as the acorn does the oak and its fortunes." Let it not be expected though, I pray, that at this stage of what I have called "Texas and the Texans," the regular order of historic recital will be attempted; as this would be both tedious and unnecessary, and might, moreover, be held by many as implying some question in reference to the merits of other writers who have already occupied this department of history with a success proportionate to their own high powers, and in a manner apparently satisfactory to the Republic of Letters.

The charming valley in which Mexico, the oldest city of the New World, is situated, is said to have been anciently distinguished by a name that is no longer applied to it, *Anahuac*,† whose meaning was beautifully typical of the singularly picturesque location of the principal cities of the valley, nine in number, along the winding margin of two lakes—which lakes, communicating with each other, by means of a canal of inconsiderable length, and gently spreading out their waters through a circumference of nearly one hundred miles, held in liquid embracement a cluster

---

* Carlyle.

† This word, in the ancient Mexican language, means "*near the water*."

3 *

of romantic islands, above whose surface were seen to rise, " as by the stroke of an enchanter's wand," those lordly and gigantic structures which asserted the majesty of the Mexican Capital : a sight of whose lofty towers, stupendous temples, and glittering palaces, overhanging the aqueous expanse below, seemed naturally to suggest to the mind of the enraptured observer the classic image of a renowned ocean-born city* of another hemisphere, which has been poetically depictured as " looking a sea-Cybele, fresh from ocean," crowned with her bright " tiara of proud towers."   The name, which was thus in the first instance applied to the *Vale of Mexico*, was subsequently much extended in its application, and, in process of time, Anahuac was recognized as embracing, with slight exceptions, all that immense tract of country afterwards known as *New Spain.*

In the year 1519, when Fernando Cortes made his first appearance in Anahuac, the country seems to have been overspread with an exceedingly dense population, outnumbering, confessedly, by many millions, the present inhabitants of the Mexican Republic. A high state of agriculture flourished throughout the dominions of Montezuma. Various arts, both useful and ornamental, had reached a point of perfection not then attained in any part of Europe, and perhaps seldom surpassed in any age of the world. Scientific knowledge, of various kinds, had. been accumulated, though the regular method of the schools was wanted to impart the dignity and clearness of systematic arrangement, and the energetic diligence of Professors set apart for the high purposes of doctrinal instruction, had not yet given a wholesome diffusiveness to Learning, nor concerted arrangements for promoting the steady improvement of intellect. Temperance, Frugality, Industry, Honesty, Truth, and even Modesty, respect for the laws, reverence for the Powers of

---

* Venice.

Heaven, with numerous household and social virtues besides, are asserted, by grave historians, to have been zealously inculcated and rigidly enforced among the happy subjects of the pious Montezuma. Forty-three distinct cities of enormous size, and of gorgeous, if not tasteful, construction, met the gaze of the spectator, and conveyed to his mind the ever-pleasing impression of advanced and still advancing civilization. Not only were Temples sacred to the Mexican Deities to be found in Towns and populous districts, but in some instances they were seen to invest with a mystic sacredness the most solitary and secluded recesses of the wilderness:—from all which, it is evident that the inhabitants of Mexico at this period were not only entitled to claim respect as a moral and refined people, but are likewise deserving of our sympathy and esteem as a race among whom the maxims of social virtue, as asserted by enlightened *policy* everywhere, had attained a subtler, as well as a more commanding influence over the sensibilities of the promiscuous multitude by being enstamped with at least a *nominal* supernal sanction,—which, though nominal only, yet being respected as real, must be regarded as only inferior, both in dignity and efficiency, to a genuine Revelation of the Divine Will. But it is the chief glory of Mexico, whilst yet enshrouded in the mists of Heathenism, that *Religion*, though her supremacy was upheld, and her authority kept in lively action through the agency of a body of chosen Priests who ministered night and day at her altars; though countless prodigies were asserted and profoundly believed to attest her celestial origin,—and good and evil prophecies, whispered from Heaven, were supposed to be in a course of constant fulfilment—some of which even affected the duration of the Mexican empire itself;—though the august images of their National Gods and Goddesses, of Herculean proportions, and decked with the most gorgeous and imposing insignia, were constantly exhibited to the view of an admiring populace in the high towers of their cloud-capt Temples,—thus making it next to impossible that their votaries could ever for an instant forget their title to affectionate reverence ;—though the style of worship maintained, was emblazoned with all the ceremonial splendour judged expedient for the enforcement of a reverend homage or the enkindlement of a pious sensibility ;—yet, under all these circumstances, may it truly be asserted, to the honour of the unchristianized subjects of Montezuma, that among them *Religion* was not absurdly, not to say barbarously, dissociated from that angelic spirit of high-souled *Toleration* and tender *Charity* which are her natural accompaniments ; but which, it must be confessed, even under a *purer* dispensation, are not always found in alliance with her.   The anecdote about to be introduced might indeed almost justify a feeling of regret that the Mexicans of the sixteenth century were not permitted to remain in a state of spiritual *darkness*, instead of being ushered into the light of the Gospel by such rude and unchristian ministrations as those with which they were alone favoured by the Catholic propagandists of that period ; and the same anecdote, though couched in phraseology far from elegant, will be found to verify most of what has been said in commendation of the social traits belonging to the original Mexican character ere it was contaminated and debased by those sword-bearing, fire-applying missionaries of Catholicism, who, during the sixteenth and seventeenth centuries, came across the ocean to force these amiable Heathens into the Christian fold, so called ; and who, with an impious and indecent presumption which cannot be sufficiently admired, assumed to perform the whole work of this constrained regeneration in the name and by the authority of a God of infinite benignity.

It is the language of one of the associates of Cortes, which I am about to cite — *Captain Bernal Diaz del Castillo*, who, in the sixteenth century, published a work entitled " A True Account of the Conquest of Mexico," and who narrates such facts as he had himself witnessed.   It seems, that on the first visit of Cortes to the Capital of

Montezuma, which was made under strong professions of amity, all the rites of an elegant hospitality were cordially administered by this amiable monarch, who evinced an earnest desire to make the sojourn of the Spanish Commander and his comrades altogether agreeable to them. On the day after his arrival, Cortes called upon the Emperor at his palace, attended by four of his captains and five soldiers—Bernal Diaz del Castillo, just mentioned, being along. Hear this same Captain : " When they entered the hall of entertainment, and Montezuma had received information thereof, he came as far as the middle of the hall to meet them, attended by his relations ; no other person being allowed to enter where he was, except on the most important business. With great ceremony on each side, the King took Cortes by the hand, and, leading him to the elevated part of the saloon, placed him upon his right, and, with much affability, desired the rest of the guests to be seated. Cortes then proceeded to say, that he came to him for the service of the *Lord God*, whom the Christians adored—who was named Jesus Christ, and who suffered death for our sakes. He also explained, that we adored the cross, as the emblem of the crucifixion for our salvation, whereby the human race was redeemed, and that our Lord, on the third day, rose, and is in Heaven, and that it was he who created heaven, and earth, and sea, and is adored by us as our creator ; but that those *things* which he (Montezuma) held to be gods, were not such, but *devils*, which are very bad things, of evil countenances, and worse deeds ; and that he might judge how wicked they were, and how little power they had, inasmuch as wherever we placed crosses they dared not show their faces. He, therefore, requested that he would attend to what he had told him ; which was, that we were all brothers, the children of Adam and Eve, and that as such, our Emperor, lamenting the loss of souls in such numbers as those which were brought by his idols into everlasting flames, had sent us to apply a remedy thereto, by putting an end to the worship of these false gods, to human sacrifices, and all other crimes; and that he now came to notify his majesty's intentions; but our Emperor would at a future time, send *holy men*, fully capable of explaining them. Here Cortes stopped, and Montezuma seemed to show an inclination to reply; but Cortes observing that this was enough for the first time, proposed to us to retire, when we were prevented by Montezuma, who spoke to him as follows: "I have already heard, through my ambassador, of those things which you now mention, and to which I have hitherto made no reply, because we have, *from the first*, worshipped the gods we now do, and considered them as *just* and *good*. *So no doubt are yours.* In regard to the creation of the world our beliefs are the same, and we also believe you to be the people who were to come to us from where the sun rises. To your great king I am indebted. There have been already persons on our coasts from your country. I wish to know if you are all the same people." To which Cortes having replied, that they were all subjects of the same king, Montezuma said, that from the first time he had heard of them, it had been his wish to see them, which his gods had now granted him; that we should, therefore, consider ourselves as *at home*, and if ever we were refused entrance into any of his cities, it would not be his fault, but that of his subjects, who were terrified by the reports they heard of us, such as that we carried with us thunder and lightning—that our voices killed men, and that we were furious teules,* with other follies of that kind; adding, that he saw we were *men*, and that we were valiant and wise, for which he esteemed us, and would give us proof thereof. For this condescension, we all expressed our gratitude. He then addressed himself to Cortes, in a laughing manner, for he was very gay in conversation, when in his state, saying, "Malintzin,† the Tlazcalans, your new friends, have, I

---

* This was the ancient Mexican word for devils or evil spirits.
† The name by which Cortes was known among the Mexicans.

know, told you that I am like a *God*, and that all about me is *gold*, and *silver*, and *precious stones*; but you now see that I am *flesh* and *blood*, and that my houses are built like other houses, of lime, and stone, and timber. It is true that I am a great King, and inherit riches from my ancestors; but for these ridiculous falsehoods, do you treat them with the same contempt that I do the stories that I was told of your commanding the elements." To which Cortes good-humouredly replied, that the accounts of enemies were not to be relied on, paying him, at the same time, a handsome compliment upon his power and grandeur. During the conversation, Montezuma had made a sign to one of his principal attendants to order his officers to bring him certain pieces of gold which he had laid apart to give to Cortes, together with ten loads of fine stuffs, which he divided among Cortes and his Captains, and to every soldier he gave two collars of gold each, with ten crowns, and two loads of mantles. The gold amounted in value to upwards of a thousand crowns, and he gave it with an affability and indifference which made him appear a truly magnificent Prince. It being now past mid-day, Cortes took his leave, observing, that it was his majesty's hour of dinner, and that he heaped obligations upon us; to which Montezuma replied, that, on the contrary, we had obliged him. We then retired, impressed with respect for the Great Montezuma, from his Princely manner, and his liberality."

A more striking contrast could not be easily imagined, than the one presented to view in the anecdote just related, between the *reverse sides* of the colloquial picture therein displayed; and in comparing the demeanour of Montezuma with that of Cortes, at this interview, one is almost tempted to exclaim, with something of dramatic emphasis, " Hyperion to a Satyr ! !" Cortes, an avaricious, presuming, ill-bred Captain of a band of rapacious and unprincipled outlaws, overleaping all the ceremonial obstructions of polished life, intrudes himself, uninvited, upon the generous hospitalities of a noble monarch, pretending to be the special representative both of the Almighty in Heaven and a great potentate beyond the ocean—which last he declares to be solicitous of establishing an intercourse of reciprocal civilities with the Sovereign of Mexico. He is received into the palace of Montezuma, and honoured with distinguished tokens of respect. At the second interview which takes place between this self-constituted Apostle and the executive head of a great empire, Cortes, in the genuine spirit of inquisitorial arrogance, and with something of a snuffling pretension to special and exclusive piety, takes it upon himself to deride the fundamental tenets which enter into the religious creed of his royal host. With a demoniac fierceness only fit to be associated with the infernal glories of a Spanish Auta-da-fé, he pours forth a sulphurous tide of contemptuous invective upon the Gods and Goddesses of Mexico, though their Deities stood sanctified by the reverential devotion of a whole people for centuries, and though Montezuma himself had been, for many years, a High Priest of the very religion he was denouncing. And then, when the monarch, who has been thus insultingly treated in his own palace, deigns to offer a fitting response, this haughty Brigand abruptly declines all further parlance, evidently apprehending that he might by possibility, if the dialogue should be longer continued, lose some portion of the advantage which he fancied himself to have gained by monopolizing, so far, the attention of those present. So much for Cortes and the Spanish politeness and liberality of that age; but what is the conduct of Montezuma, under such provocatives to wrath? The urbane monarch puts forth his hand and gently detains the ill-mannered guest a few moments longer in his presence. This is apparently not done with a view to angry recrimination; nor even for the vain purpose of presenting an elaborate vindication of the creed in which his infancy had been nurtured, his manhood confirmed, and which he heard now, doubtless for the first time, profanely called in question. He begins to speak. A grave and impressive dignity marks his manner at first, which mellows, as he proceeds, into the most winning suavity. Exquisite good-breeding altogether withholds his tongue from the language of retaliatory revilement. He contents himself with a mild but decided affirmation of his own creed, and a firm and composed announcement of his determination not to abandon the Gods of his forefathers, at the unauthorized bidding of this rude stranger; acknowledging, at the same time, the merits which he doubted not belonged to the creed which he had heard unfolded, and even graciously deigning to suggest certain points of similitude which he discovered to exist between the two creeds which had been thrust into such rude collision with each other. He then skilfully directs the stream of conversation to topics less exciting, pleasantly observing upon the superstitious notions entertained in regard to himself by the barbarians who surrounded his empire—to whom, with a pardonable irony, he alludes as " the new friends" of Cortes — aptly likening these notions to certain absurd fancies taken up by some of the more ignorant of his own subjects relative to the Spaniards; and at last gracefully brings this disagreeable dialogue to a close by a singular display of munificent liberality towards Cortes and his grim associates. The pages of history have been seldom illumined with a finer instance than this, of that perfect *Charity of heart*, which patiently and affectionately extends to others the sacred privilege of independently entertaining and unrestrainedly avowing adverse religious sentiments: and the people among whom such an example of *Philosophic toleration* could occur, if standing in need of the purifying grace of a more orthodox piety, may be well said not to have lacked such moral teaching as the Priesthood of inquisitorial Spain was capable of affording. The scene

which has been described, with many others of a kindred
nature which were exhibited about the same period in Mexico, fully authorizes the assertion, that, whatever other deficiencies may have been apparent in the subjects of Montezuma, the Mexicans of the 16th century were at least exempt from everything like a stupid and unreasoning *Bigotry*, or a barbarous and blood-seeking *Proscriptiveness
of spirit ;*—such as at the very time in question, under the
direction of the celebrated Charles V., was hurrying one
hundred thousand of his Protestant subjects in the Nether-
lands to martyrdom for presuming to exercise freedom of
conscience.   Enlightened reason is shocked at the indecent
presumption of such men as Fernando Cortes, his associates, aiders, or abettors, whether priests or laymen, in
attempting to reform the moral institutions of Mexico.

Indeed, there is good evidence in support of the position,
strange as its assertion may appear to some, that the Mexicans of the sixteenth century were decidedly superior to the
Spaniards who succeeded in enslaving them, in most of those
points which serve to discriminate the savage from the civilized condition.   They undeniably possessed more softness
and amenity of manners in social intercourse ; were more
chaste and refined in their general sentiments ;—they were
juster as well as more benevolent in all their dealings with
their fellow-men ; were more orderly and obedient to law ;
more faithful to individual engagements of every kind ; and
less disposed, in all respects, to encroach upon the rights
of others.   It is true, that several things which have been
pronounced by some speculative writers as necessarily ap-
purtenant to a state of complete *civilization*, were to be me*
with in Spain and not in Mexico.   For instance : *Gunpowder*, by whose malign agency the terrors of War have been
so greatly multiplied, had not yet caused the hills and valleys of the New World to rebellow with artificial thunder.
Cavalry, so efficiently wielded by Cortes against the valo-

rous infantry of Mexico, had never yet trampled the luxuriant herbage which everywhere carpeted the fair plains of Anahuac. No Cadmus had yet landed on her shores, bringing with him the invaluable gift of *Alphabetical Symbols*. The use of *Iron* was not known in Mexico; nor, perhaps, *Money*—understood in the ordinary acceptation of that imposing word—as a metallic representative of value, and medium of commercial exchange. Nor had the subjects of Montezuma any *ships*, with which they might navigate the perilous ocean, and sail, if need be, beyond their own hemisphere. But notwithstanding all these confessed deficiencies, much might be said to prove that the disadvantages resulting therefrom were more imaginary than real. I shall not enlarge upon this topic, because it is merely collateral to the object which I have in view; but perhaps a remark or two on some of the points suggested would not be altogether unseasonable. In the present age of the world, when Political Philosophers are confidently asserting the doctrine that *War*, with all its horrible concomitants, is but a relic of departing barbarism; and that indeed its occurrence should, if possible, be altogether prevented, if by no other means, by compelling disputant nations to submit in all cases to neutral arbitrament — no conjectures very unfavourable to the Mexicans of the sixteenth century, are likely to be grounded upon their want of either *Gunpowder* or *Cavalry*. A conclusive answer to all such conjectures would certainly be, that the Mexicans of the *nineteenth century* abound much in both the articles named, and yet no sensible man in either hemisphere would undertake, at this time, to sustain their claim to thorough civilization. It will not be disputed that the use of Alphabetical characters has been generally regarded as indispensable to any signal advance of mind; but various nations have been in the enjoyment of this grand auxiliary of Science without becoming at all distinguished in the higher departments of Learning; and several have relapsed into utter barbarism in spite of any magical influence which the mere use of Alphabetical sym-

bols was capable of yielding. Besides, it is a fact not at all
contested, that the Mexicans, at the period of their history
now under examination, had at least passed through all those
stages supposed to be naturally precedent to the formation
of a regular Alphabet. They could exhibit numerous *Paintings*, many of which were executed with admirable skill ;—
which Paintings, it is evident, were made to answer, with
tolerable convenience, nearly all the purposes of writing.
Some of these, we learn, were of an *historical* character, and
were faithfully and even minutely preservative of the memory
of past transactions ; whilst others of the same class were
perspicuously delineative of current events. There were
pictorial productions, also, of a moral cast, illustrative
of the surpassing glories of virtue, and the deleterious
consequences of vice, or the unrestrained indulgence in
luxurious pleasures. Some of these ancient Paintings
have been found to supply copious and valuable materials for authentic printed history, and from these alone have
been compiled several voluminous works which have obtained considerable respect in the literary world ;—and in
them will we find the ancient usages of the Mexican race
traced out and exhibited in a manner which leaves little information unsupplied that Philosophic curiosity would be
likely to demand. It is known that these same Paintings
have been often introduced before Judicial tribunals in Mexico, during the last two centuries, and have been unhesitatingly admitted as muniments of title to real estate of a quality entirely satisfactory. But in addition to the Paintings
described, the Mexicans, in the age of Montezuma, and long
before, were in the habit of employing *hieroglyphics, alle-
gorical symbols*, and *arbitrary characters* of different kinds,
by means of which they were able both to interchange and
perpetuate ideas, either useful or agreeable, almost as conveniently as if they had been blessed with the Alphabet
self.

Now, though the art of Printing had gained admittance

in Spain anterior to the arrival of Cortes in Mexico, yet, as has been already observed, for certain reasons of state, it had not been permitted, and never has been permitted since, to become, to any considerable degree, an efficient agent in spreading information among the popular mass ; and the gross illiteracy of most of those *soldiers of fortune*, as they called themselves, by whose efforts the power of Spain in the New World was violently established, is too well ascertained to authorize a presumption of literary accomplishment in regard to them, by reason of their having left behind them in some of the large cities of Spain, a few individuals who imperfectly understood the ingenious collocation of types.

In reference to the want of money in Mexico, if it is indeed a point worthy of serious notice in this examination, it should be mentioned that we have the authority of Cortes himself, in support of the position that *metallic coin* was not, as several writers have asserted, wholly unknown in Mexico at the period of the Conquest : in one of his letters to the Emperor Charles V., which is still extant, he expressly declares that he found money employed in several provinces of the Empire which he visited in aid of commercial dealings. But, discarding this statement entirely, yet will it not be necessary to admit that the Mexican people had ordained no *regular standard of value :* for, not only was the famous nut of the Cacao everywhere used as a medium of commercial exchange, but Gold-dust, enclosed in goose-quills, and certain pieces of a valuable cotton-cloth, called *Patolquactotli,* helped to swell the circulation. All this, it must be confessed, would constitute but a slender provision for such a commerce as England now possesses ; but it remains yet to be proved that a traffic so extended is at all necessary to the moral advancement of the English people, and that learning and refinement in the British Isles have at all kept pace with the extension of commercial traffic. Those inclined to pronounce the Mex-

4 *

icans of the 16th century to have been barbarians on the ground of their not having yet organized a perfectly convenient metallic currency, would do well to recollect that Rome, in the days of Servius Tullus, was in a similar condition, and that the Lacedemonians, for more than seven hundred years, even whilst dominating over all Greece, were little better off in this particular.   But, with all men of classical research, an instance still more ancient will be held absolutely conclusive of the point in question; since the immortal poems of Homer have depictured all the states of Greece, whose chivalry was congregated before the walls of Troy for the destruction of that proud city, as having formed no conceptions of traffic beyond a simple *barter of commodities.*

It has been occasionally urged, in depreciation of the people of Mexico, that they had not, anterior to the invasion of their country by the Spaniards, ascertained the use of *iron :* and this is even strictly true in point of fact; for utensils made of this metal were certainly unknown to this ingenious race; yet, to make amends for this seeming deficiency, it is to be mentioned, that they had found in the bosom of their soil two kinds of *copper*, " the one hard, which was used instead of iron, to make axes, hatchets, and other instruments of war and agriculture, — and the other, flexible, which was used to make pots, basins and other vessels for domestic use."   Such is the statement of a writer* whose volumes have been long regarded as of unquestionable authenticity, and whose fidelity has been praised by a personage no less distinguished than the celebrated Thomas Jefferson.   The same writer continues to state on this subject as follows :—" The Indians, (says Oviedo, an eye-witness, and who is asserted to have been specially skilled in metals,) know very well how to gild copper vessels, or those of low gold, and to give them so excellent and bright a colour, that they appear to be gold

---

* Abbe D. Francesco Saverio Clavigero.

of twenty-two carats or more; this they do by means of certain herbs. The gilding is so well executed, that if a goldsmith of Spain or Italy were possessed of the recipe he would esteem himself very rich." Captain Bernal Diaz del Castillo, in his account of the siege of Mexico by the Spaniards and their native allies, in which, as heretofore mentioned, he was himself a participant, informs us that " Cortes issued a circular to all the districts of his alliance in the neighbourhood of Tezcuco, to send him each, within the space of eight days, eight thousand arrow-heads, made of copper; also an equal number of shafts made of a particular wood. By the expiration of the given time, the whole number was brought, executed to a degree of perfection which exceeded the pattern."

In reference to the entire want of vessels of marine construction in Mexico, capable of encountering the dangers of the ocean, it may be fairly urged, that, however useful such vessels might have proved in forwarding the operations of general commerce, and thus, perchance, incidentally multiplying the number of ideas in circulation; yet is it apparent that the intercourse of exterior trade was by no means so necessary to Mexico, on the score of mere social and domestic comfort, as to most other countries; since her various climate and bounteous soil plenteously supplied her crowded population, at all seasons, with every thing requisite for either healthful or luxurious accommodation. It may be here remarked in passing, that it has been strongly doubted by men of enlightened minds, in all ages of the world, whether the aggregate influence of commerce has not been more baneful than propitious to the moral interests of mankind; and, without adopting the language of a gifted poet, and asserting that " Honour sinks where commerce long prevails," I feel authorised to say, that, in all countries it has been found, that the simple virtues of social life flourish best in districts somewhat remote from the dexterous sons of traffic; and I am even strongly tempted to assert, that *science flies, with instinctive alarm, from the clamour of mercantile exchanges.* The glory of Rome was almost at its meridian height ere she could claim a single bark upon the Mediterranean; and the cause of freedom gained far less than it lost by every naval victory which graced her conquering arms.

So much of the moral condition of the people of Mexico, when first visited by the Spaniards, and of the comparative merits of the conquerors and the conquered: a few observations remain to be offered in order to present a complete picture of Mexico as a nation, at this Augustan period of her annals. The original government of the Mexican people is supposed to have been an elective aristocracy;—about twenty individuals among the nobility, of approved valour and wisdom, being chosen, at stated periods, to administer the national concerns. It was not until the year 1352, of the Christian era, that the aristocratical frame was judged too feeble to supply the necessary energy to the government to enable it to repel the continual encroachments of surrounding tribes or nations, and an elective monarchy was substituted in place of the rule of nobles. Eight sovereigns had successively mounted the throne before the elevation of Montezuma II., in 1502, whose reign was in progress at the arrival of the Spaniards, seventeen years thereafter. The government still retained its original *elective* feature; and upon the death of the reigning monarch, it was a settled and well-understood principle that a successor should be called to the throne by the free suffrages of a specified body of *Electors*, who were recognised as representing the wishes of the whole nation. These elections are stated to have been uniformly conducted in a peaceful and orderly manner, and never to have been marked, as has been, unhappily, sometimes the case in other countries where similar proceedings have occurred, by tumults, bloodshed, or corruption; all of which must be admitted to administer valuable evidence in proof both of the purity of the Electors, and of the general virtue of the popular mass.

We learn, from the pages of Clavigero, that the predecessors of Montezuma II. upon the throne of Mexico, had been all somewhat distinguished for those qualities which give true dignity to monarchs whilst living, and secure to them the lasting affection of their subjects after death ; but none of them had testified higher qualifications for government, or manifested a more paternal regard for their people, than the second Montezuma himself. Before the Electoral suffrages had fallen upon him, he had acquired much fame as a military commander, and had likewise officiated for several years, in one of the Great Temples of Mexico, as a Sacerdotal functionary. He is described by Clavigero, in his capacity of High Priest and Warrior, as " a man of taciturn temper, extremely deliberate, not only in his words, but also in his actions ;" and it is said, that " whenever he spoke in the Royal council, of which he was a member, he was listened to with respect." He is represented as having been occupied in the performance of his Priestly functions, at the moment when he received intelligence of his having been chosen to reign over his fellow-citizens ; from which it is perhaps inferrible that he did not earn this high promotion by personal solicitation, or intrigue of any sort. A curious address is extant, which is supposed to have been delivered to Montezuma on the occasion of his *inauguration*, by the King of Acolhuacan, who had now become one of his subjects, and which will be found interesting in several points of view. It contains much sound counsel suited to the present age of the world. " The great good fortune (said the patriotic Orator) of the Mexican people is made manifest by the unanimity of your election, and the uncommon applause with which it is celebrated by all. All have in truth reason to celebrate it ; for the Kingdom of Mexico is arrived at such greatness, that no less fortitude than your invincible heart possesses, no less wisdom than that which in you we admire, would be sufficient to support so great a load. It is most evident how strong is the love which the Omnipotent God bears to this nation; as he has enlightened it that it may choose that which is most beneficial to it. Who is able to persuade himself that *He*, who, as a private individual, has searched into the mysteries of Heaven, will not now, when a monarch, know the things of this earth which will preserve the happiness of his subjects? That *He*, who, on so many occasions, has shown the greatness of his soul, will not now retain it, when it is become most necessary to him? Who can imagine, that where there is so much *courage*, and so much *wisdom*, the widow or the orphan will ever apply without relief? The Mexican Empire has unquestionably attained the height of its power, and the Creator of Heaven has been pleased to invest you with so much power as to inspire all who behold you with awe and respect. Rejoice, therefore, O happy land! that thou art destined to have a Prince who will not only be thy support, but will, by his *clemency*, prove a *Father* and a *Brother* to his subjects. Thou hast a King who will not seize the occasion of his exaltation to give himself up to *Luxury*, and lie sluggishly in bed, abandoned to pastimes and effeminate pleasures; his anxiety will rather wake and agitate his bosom, in the softest hours of repose; nor will he be able to taste food, or relish the most delicious morsel, whilst thy interests are oppressed or neglected. And do you, noble Prince and most powerful Lord, be confident, and trust that the Creator of Heaven, who has raised you to so high a dignity, will give you strength to discharge all the obligations which are annexed to it. HE who has been hitherto so liberal to you, will not now be niggardly of his precious gifts, having himself raised you to the throne on which I wish you many years of happiness." Little did the King of Acolhuacan anticipate the tragic catastrophe which should mark the reign of Montezuma as the most disastrous in Mexican annals; little did he suspect that the Powers of Heaven to whom the Mexicans piously trusted, would be found too feeble to resist the champions of a more Orthodox Faith, who should come across the great waters armed with physical and moral energies of Invincible might, and who would quickly shroud the glories of an ancient and magnificent empire in a night of endless darkness and despair.

Captain Bernal Diaz del Castillo has delineated the person and manners of Montezuma when he first beheld him, in a coarse but graphic style, as follows : " The great Montezuma was at this time aged about forty years, of good stature, well-proportioned and thin : his complexion was much fairer than that of the Indians ; he wore his hair shoit, just covering his ears—with very little beard, well-arranged, thin, and black. His face was rather long, with a pleasant countenance and good eyes." All writers concur in attributing to Montezuma abilities of no common order, both as a commander of armies, and as a judicious and faithful manager of civic affairs. Though encircled by splendours such as no modern Potentate has been permitted to behold, he appears never to have forfeited his native modesty of soul, or to have evinced by his demeanour that he held himself released in the least degree from the essential and indispensable obligations of humanity. Though surrounded by luxuries whose delicacy and profusion left naught for the most refined or most rapacious voluptuousness to desire, he was never accused of having, on any occasion, postponed the practical duties of his station to schemes of mere pleasurable indulgence ; and whilst with the polished and enlightened nobles of his Empire, he delighted to cultivate an intercourse reciprocally cordial and respectful, yet, as we are assured, his ear was ever open to the complaints of the humblest of his subjects, and his benevolence ever in action to alleviate their distresses. There must have been certainly a peculiar charmfulness about his manners, when even one who sanctioned all the cruel and unprincipled artifices by which he was ultimately betrayed to ruin and death, (I allude to Captain Bernal Diaz del Castillo) has acknowledged that " he delighted all by his affable and friendly behaviour," and adds : " nor is it possible to describe how noble he was in everything he did, nor the respect in which he was held by every one about him." Montezuma is reported by historians as having had personal cognizance of all the important operations of government, and is said never to have suffered oppression, or fraud, or even gross neglect to go unpunished in his most trusted functionaries. Numerous counsellors, alike recommended by their wisdom and their virtues, remained constantly in his presence, ready to assist by their counsels in the decision of questions either of high public moment, or of peculiar complexity ; whilst couriers were continually arriving from the most distant parts of his dominions freighted with authentic intelligence of all important events which had recently transpired. Over the fiscal interests of his Empire he exercised a sober and steady vigilance ; the commanders of his armies were subjected to a constant and rigid responsibility ; and a Judicial tribunal, composed of three Judges, profoundly versed in the laws and usages of Mexico, held its solemn sessions throughout the year, with slight intermissions, near the precincts of the Royal palace. A brighter picture of National happiness has rarely been presented on earth than Mexico exhibited early in the reign of Montezuma : the domestic quiet and prosperity of the nation seemed complete ; and the happy subjects, of the happy monarch, uttered unanimous jubilations over the illustrious virtues of their chosen sovereign, and the fair prospect which seemed to expand before their view of social beatitude——ever to continue on the increase, and national glories multiplying without end. And no one can say that these rejoicings were unreasonable : for, in addition to the institutions which the wisdom of their ancestors had ordained in their behalf, and, which their own

virtues had hitherto maintained inviolate, did they not behold themselves the fortunate occupants of a region where
Nature had scattered her choicest gifts, with a lavish liberality nowhere else to be discovered? and was it not indeed true of this Paradise of theirs, that,

> " Whatever fruits in different climes were found,
>   That proudly rise, or humbly court the ground;
>   Whatever blooms in torrid tracts appear,
>   Whose bright succession decks the varied year;
>   Whatever sweets salute the Northern sky,
>   With vernal tints, that blossom but to die,
>   These, here disporting, own the kindred soil,
>   Nor ask luxuriance from the planter's toil,
>   While sea-born gales their gelid wings expand,
>   To winnow fragrance round the smiling land."

But alas! all sublunary hopes of permanent and unalloyed
felicity are but illusory at last, and man, both individual and
aggregate, is oftentimes upon the very brink of destruction
when he imagines himself most secure.   It remains to be
mentioned, that the people of Mexico, blessed so richly with
moral and physical advantages as has been described, were
yet not altogether exempt from the harassment of exterior
foes; indeed, the persevering enmity of certain contiguous
Indian tribes, and the marauding and cannibal hostility with
which they delighted to vex the frontiers of the Empire,
called for the exercise of a vigilance ever in action, and had
several times provoked signal chastisement at the hands of a
valorous and patriotic soldiery.   Like Marseilles of old, Mexico chanced to be a solitary civilized nation in the midst of in-
numerable savage hordes, who proved, as was perhaps quite
natural, alike envious of her superior social cultivation, and
rapacious of that prodigal abundance which crowned the
regular industry of her citizens.   But, unlike Marseilles in
one respect, no generous sister nation, no Rome of the New
World, affiliated by the endearing ties of a common and
participated refinement, stood ever ready to sympathize in
her perils, and "awe back" those modern Ligurians "who

sought to shed her blood." Mexico had to fight her battles alone,—and hitherto she had fought them successfully. But it was evident that her future safety would depend upon the continued want of consentaneous action among her scattered and tumultuary enemies,—a state of things not unreasonable to be looked for among wholly uncultivated, and of course entirely unsocial barbarians. Until these ferocious myriads should, in some way not to be expected, be brought into *union of thought and action,* and a judicious system of co-operative measures be matured and executed among them, no serious injury was to be apprehended from the irregular and unsupported inroads of separate and unconnected portions of them;—and the season of halcyon prosperity in which the Mexican nation was then reposing would be in no danger of a rude and abrupt termination. But lo! "a cloud no bigger than a man's hand," is seen faintly to dot the eastern horizon; and in the bosom of that same cloud a *Tempest* is engendering whose fury will not be allayed until a great and glorious nation shall be swept into irretrievable Ruin.

CHAPTER III.

View of the Conquest of Mexico by Fernando Cortes, with some notice of the leading historic facts connected therewith.

DETAILS heretofore given seem fully to justify the following propositions. The Mexican population of the sixteenth century had clearly emerged from the condition of primeval barbarism. They had made great and solid advances in the amelioration of their social state, and were yet steadily and actively prosecuting the career of improvement begun by their forefathers. As a people, their stock of general knowledge was considerable, and the desire of additional knowledge was everywhere manifest. The remarkable *docility* evinced by the Mexican race is even attested by the Catholic Priests of the period,—a body of men never accused of overrating the capacity of the Aborigines of the New World, or of lauding them beyond the sober requisitions of Truth and Justice.

It is time now that Fernando Cortes and his comrades in iniquity should be more formally presented to the view of the reader. It may, without extravagance, be said of this Captain General of the Inquisition called *Holy*, that his very name is suggestive of all that is mean and disgusting in sordidness and knavery, as it is equally of all that is shocking and detestable in scenes of high-handed violence and cruelty. He came to Mexico as the avowed representative of a fierce Saracenic *Fanaticism*,—eager to enforce its behests by the uplifted sword and blazing fagot; and he brought with him an excited and unscrupulous *Avarice*, whose abominable cravings could only be satisfied by the fruits of Robbery and Fraud, the destruction of Kingdoms, wide-sweeping murder, and unsparing devastation. The melancholy fate which was soon to engulf the Mexican Monarch and his people was by no means unexampled in history; a similar fate, by very similar means, had long before signalized the triumphs of the Crescent in the most refined and populous districts of Asia. But Cortes was no Mahometan in *creed*, whatever he was in conduct; and the pious votaries of Christianity have much reason to regret the perpetration of misdeeds in the name of a religion of *Peace*, which it would be indecent to suppose sanctioned either by scriptural authority or example.

It would be difficult to imagine a man better fitted in all respects for the work which lay before him, than was this same Fernando Cortes. He was born, as we are informed, in Estremadura, of Old Spain, about the year 1485—and was placed, at the early age of fourteen, under regular Ecclesiastical tutelage, at the celebrated school of Salamanca, where he is supposed to have acquired a superficial acquaintance with the Latin tongue. An exorbitant thirst for gold, with an immoderate ambition for the renown of arms, transported him first to St. Domingo, and afterwards to Cuba. In these two islands he remained long enough to become versed in all the arts of rapacious violence there prevailing, and to have the native cupidity of his heart roused to vehement action, by the tokens which he saw about him on all sides, of opulence suddenly acquired by means in the highest degree unworthy. He is reported to have been married upon one of these islands, to a woman with whom he lived for a few months unhappily; and from whom he soon separated. Some have even suggested that he owed, in part, the energetic development of his heroic attributes to the stimulus of *nuptial discord :* if this be true, it would not perchance present the only instance of a similar nature recorded in history ; though it would certainly be unreasonable to expect much of virtuous renown to be earned by a Hero who is able to boast only the vulgar inspiration, not unfrequently supplied to the most ignoble bosoms, from the turbid fount of *Disappointment.*

Such were the leading circumstances under which Cortes sought and obtained authority to take command of the expedition which the Governor of Cuba had resolved to despatch to the coast of Mexico, " in search of gold and *precious stones.*" Before any thing farther is said in reference to this same expedition, out of which events the most momentous are soon to arise, one or two additional remarks will be offered upon the character of Cortes. It is evident that he was a man of uncommon quickness of intellect ; and that, though deficient in the learning to be educed from books, he was conversant with all the ordinary springs of human conduct. He was bold, even to fearlessness, and was noted for his expertness in the use of arms of all kinds ; but, with his boldness, was associated a cool and calculating discretion, whose influence was never for an instant intermitted—save, probably, on some unexpected occasion, when his fierce passions chanced to be suddenly thrown into commotion.   He was artful in the extreme; and could ply, with wonderful dexterity, all those coarser implements of *ingratiation*, by which the sensibilities of uncultivated soldiers are ever to be swayed and directed.   His Avarice and Fanaticism have been already spoken of, as exercising a sort of joint mastery over his soul; now, just in the rear of these capital traits, came *Amativeness*—or rather a brutal, unsentimental, and undiscriminating fondness for women.   In illustration of his excessive devotion to libidinous pleasures, it may be mentioned that ere he left Cuba, his unauthorised amours had several times placed his life in serious jeopardy; and whilst on his march to Mexico, (as is recorded, with much sang-froid, by his friend and fellow-soldier, Castillo,) he was actually married, in rapid succession, to three or four different maidens, the daughters of Barbarian chieftains; and the matrimonial ceremony was most indecently administered in each case, by pious Catholic Fathers who accompanied the expedition.   Very few will feel much curiosity about the person of such a wretch; those who happen to do so, will be perhaps content to read, in the words of the Abbe de Francesco Saverio Clavigero, as follows: " Cortes was of good stature, and well proportioned, robust and active.   His chest was rather prominent, his beard black, and his eyes sparkling and amorous."

The writer just cited has thought proper to describe several of those who co-operated prominently with Cortes in the conquest of Mexico, and I again avail myself of his aid as follows: " *Alvarado* was a young man of handsome shape, and extreme agility, fair, graceful, lively, popular, addicted to luxurious pleasures, fond of gold, of which he stood in need to support his love of grandeur, and, as some authors affirm, was unscrupulous how he obtained it.   He was inhuman and violent in his conduct in some expeditions.   *Olid* was stout-limbed, dark, and double.   Both of them were very serviceable to Cortes in the Conquest; but

5 *

they proved ungrateful to him afterwards, and met with a tragical end. Alvarado died in New Gallicia, being killed by his horse, who tumbled down a precipice. Olid was beheaded by his enemies, in the square or market-place of Naco, in the province of Honduras. *Sandoval* was well-shaped, manly in stature, and of a healthy complexion. His hair was of a chestnut colour, and curly ; his voice strong and thick. He was a person of few words, but striking deeds."

The whole armament of Cortes, when he departed from Cuba, was eleven vessels, five hundred and eight soldiers, one hundred and nine seamen, sixteen horses, ten pieces of cannon, and four falconets. The sweeping observation may be here hazarded, that there was not a single man, among those above enumerated, who was not prepared in heart for the commission of criminal deeds, of whatever grade or complexion, which, in the judgment of their chosen leader, might be supposed necessary to the accomplishment of his nefarious designs.

I shall not stop to describe the difficulties which were thrown in the way of the expedition by the Governor of Cuba, in consequence of that officer's having been induced to suspect the perfect good faith of Cortes towards the Spanish Government, and himself personally ; nor do I care about dwelling upon the extraordinary address with which Cortes is said to have overcome all impediments thus arising, and to have gone forth upon the contemplated voyage to Mexico, in despite of all attempts of the civil officers to arrest his movements. All this will be found minutely explained in other books with which every one is familiar.

The reader is requested to consider Cortes and his brother adventurers to have arrived at the island of Cozumel, on their way to the Mexican coast. The 19th of February, 1519, was the day of their departure from Cuba, since which occurrence only a few other days had elapsed. And now, says the valiant Castillo, " Cortes began to take the command upon him in earnest, and our Lord was pleased to give him grace, that whatever he undertook he succeeded in." Whilst the adventurers yet tarried at Cozumel, a curious incident occurred, which will be described in the precise words of an eye-witness.* " There was, on the island of Cozumel, a Temple, and some religious idols, to which all the Indians of the neighbouring districts used to go frequently in solemn procession. One morning the courts of the Temple were filled with Indians, and curiosity having also drawn many of us hither, we found them burning odoriferous resins, like our own incense; and shortly after an old man, in a large loose mantle, ascended to the top of the Temple, and harangued, or preached, to the multitude for a considerable time. Cortes, who was present, at length called Milchorejo to him, to question him in regard to the evil doctrines which the old man was delivering. He then summoned all the caciques and chief persons to come to him, and, as well as he could, by signs and interpretations, explained to them that the idols which they worshipped were not Gods, but evil things, which would draw their souls down to hell, and that if they would remain in *brotherly* connection with us, they must pull them down, and place in their stead the crucifix of our Lord, by whose assistance they would obtain good harvests, and the salvation of their souls; with many other good and holy reasons, which he expressed very well. The priests and chiefs replied, that they worshipped those gods, as their ancestors had done, because they were kind to them; and that if we attempted to molest them, their gods would convince us of their power by destroying us in the sea. Cortes then ordered them to be prostrated, which we immediately did, rolling them down some steps. We next sent for lime, of which there was abundance in the place, and Indian masons, by whom, under our direction, a very handsome altar was constructed, wherein we placed an image of the holy

---

* Captain Bernal Diaz del Castillo.

virgin, and the carpenters having made a crucifix, which was erected in a small chapel, close to the altar, mass was said by the Reverend Father Juan Dias, and listened to by the Priests, chiefs, and the rest of the natives, with great attention." Thus was the proselyting sword of the Holy Office first unsheathed in the hands of that meek and lowly " Soldier of the Cross," Fernando Cortes ; and a practical exemplification was afforded of his determination to subject the moral world to the physical ; and, in the event of its becoming at all necessary, to resort to that very compendious method of argument, by means of which a man is able to

> " Prove his doctrine orthodox
> By Apostolic blows and knocks."

The plan of this work, as already indicated, forbids the presentation here of a minute and regular account of the wasting and sanguinary career of Cortes in Mexico. It is believed that such as have made themselves acquainted with its incidents will not be surprised by the assertion, that the conqueror held steadily in view, from the day of his landing at St. Juan de Ulloa, up to the consummation of his diversified projects, two grand objects — *the acquisition of enormous wealth for himself and his associates, and the complete establishment of the Catholic Faith in the New World.* Whether fighting, or negotiating ; alarming the natives with the thunderings of his cannon, or enforcing discipline among his rude soldiers ; revelling amidst the joys of wine, or wallowing in coarse venereal pleasures ; sojourning in the villages of his barbarous allies, or luxuriating in the polished hospitality of the imperial Montezuma,— still, still did the two great objects mentioned, command the attention of his understanding and dominate over the sensibilities of his soul. Though a professed champion of Messiah, and, as a faithful believer in his divine teachings, should have doubted the possibility of serving God and Mammon, *conjunctirely ;* yet it is evident that he had formed no conception of any scheme of Piety which excluded either the one or the other from the reception of his fervent homage.

Cortes had not been many days on *terra firma,* before his sagacity detected the true condition of things around him. He perceived clearly that no serious impression could be made upon the solid fabric of Mexican power, save in one mode : it was indispensable to bring about a perfect *consociation* of the energies of all the various native tribes, who happened at the time to be either openly at war with Montezuma, or had grown somewhat restive under his authority by reason of the large tribute which he annually exacted from them. With that extraordinary decision of character which certainly belonged to him, and that dexterity in contrivance which marked his whole course, he instantly set about the project of *uniting* all the separate fragments of hostility about his own person, as a sort of *nucleus,* or common centre; designing, of course, as soon as the whole Barbarian strength could be consolidated into a mass of sufficient magnitude, to precipitate it, as an avalanche of ruin, upon the Mexican Capital. — The means which he employed for the attainment of this purpose of *concentration* were diversified according to circumstances. Some of the native tribes are said to have been terrified into obedience to the Spanish Commander by the roaring of his artillery, which they mistook for celestial thunder ; and they are described to have been little less affected by the furious movements of the cavalry—supposing the horse and his rider to constitute but a single animal. Many of the Aborigines were captivated by extraordinary professions of amity and promises of protection against the power of the Mexican Monarch. Some were won over to the interest of the invaders by vivid pourtrayals of those scenes of bloody *revenge* to which Cortes engaged to lead them. Luxurious enjoyments, without stint or limitation, and inexhaustible treasures were held forth to all ; whilst

some of the most influential of the Barbarian chieftains were
conciliated by the cheap honours of intermarriage with their
daughters or other female relatives—the principal officers of
the Spanish army proving quite as accommodating on this
head as Cortes himself is already described to have been.
Nor did this astute *manager* decline availing himself of such
expedients as might bring the *Superstitious* notions preva-
lent among the natives to his aid ; for we learn, that through
the instrumentality of certain Catholic Priests, he was able,
without difficulty, to diffuse a very general impression among
the untutored savages, that he came among them as a special *Missionary* of Heaven, for the fulfilment of several prophecies long familiarly known to them, and which he had
discovered to be associated with their strongest religious sensibilities.   It will not be regarded as at all surprising, that
by means of the exertions described, Cortes found himself,
in the course of a few months, at the head of *two hundred
thousand* Barbarian soldiers—all eager to participate in the
conquest of a city more opulent than any other then existing ; and that, with such an army, he was able, after a siege
of seventy-five or eighty days, to take possession of that city
and to recognise himself as the undisputed master of a great
Empire.

The scenes of outrage and brutality which succeeded the
downfall of the Mexican Capital are far too hideous and
multiplied for specific recital here ; but they cannot be said
to have at all exceeded in enormity many of those presented
during the progress of the siege ; nor are we likely to survey them with stronger feelings of horror than are awakened by various acts of Cortes, recorded in regular historic
works, which were perpetrated before the formal commencement of hostilities.

From the dark catalogue of criminal acts committed in
Mexico under the direction of Cortes, a few may be arrayed
here, as more plenteously surcharged than others with the
fell spirit of the Holy Office, and of a nature, in other respects,

demanding peculiar reprobation;—such as the abominable *treachery* practised for the decoyment of the confiding Montezuma into captivity ; the tyrannous coercion resorted to with a view to extracting orders from the unfortunate Monarch to his own subjects, whose execution involved the ruin of his country; his atrocious murder ;—the indiscriminate massacre of men, women, and children ;—the sanction expressly afforded by Cortes to the most disgusting *Cannibalism* known at any time to have been practised even among savage nations ; the forcible demolition of Temples of Mexican worship, in order to make way for the establishment of Catholic Christianity.

The condition of the city when it fell into the hands of Cortes is thus described by Captain Bernal Dias del Castillo. " Guatimozin now requested of Cortes that permission should be given to clear the City entirely of inhabitants, in order to purify it and restore its salubrity. Accordingly, they were ordered to remove to the neighbouring towns ; and for three days and three nights all the causeways were full, from one end to the other, of men, women, and children, so weak and sickly, squalid and dirty, and pestilential, that it was misery to behold them. When all those who were able had quitted the City, we went to examine the state of it, which was as I have described. The streets, courts, and houses were covered with dead bodies, and some miserable wretches were creeping about in the different stages of the most offensive disorders, the consequences of famine and improper food. The ground was all broken up to get at the roots of such vegetation as it afforded, and the very trees were stripped of their bark ! There was no fresh water in the Town. During all their distress, however, though their constant practice was to feed on such as they took prisoners,* no instance occurred of their having preyed on each other ; and certainly never existed since the creation a people who suffered so much through hunger, thirst, and warfare."

---

* This last is a fact of which it would seem the Captain could hardly be certified by sufficient evidence.

The same writer thus recounts the closing scene of the Conquest : " After having returned thanks to God, Cortes determined to celebrate his success by a festival in Cuyoacan.   A vessel had arrived at Villa Rica with a cargo of wine, and bags had been provided from the island of Cuba. To this entertainment he invited all the officers of his army, and also the soldiers of estimation ; and all things being prepared, we waited on our General.   When we came to sit down to dinner, there were not tables for one half of us ; this brought on great confusion in the company, and indeed for many reasons it would have been much better let alone. The plant of Noah was the cause of many fooleries and worse things ; it made some leap over the tables, who could not afterwards go out at the doors, and many rolled down the steps.   The private soldiers swore they would buy horses with golden harness ; the cross-bowmen would use none but golden arrows.   All were to have their fortunes made. When the tables were taken away, the soldiers danced in their armour, with the ladies, as many of them as there were, but the disproportion in number was very great.   The scene was truly ridiculous.   I will not mention the names, suffice it to say, a fair field was open for satire.   Fra. de Olmido thought what he observed at the feast, and in the dances, too scandalous, and complained to Sandoval ; and the latter directly told Cortes how the reverend father was scolding and grumbling.   Cortes, discreet in all his actions, then came to him, and affecting to disapprove the whole, requested that he would order a solemn mass and thanksgiving, and preach a sermon to the soldiers on their religious duties.   Fra. Bartholome was highly pleased at this, thinking it had originated spontaneously from Cortes, and not knowing that the hint had been given him by Sandoval. Accordingly, the Crucifixes, and the images of our Lady, were borne in solemn procession, with drums and standards ; the litany was sung during the ceremony. Fra. Bartholome preached and administered the sacrament, and we returned thanks to God for our victory."   *   *   *   *   *

" Cortes now took leave of his allies, the Tascallan chiefs, and also of Tuchel, otherwise Don Carlos, a very brave man, as was another a Captain of some city near the lake, the name of which I forget ; but he did wonders. Many others who had rendered us most important services departed at the same time. Cortes dismissed them all to their homes with many embraces, thanks and compliments, promising that he would soon make them rich and great lords, and give them lands and vassals, so that they took their departure in high spirits. They had, however, secured something more substantial than promises, for they were well loaded with the plunder of Mexico ; nor were they behind the* enemy in their cannibal feasts, carrying with them portions preserved to supply their friends on their return home." Such was the sad downfall of the most ancient City of the New World, whose inhabitants had, only a few months earlier, presented that picture of serene and innocent felicity which has been faintly delineated in these pages, and which it is refreshing to contemplate even at the distance of centuries. Such was the woeful termination of a splendid sovereignty, whose greatness had been the slow work of many successive generations,—of generations, too, distinguished by the arts of enlightened industry, and embellished by high displays of heroic virtue. Such, in fine, was the dismal and hopeless ruin which had come upon a singularly moral and magnanimous people, who had earned the dominion which they wielded chiefly by the exercise of a modest and sedate wisdom, and by rigidly adhering to those judicious and wholesome principles of social polity, which, under different names, more or less

---

* So far as the suggestion of *Cannibalism* is applicable to the *Mexicans*, it must be obviously received with some allowance, since the valiant Castillo had no means of *absolute knowledge.* If human flesh was devoured by the Mexicans at all, it must have been done in obedience to the imperious necessities of famine ; as has oftentimes happened in besieged cities where the existence of civilization and humanity could not be questioned.

imposing, have been, in all ages, found, either sooner or later, to constitute the only foundation upon which the fabric of national happiness and honour can be expected permanently to repose.

Who is prepared to assert, that the Mexican people of the 16th century deserved all the sufferings imposed on them by their Spanish oppressors? who will dare even to suggest an idea so monstrous, in this enlightened age of the world,—when a mild and literate *Philosophy* has almost everywhere proved triumphant over the absurd and mischievous dogmas of a gloomy and malignant *Superstition*, and a lofty and expansive *Philanthropy* is chasing into outer darkness the deformed and monstrous brood of a rayless and unreasoning Fanaticism?

The period has gone by when such atrocities as stain the character of Fernando Cortes can be mentioned in the language of approbation; and the modern *Spoiler*, who affected to *rob* and *murder*, by the *grace of God*, and for the good of the Holy Catholic Church, can be now recognized only as a sort of " *bastard* " ALARIC, — " following him of old, with steps unequal;" exhibiting the most offensive attributes of the Gothic chieftain with aggravated hideousness, and without any of those redeeming traits which have in some degree rescued the name of Alaric from the unmitigated execration of mankind. For does not the historic page inform us that the Barbarian Commander was not without some plausible pretexts for his career of devastation? Was not the *golden tribute*, which a pusillanimous Roman Emperor had engaged to pay, as *the price of peace*, most obstinately withheld? Was not the friend of Alaric, the heroic Stilicho, most treacherously assassinated by degenerate Romans? And did not the Gothic King march against the ancient capital of the world at the bidding of myriads of his brothers in arms, who were vociferating clamorously for the necessaries of life? It is true that Alaric plundered Rome of a portion of her superfluous wealth ; it is equally true, that his soldiers committed much havoc upon private and public property during their short sojourn in Rome ; but did he not, in a few days, withdraw his barbarous legions, and permit the unhappy Romans to repair the ruin which he had caused, and once more to enjoy that repose which he was content thus transiently to have disturbed ? We are nowhere told that Alaric, like the conqueror of Mexico, plunged the whole people of Rome into a state of debasing vassalage, or that he attempted to secure to himself and his brother Goths, *in perpetuum,* all the private and public wealth of the country over which his arms had prevailed. Now, it is quite a remarkable fact, that this same Alaric, severely and *justly* as he has been denounced by various historians, was never known, in a single instance, to order or to sanction such a scene of indiscriminate massacre as that which we have just seen proceeding in Mexico ; and that the King of the Goths, though a *barbarian acknowledged*, had the *decency,** when Rome and every thing Roman lay at his mercy, to save the Christian churches of St. Peter and St. Paul from all danger of *desecration* at the hands of his rude soldiers. What must those who call Alaric a Barbarian, think of Fernando Cortes and those foul deeds of his which have been passed in review ? And yet is this same Fernando Cortes destined, in a short time, to rise into high favour at the court of Charles V., to become a noble of Spain, and, as we shall presently see, a special and confidential friend and agent of the then head of the Christian Church, the Pope of Rome.

Had Plutarch flourished in the present age of the world, and that graphic and impartial delineator of character had

* Mr. Gibbon says, in reference to the conduct of Alaric above alluded to, that whilst " he encouraged his troops boldly to seize the rewards of valour, and to enrich themselves with the spoils of a wealthy and effeminate people, he exhorted them, at the same time, to spare the lives of the unresisting citizens, and to respect the churches of the Apostles, St. Peter and St. Paul, as inviolable sanctuaries."

been requested to designate the person who, more than all others of ancient or modern times, seemed to him to resemble, both in his attributes and exploits, the famed Conqueror of Mexico, it is hardly to be doubted that the good old Grecian, of Biographic renown, would have been heard to announce the dread name of a Chieftain whose bustling and bloody career had its progress in the fifth century of the Christian era; and GENSERIC, the murdering and plundering King of the ferocious, but *fanatical* Vandals, might have been carried through a regular *comparison*, such as Plutarch delighted to institute, and in the execution of which he is acknowledged to have been so eminently successful. One who has neither desire nor expectation to be thought the Plutarch of the current generation, may be allowed to suggest that Cortes, like Genseric, as we have just seen, was an avowed and zealous champion of Christianity, and, in his capacity of a devout disciple of the religious school christened with the name of *Athanasius*, he shed at least as much blood as is supposed to have flowed at the bidding of Genseric in the maintenance of the then more approved tenets of *Arius*. Both of these *Scourges of God*, (if the self-adopted title of Attila may be applied to them,) gave evidence of the same insatiate cruelty of temper, and the same all-grasping, Crœsus-like avarice. It is quite a curious fact that both Genseric and Cortes were natives of the same country, *Spain;* and it is perhaps a circumstance not less striking, that each of them fell upon the same plan of employing uncultivated barbarians to execute grand schemes of Conquest in civilized countries; insomuch, that when we behold the Vandal monarch before the gates of Carthage, surrounded by that swarthy army of Moors, whom he had suddenly congregated from the neighbouring desert —we could almost imagine that we saw Cortes himself, at the head of his two hundred thousand cannibal Warriors, ready to pour a tide of blood and fire over the walls of the Mexican Capital. The memorable pillage of Rome by Genseric, in the year four hundred and fifty-five, of the Christian era, may be not unaptly likened to the pillage of Mexico more than a thousand years thereafter ; and when we read that Genseric diligently transported to the African Kingdom which he had lately founded, all that yet remained in Rome of sacred and profane treasure ; that he demolished the statues of Gods and heroes in his fanatical course of desolation, and that he even tore from the venerable Roman Capitol its splendid roof of *gilt-bronze*, whose fabrication had cost the enormous sum of two millions two hundred thousand pounds sterling, we find the parallel suggested to be most curiously strengthened. It is even true, that language descriptive of the characteristics of either one of these personages, will be discovered to be almost equally applicable to the other ; for it can be most correctly said of Cortes, as a distinguished modern historian* has elegantly observed in relation ' to his terrible *Prototype*, that he " could dexterously employ the dark engines of *policy* to solicit the *allies* who might be useful to his success, and to scatter among his enemies the seeds of hatred and contention ;" that " his slow and cautious speech seldom declared the deep purposes of his soul ;" that " careless of the distinction of age or *rank*, he employed every species of indignity and *torture*† to force from the captives a discovery of their hidden wealth." Throughout his whole course, Cortes was evidently sensible of no responsibility, either to the opinions of the truly upright of his own generation, or to the unbiassed judgment of posterity. He looked to the *cotemporaneous* applause of the *vicious* and the *interested* alone ; and his well-disciplined conscience was not apt to give him annoyance, provided he could succeed in the duplicate, but not at all difficult task, of conciliating both the

---

* It is perhaps unnecessary to state that this is the language of Gibbon.

† Who is not reminded in this instance of the sufferings inflicted by Cortes upon the gallant Guatamozin ?

6 *

Sovereign to whom he owed temporal allegiance—and the
Roman Pontiff, to whose hands, he devoutly believed, those
Keys had been committed which would infallibly secure
his honourable entrance within the portals of Spiritual Paradise.   Now it is known that Cortes was fortunate
enough to possess himself of the confidence and regard of
Charles V. by *gifts* of extraordinary value — a part of
the *spoils* which he had torn from the unhappy Mexicans ;
and that the monarch in question was actually *bribed* into
an avowal of respect for proceedings *confessedly* carried on
in direct opposition to *legal** authority, and, what is still
more opprobrious, shortly after showered honours and pre-
ferments upon that most magnificent malefactor, by whose
offences he now discovered he was himself about to profit
so largely.

The Pope of Rome, who arrogantly assumed to be God's
vice-gerent on earth, was won over to the interest of Cortes
with equal facility ; and as the particulars connected with
this achievement are rather curious, I choose to give them
in the very words of a cotemporaneous author† ; who
writes as follows : " Cortes now sent a gentleman to Rome,
to kiss the feet of his Holiness Pope Clement, with a rich
present of gold, and silver, and jewels. . He also sent some
of the Indians who played with the stick, and a full memorial of all the circumstances connected with the newly discovered country.   He also took this opportunity to sup-
plicate for a partial remission of tithes in New Spain.   His
Holiness, on the receipt of the letters, returned thanks to
God, for the opportunity of making so many thousand converts to the holy faith.   He also praised the services ren-

---

* This will be perfectly comprehended by those who have read, in
Robinson and other authors, who have given a regular history of Mexico, how Cortes not only came off from Cuba without the consent, and
in opposition to the wish of the Governor of that Island, but how he
actually *made open war* upon a body of soldiers sent to Mexico by that
officer for the purpose of arresting his operations.

† Captain Bernal Diaz del Castillo.

dered by us to the Church and to our Monarch, and sent us Bulls of Indulgence from penalties of our sins, with others for churches and hospitals. * * * * ** The Indians were brought to *dance* before his Holiness and the Cardinals, who expressed their high satisfaction at their performances."

The extraordinary events which had occurred in the New World were not kept long concealed from the general population of Europe ; and the fame which spread quickly through Spain in particular touching the prodigious treasures supposed to have been acquired by Cortes and his brother adventurers, very soon despatched to Mexico a vast crowd of enterprizing *soldiers of fortune,* whose numbers were almost at once sufficient to overcome all resistance which the undisciplined natives of the country were able to present to their progress. Thousands on thousands flew to a region in which Fortune was described as eager to cast her choicest gifts upon her votaries, without exacting from them any of those tedious forms of solicitation elsewhere in use. Many of these were men who had led a life of riotous debauchery in Spain ere they had left her confines, and who having exhausted all their fiscal means in dissolute pleasures, were anxious to get these means renewed again as expeditiously as possible, that they might live over once more the life so dear to them. The greater part of the emigrants were persons of the most depraved character, and had sought a residence in Mexico in order to give unrestrained license to coarse and beastly passions, in a country where they would be free from the dread of legal punishment, or even of social dishonour. The notions which all brought with them relative to the efficacy of those *plenary indulgences* then afforded to her votaries by the Church of Rome, took away one of the strongest motives which a Christian believer can feel for the performance of virtuous conduct of any kind; since they seem in the New World, however they were considered in Europe, to have had an operation,

both retrospective and prospective, and could in the twink-
ling of an eye, that is to say as soon as they were purchased
and paid for, absterge the guilty conscience of man or woman from sins of any number or complexion which had
been already committed, and yield a generous latitude for
the time to come.   The Church of Rome had promulgated
to all her spiritual vassals for several centuries, and did so
at this period with especial emphasis, that the warfare committed upon any *unbelieving* people was in no respect either
impious or censurable, but, on the contrary, was doing God
service and strengthening the walls of Zion in a manner
altogether commendable.   With a view to the facilitation
of these labours of love, a concourse of accommodating
Ecclesiastics stood ever ready to bring the powers of Heaven to the aid of a pious soldiery; and on several occasions, in the progress of those conflicts with the natives of
Mexico which the Spaniards carried on, it was devoutly
believed, or at least boldly asserted, that the Apostles St.
Peter and St. Paul had been *seen* to turn the tide of battle
against the *idolators* of a continent unknown to their
earthly ministrations.

Under all the circumstances detailed, it is easy to understand how the Spanish invaders of Mexico were able very
soon to recognize themselves the undisputed possessors of
an extensive territory, and could boast of having reduced
to unmurmuring subjection the whole of that savage multitude, who, after the downfall of the Mexican Empire,
alone opposed the progress of Spanish arms, and between
whose scattered and unsocial tribes, no principle of *confra-
ternity* existed which could lead to a concentration of their
strength against the *common foe.*   It should be here explained, that though Cortes had pledged his undying amity
and sure protection to that portion of the Aboriginal tribes
who had aided him in the war against Montezuma, yet that
the *Punic* faith of those *Christian barbarians* who followed
his crimson standard, did not hesitate to involve the whole

of them, and speedily, in a fate as onerous and destructive as that which had been fastened upon the remnant of the Mexican nation. Even *congeniality of wickedness* could not furnish to the late allies of Cortes a shield of security; and they were soon compelled to atone, in rigorous servitude, for the unnatural and, as they now found, *impolitic* association which they had formed with those guileful strangers, who had deluded them into a compact of iniquity and blood, from whose execution *they* were allowed to derive none of the promised advantages.

The readers of this work will be spared the pain of perusing a sickening detail of all the outrages which preceded and succeeded the establishment of New Spain as a Province of the Spanish Monarchy, to which, in fact, no human pen could do perfect justice, and a faithful picture of which, would, perhaps, require colourings fitted to reflect the horrors of Pandemonium itself.* For it is true, as an accomplished British historian has declared, that " in almost every district of the Mexican Empire, the progress of the Spanish arms was marked with blood. In the country of

---

* It is worthy of observation, that precisely such scenes as the Spaniards are accused of contriving, for the benefit of the New World, the most eloquent historian that Spain has yet produced, describes as having been brought on that country itself early in the fifth century, by the Suevi, the Vandals, and the Alani; and the language of Idatius may be applied, without danger of exaggeration, to the conduct of his own countrymen in another hemisphere. " The irruptions of these nations," says Idatius, " was followed by the most dreadful calamities: as the barbarians exercised their indiscriminate cruelty on the fortunes of the Romans and the Spaniards; and ravaged, with equal fury, the cities and the open country. The progress of famine reduced the miserable inhabitants to feed on the flesh of their fellow-creatures; and even the wild beasts, who multiplied without control in the deserts, were exasperated by the taste of blood, and the impatience of hunger, boldly to attack and devour their human prey. Pestilence soon appeared, the inseparable companion of famine; a large proportion of the people were swept away; and the groans of the dying only excited the envy of surviving friends. At length the barbarians, satiated with carnage and rapine, and affected by the contagious evils which themselves had introduced, fixed their permanent abodes in the depopulated country."

Panuco, sixty caciques, or leaders, and four hundred nobles were burnt at one time; and to complete the horror of the scene, the children and relations of the wretched victims were compelled to be spectators of their dying agonies."*

It surely could not be reasonably expected, that an empire, purely *physical*, established by such vile means, and upheld by arts repugnant to all the principles of natural justice and humanity, could become animate with an enduring vitality, or that it could, by any possibility, prove wholesome in its influence upon any portion of those located within the circle of its action. Even the dreadful memory of such inordinate and astounding crimes as have been either related or alluded to, diffusively retained among a whole people, could not but degrade the sense of public honour, extinguish all generous aspirations for virtuous renown, and ultimately make *vice* and *vicious men* triumphant over the best and most enlivening hopes which belong to man in this uncertain and troublous state of being.

It is possible that the view just presented may appear to some minds somewhat more fanciful than solid; it will, therefore, be expedient, in due season, to specify certain well-attested causes, whose efficacy was early felt in Mexico, after it became an appanage of the Spanish crown, which continued to operate, with undiminished energy, for centuries, and the unpropitious influence of which is even yet plainly exhibited. A careful and dispassionate examination of the causes alluded to will be necessary, to enable us to account, upon rational principles, for various strange moral phenomena hereafter to be noticed; and will, perchance, also open to the view of some, what they have not heretofore distinctly perceived, *certain grand consequences, now in a course of active developement, the progress of which no earthly power will probably be able to arrest, and no sophistry, on either side of the Atlantic, can succeed much longer in concealing or mystifying.*

* Robinson.

CHAPTER IV.

Comparative view of various instances of National Conquest; with special observations on the General Moral Effect of the Conquest of Mexico upon the Aboriginal or Native population.

HUMAN good and evil being chiefly *comparative*, and the transactions of men, so far as they constitute suitable materials for public history, presenting to the view only different mixtures of *Vice* and *Virtue*, of *Ignorance* and *Wisdom*, it is plain that we must be greatly facilitated in our efforts to fix the merit or demerit, the glory or the infamy of particular measures, or systems of measures, by taking a sort of *collective* retrospect of the admonitory *Past*, and appropriately arranging, for the purpose of *relative* examination, such capital occurrences as belong to the same generic class or order, without special regard to the place *where*, or the time *when* such occurrences may have severally had their progress in the world. *Then*, if we take care to shut out the Syren *Prejudice* from our councils, we may reasonably hope that the conclusions which we shall attain may prove not wholly valueless to ourselves and to others. In such a comparative survey as has been suggested, no portion of human history is better calculated to awaken and reward a rational and liberal curiosity than that which presents noted instances of the sudden overthrow of nations and dynasties, of political institutions and religious systems, and the establishment of others in their place, by the agency of *causes* whose efficiency, both in the work of demolition and re-construction, has been chiefly derived from *Arms*. Sesostris of Egypt is acknowledged to have figured as the earliest projector of extensive schemes of conquest by the sword, of whom authentic intelligence has reached the present age. His soul was inflamed with the wild and absurd ambition of forcing the entire human race to confess his supremacy; he was vain enough to covet the glory that he imagined to belong to the character of a *Universal* CONQUEROR; and if the accounts which we have received of him be correct, he was quite as successful as any of those Demigods of fame who have sought to imitate his example in subsequent times; for, commencing his terrible career amidst the arid sands of Ethiopia, he rapidly extended his sway in every direction, and in the short space of nine years received homage as the Lord of Lords, and the Sovereign of Sovereigns, from the Ganges in Asia to the European Danube. But it is worthy of observation that Sesostris did in no instance sweep away or even seriously modify the civil and social regulations which he found prevailing among the nations whom he subdued; he reduced not a single people to unconditional servitude; and with a moderation doubtless inspired by satiety of conquest, he contented himself finally with reigning peacefully and paternally over Egypt and a few adjacent provinces, beyond the limits of which, even in the generation which followed his decease, no vestiges of his triumphant career were anywhere to be discerned.

The ancient Kingdom of *Assyria* presents a picture not dissimilar in reference to the point under consideration : the various dynasties which there succeeded each other, from Nimrod to Sardanapalus, from Sardanapalus to Nebuchadonazor; from the conquest of Babylon by Cyrus the Great, up to the dethronement of his degenerate descendant by Smerdis, and the elevation of Darius Hystaspes as victor over the Magian usurper; are alike exempt from the dark dishonour of involving at any time a whole people in the nameless woes which wait upon a state of absolute servitude; except, indeed, so far as the inhabitants of Palestine may be regarded as forming an exception. But it may be observed in passing, that the unfortunate posterity of Abraham were not so circumstanced as to be allowed the privilege of consoling themselves under the sufferings which fell upon them, by the arraignment of their *visible oppressors* before the bar of moral justice; for all the evils which assailed them were attributable to the *direct agency of Heaven*—had been distinctly shadowed forth beforehand by repeated prophecies, and must be probably, therefore, viewed only as the meet retribution imposed by Almighty vengeance for *peculiar offences.* In a merely *temporal* point of view, it may be remarked, that the *geographical position* of Palestine was particularly unfortunate,—being situated between Syria and Egypt — and without the supposition of supernal agency, it is not difficult to understand how a country so desirable in many respects, should have become a subject of continual strife—first between the earlier Kings of Egypt and Assyria, and subsequently between the Ptolemies and Seleucidæ; nor is it at all surprising, either, that so desirable a prize, seized upon first by one and then by the other of these ambitious powers, should suffer somewhat from the alternate fluctuations of dominion, and that the favourite people of God were thus made to endure grievances beyond the ordinary experience of subject nations.   But even the *Babylonish captivity*,—that copious theme of inspired lamentation and declamatory rhetoric, does not seem to have approximated to the condition of unmitigated bondage: the pious dwellers in Jerusalem, it is true, were forbidden to abide in the city of their fathers, and were constrained to sojourn for a season among *idolators* whom they hated; but even these abhorred idolators permitted them still to enjoy many valuable civil rights; they were allowed, in spite of their own unbending *intolerance*, freely and publicly to worship the God of Abraham, of Isaac, and of Jacob; they exercised with impunity the precious privilege of denouncing and ridiculing their heathen enemies even in their midst; and the sacred Prophets were heard to vaticinate, with terrible energy and boldness, and in high places, in advance of coming evils; whose approach was doubtless quickened oftentimes by the magic influence of Heaven-taught prediction. Many of the Jews in Babylon were admitted to the seats of municipal rule; and the Prophet Daniel in particular, during the successive reigns of Nebuchadonazor and Cyrus, was armed, as prime minister of a great Empire, with a power and patronage which raised him almost to a level with the throne itself in point of influence and authority.

When the Persian monarchy tumbled into ruin before the irresistible genius of the Macedonian Conqueror, and the sceptre of universal dominion was transferred to the hands of the victorious Greeks, the new governments which were soon after organized by the successors of Alexander, were of a character altogether benignant; and though full equality of privileges could not be prudently acceded at once to the vanquished subjects of Darius, yet were they not despoiled of all civil freedom: their religious institutions, however absurd, were sacredly respected; and the social deprivations which they were made to feel were not more grievous than they had frequently experienced under the rule of their native monarchs. After the lapse of one or two generations only, we find the conquerors and the conquered mingling fraternally together as *one people*, claiming and enjoying the same rights and immunities in every respect, and scarcely indeed exhibiting the faintest tokens of that fierce and bloody struggle through which their fathers had so recently passed.

The revolution of a few centuries brings to our view the triumphant Eagles of all-conquering Rome, soaring with majestic impetuosity over Europe, and Asia, and Africa, and the innumerous isles which bespangle the surface of the bordering seas, " until the o'er-canopied horizon failed their rushing wings," and the august Republic was everywhere " Almighty hailed." And now were institutions founded among the prostrate nations, and principles disseminated, which quickly wrought a decided improvement in the moral condition of most of them, and were productive of a beneficial expansion of their civil liberties. The rendition of tribute was the only badge of subjection which Roman magnanimity could demand; and this tribute in most instances but little exceeded that fair recompense which the most paternal government might honourably demand in requital for protection afforded and order guarantied.

So far, the instances reviewed have been those of civilized nations falling by the fortune of war under the rule of other nations, themselves more or less civilized. The destruction of Roman power by the barbarians of the North, whose successive multitudes gradually overran and conquered the finest provinces of the Empire, offers to our contemplation a conjunction of circumstances very different. One might naturally conjecture, that the Franks, who acquired the mastery of Gaul, the Lombards, who seated themselves in Italy, and the Visigoths, who succeeded in occupying Spain, may have accompanied their respective acts of conquest with striking displays of violence and injustice; and that by them, if at all, such examples were afforded as might lend some slight show of palliation to the unmeasured atrocities which marked the progress of the Spaniards in Mexico. But in vain do we look even among the gloomy records of those times for appropriate precedents. We might almost use the language of Pyrrhus, when he first beheld a Roman army : *Among these Barbarians we discover no barbarism.* Anterior to the conversion of Clovis to Christianity, he indulged his recently acquired subjects in perfect freedom of religious faith ; and whilst the Salic and the Ripuarian usages supplied materials for the *double Code* prepared for the control of the Franks themselves, " the rude institutions of the Alemanni and the Bavarians were diligently compiled and ratified by the supreme authority of the Merovingian Kings." Clovis and his successors, " instead of imposing a uniform rule of conduct on their various subjects, permitted each people and each family of the Empire freely to enjoy their domestic institutions ;" and even the Romans themselves were not excluded from the common benefits of this legal toleration. "Every citizen, in the presence of the Judge, might declare the law under which he desired to live, and the national society to which he desired to belong."

The same accomplished historian,* from whose pages the extracts just given are drawn, informs us, that "so rapid was the influence of climate and example, that the Lombards of the fourth generation surveyed with curiosity and affright the portraits of their savage forefathers. Their heads were shaven behind, but their shaggy locks hung over their eyes and mouth, and a long beard represented the name and character of the nation. Their dress consisted of loose linen garments, after the fashion of the Anglo-Saxons, which were decorated, in their opinion, with broad stripes of variegated colours. Their legs and feet were clothed in long hose and open sandals, and even in the security of peace, a trusty sword was constantly girt to their side." But even the Lombards, savage as they unquestionably were, were not devoid of certain high moral qualities, for "this strange apparel, and horrid aspect, often concealed a gentle and generous disposition; and as soon as the rage of battle had subsided, the captives and subjects were sometimes surprised by the humanity of the victor. The vices of the Lombards were the effect of passion, of ignorance, of intoxication; their virtues are the more laudable, as they were not affected by the hypocrisy of social manners, nor imposed by the rigid constraint of laws and education."† When the Italians were able to present no further opposition to these conquering barbarians, all who survived were "divided among the strangers, and a tributary obligation was imposed, (under the name of *hospitality*), of paying to the Lombards the third part of the fruits of the earth. Within less than seventy years, this artificial system was abolished by a more simple and solid tenure. Either the Roman landlord was expelled by his strong and insolent guest; or the annual payment, a third

---

* Gibbon.   † Ibid.

of the produce, was exchanged, by a more equitable transaction, for an adequate proportion of landed property."*
The succession of Lombard " Kings is marked with virtue
and ability ; the troubled series of their annals is adorned
with fair intervals of peace, order, and domestic happiness ;
and the Italians enjoyed a milder and more equitable government than any of the other kingdoms which had been
founded on the ruins of the Western Empire."†

To the mind of an *over-orthodox* Christian, it might almost seem indecent to seek the illustration of grave moral
principles by the citation of Heathen examples ; and in the
mental scales of a *bigoted sectary*, even the precious dia-
mond of truth must submit to lose some of its weight, when
it chances to be cast into the balance from *infidel* hands.
But I am not afraid of giving offence to judgments, which
if more *profane*, are at least as *philosophic*, by invoking a
transient attention to the fierce career of the great Arabian
Prophet, and his thrice-valiant successors. We are told
that " Mahomet, with the sword in one hand and the Koran
in the other, erected his throne on the ruins of Christianity
and of Rome."‡ We know that the extirpation of obstinate unbelievers was one of the leading maxims of the
faith which he prescribed ; yet we learn with gratification,
that when the enemies of the Koran had once professed the
creed of Islam, " they were admitted to all the temporal
and spiritual benefits of the primitive disciples, and marched under the same banner to extend the religion which they
had embraced. The *clemency* of the Prophet was decided
by his *interest*, yet he seldom trampled on a *prostrate*
enemy ; and he seems to promise that on the payment of a
tribute, the least guilty of his unbelieving subjects might be
indulged in their worship, or at least in their imperfect
faith. The disciples of Abraham, of Moses, and of Jesus,
were solemnly invited to accept the more perfect revelation
of Mahomet ; but if they preferred the payment of a mo-

---

* Gibbon.   † Ibid.   ‡ Ibid.
7 *

derate tribute, they were entitled to the freedom of conscience and religious worship."* The Mahometan conquerors of Hindostan spared the Pagods of that devout
and populous country ; and when the son of the renowned
Musa had overthrown the Gothic power of Spain, and the
defenders of Christianity were compelled to imprecate the
clemency of their Mussulman conqueror, we find that the
magnanimous Abdelaziz agreed to a treaty with Prince
Theodemer, by which it was guarantied that " no injury
should be offered to the life or property, the wives and
children, the religion and temples of the Christians ;"† the
Gothic Prince stipulating only that " himself and each of
his nobles should annually pay one piece of gold, four
measures of wheat, as many of barley, with a certain proportion of honey, oil and vinegar, and that each of their
vassals should be taxed one moiety of said imposition."‡
The prosperity of Spain under the sway of the Saracens,
— the flourishing state of her agriculture, commerce, and
manufactures, constitutes the most satisfactory evidence of
the wisdom and humanity of her infidel rulers ; and seems
at least to authorise a doubt, whether the prevalence of orthodox tenets is indispensable to civil happiness. At least,
the wholesome instruction to be drawn from this domestic
example should not have been unproductive of advantage
to Spaniards of the Christian faith, in a generation not remote from it in subsequent time. But it is evident, that
the Spaniards of the fifteenth and sixteenth centuries were
unmindful of all *experience*, both Christian and profane ;
the mind of the whole nation was encrusted with a barbarous *bigotry*, which rendered it impervious to the rays of
truth of every kind ; else they surely might have reaped
some little edification from those scenes of wretchedness
which their own intolerance in religious matters was at that
moment rapidly spreading abroad among millions of their
own countrymen.

---

* Gibbon.   † Ibid.   ‡ Ibid.

Had Fernando Cortes been, *in truth*, another *Moses*, as he pretended to be, or had he been *sanctioned from Heaven*, as were the Kings and Judges of Israel in olden times —when Jehovah accompanied the march of armies to push forward the execution of his own dread mandates upon the impious Canaanites ; the simple-hearted piety which has been able to justify in the case of that *meekest* of men, who led the Israelites from bondage, the indiscriminate butchery of all the *males* found in the infidel cities, as well as the destruction of every creature bearing life, might discover much in the scourgeful career of Cortes himself worthy of special admiration and esteem. But as his claim to Apostleship, however impudently asserted, has been long since exploded, it is time that human justice should affix a proper sentence of condemnation to acts which are far beyond the reach both of vindication and atonement.

A philosophic historian,* taking a view of the Spanish character about this period, uses the following language : " At the same era, the Spaniards were the terror both of the old and new world ; but their high-spirited valour was disgraced by gloomy pride, rapacious avarice, and unrelenting cruelty. Indefatigable in the pursuit of fame and riches, they had improved, by repeated practice, the most exquisite and effectual methods of torturing their prisoners." This delineation is fully warranted by what has been already disclosed in this work ; nor is there anything hereafter to be stated calculated to relieve the general aspect of a picture far too sombre already, for pleasurable or respectful inspection.

The *leading fact* in the conduct of the Spaniards towards the Aborigines of Mexico was the indiscriminate *slavery* to which these unfortunate people were consigned ; a slavery which comprehended all the evils that could possibly accompany the deprivation of freedom ; which ex-

---

* Gibbon.

tinguished the independent exercise of the will in regard to
all affairs whatsoever, whether spiritual or temporal, political, social, or domestic; which bore equal sway over the
minds and bodies of men, demanding from its subjects not
only unremitted physical toil, but absolute obedience also in
the inner thoughts and emotions of their minds and hearts.
The work of spiritual regeneration, as it was called, certainly advanced with remarkable rapidity, if the statement
handed down to us can be confided in; for it is recorded
that in a few years more than four millions of the natives
had been dragged through the baptismal font; and that the
Catholic Fathers were active in their vocation, may be inferred from the striking instance of one of their number
having been heard to boast that he had himself baptized
five thousand converts in a single day, and had even then
desisted from his pious labours in consequence of bodily
exhaustion.   Nothing seems to have occurred to tarnish
the splendour of the triumph thus in a course of achievement over the powers of darkness, save the invidious doubt
suggested by some of the missionaries who had not been
quite so successful in proselyting as others of their brethren,
relative to the capacity of the natives to digest the complex
plan of salvation expounded to them.   It is even said, that
one or two of these sceptical Fathers went so far, on several occasions, as publicly to declare the new recipients of
Gospel grace to be more nearly assimilated to *brutes* than
men, in their moral conformation; and that they even denied
to them the honour of a lineal descent from the illustrious
pair who erst reigned in Paradise.   It is certain that a council of Ecclesiastics, who convened at Lima, some years
after, determined the whole Aboriginal race to be too deficient in understanding to be allowed the privilege of participating in the Eucharistic celebration.   Happily though
for the spiritual interests of the natives, as well as for the
peace of the Catholic Church, Pope Paul the Third thought
proper to terminate all controversy on a point so exciting

by a solemn declaration, that the Aborigines of America were, one and all, rational creatures, and as such, must be held entitled to all the privileges and immunities of the most favoured Christians.

It is almost unnecessary to state, that the extraordinary rapidity with which the natives were brought into the pale of Christianity, was the effect, in a great degree, either of *force* actually put in exercise, menaces of intended violence, the seductive promise of reward, or the bestowal of contemptible donatives.

But the subjugation of the *moral* man is never complete, nor can such a subjugation prove at all permanent, whilst the *physical* man remains in the possession of unrestricted freedom of action. And this truth was well known to those who controlled the early colonial concerns of Mexico; which explains, in some degree, why it was that the whole body of the native population were apportioned out among tyrannical task-masters, as so much live stock, and coerced, by repeated and severe chastisements, to the performance of services degrading to their sense of self-respect, revolting, in some instances, to the best affections of the soul, and deeply perilous in others to their bodily health. It is undeniably true, that they were not allowed to hold any property, either real or personal ; were not permitted to enter into pecuniary contracts of any kind whatever ; nor were they recognized as capable of performing civil acts of the most inferior grade, without the consent of their rigorous owners. I shall not undertake to discuss the odious system of the *Repartimientos ;* nor shall I endeavour to ascertain to what precise extent the iron bonds of slavery were relaxed, by the substitution of what is called the *Encomiendas.* Humanity shrinks from the melancholy pursuit of the wretched victims of Spanish cupidity into the gloomy caverns of the earth, where they died by thousands in digging for mineral treasures ; and it is sufficient to state, in general terms, that the shackles of oppression, imposed on

the Aboriginal inhabitants of Mexico, continued to hold
them in cruel servitude for full three centuries; that during
this whole period, they were cautiously retained in the most
debasing ignorance, and excluded from the enjoyment of
all civil rights; and that their descendants, who now constitute so large a proportion of the eight millions confusedly
spread over the surface of the miscalled Mexican Republic,
Christians and Catholics though they claim to be, in regard
to all the graces and capabilities which belong to the truly
civilized condition, are far inferior to those of their ancestors, who tenderly wept over the sufferings of the imperial
Montezuma, or who rushed to a desperate revenge, at the
bidding of the gallant Guatamozin. Their general character is marked with a thousand incongruities which de-
note its *embryon* state; and strange and startling repug-
nancies bear witness of the violent action of numerous antagonizing influences. They are, at the same time, servile
and licentious; timid and irresolute, yet impetuous and sanguinary; mean and grovelling, yet vain and ostentatious;
profoundly obedient to military power, yet utterly regardless of legal or moral obligation; savagely superstitious,
yet dissolute and profane beyond any people now known in
any part of the world.

CHAPTER V.

Examination of the Spanish Colonial Policy, and its effects, in a moral
point of view, upon the general colonial population. Rapid citation
of leading historical particulars connected with the Revolution in
Mexico, resulting in the establishment of the Federal Constitution
of 1824.

VIRTUE secures its own reward, and vice provides its
own punishment in more than one sense: and perhaps

there has never been an instance of sweeping and deliberate injustice inflicted upon a whole race of human beings, which has not been, sooner or later, in one shape or another, succeeded by the outpouring of retributive vengeance. Even-handed justice may, and doubtless often does, defer the promulgation of her sentence for a season; but she never fails, ultimately, to commend the poisoned chalice to the lips of the guilty, who are often seen to quaff the destructive draught prepared for their intended victims, without a due percipience of the baleful ingredients which have entered into its composition. The enslavement of a great and heroic people, as were unquestionably the subjects of Montezuma — the perpetuation of their servitude through a long course of generations, unbrightened by a single ray of comfort or consolation — the habitual exercise of grinding oppression and wanton cruelty, which was one of the natural incidents to such a system as had been established by the Spaniards in Mexico — could not be otherwise than deeply degrading to all the immediate actors in this nefarious abuse of power; and the brutifying influence of such scenes as Mexico was by such means made to present to view continually, rendered it almost impossible that many, even of those who were mere spectators of these horrors, could escape from that dark gulf of social pollution which the cupidity and cruelty of the early Spaniards were rapidly digging beneath their own feet. The immutable principles of natural equity could not be expected to gain ascendancy, or long command even a nominal regard, among wretches already in open rebellion to their sacred authority. The sentiments of a refined and generous Philanthropy had no opportunity of taking root and flourishing vigorously in a region where all enlightened notions of *order* and *right* had been already completely obliterated, and in which the disruption of all those ties of good-fellowship which knit and affiliate members of the same social community with each other, was constantly occurring. The restraining, though inspiring sense of *individual honour*—that efficient auxiliary of virtue in noble bosoms—was never for an instant domiciliated in Mexico; nor was it even indeed possible that a principle so elevated could obtain sway among miscreants who imagined the highest glory of man to consist in his capability of successfully accomplishing exploits of violence and knavery. It is true, that the Spaniards who first settled in Mexico had little to apprehend from the contaminating influence of scenes which they might chance to encounter, after leaving their natal land: they had departed not from the limits of Spain, to try the chances of a new hemisphere, ere they had become thoroughly accomplished, according to the manner of their country, in all that was necessary to fit them for the grand emprise before them. The names of most of them had long been high enrolled upon the lists of infamous renown; and they had nothing more to learn of *vice* in any of its modes; and were, perhaps, better qualified in all respects than any body of men besides who have yet figured in history, to organize and take charge of a regular *Pandemonean University,* (if it be not too great a stretch of fancy even to imagine such a monstrous institution,) which being divided into numerous Professorships — correspondent with the various Departments of Crime, should be kept open night and day for the indoctrination of men of all nations in the manifold mysteries of *Iniquity.* Such were the Spanish emigrants on *their arrival* in Mexico, as they have indeed been more than once described. It remains to be stated, that they seem afterwards to have been occupied, from day to day, and from year to year, in swelling the dark catalogue of offences, with the consciousness of whose commission their inmost souls were embruted; and thus did they necessarily grow every moment less capable of appreciating the precious, but perishable treasures of social concord, or of aspiring to compass for themselves and their posterity, the priceless blessing of *organized Civil Liberty.*

But there were other causes of a more substantive and definite nature, which contributed still more powerfully to impress upon the general mass of Mexican population, characteristics highly unfavourable to their eventual advancement in the pathways of social honour, and to involve them, as a people, in a destiny of woe and degradation, in the iron grasp of which they will, in all probability, remain to the end of time—contemptible in the estimation of civilized nations, and powerless for all purposes of good ; flashing out perchance, now and then, with a sort of fitful convulsive energy, but unable to make a regular and healthful progress in any design of true *practical utility ;*—not unlike the fabled Giant of antiquity, who, whelmed by Jupiter beneath Mount Etna, and firmly chained within the precincts of his dungeon, is supposed to disclose his tenacious retention of muscular vigour, by forcing the superincumbent mountain, as he rolls from side to side of his huge prison-house, to evomit dark clouds of sulphurous smoke and streams of consuming fire. The additional causes alluded to will be now briefly noticed ; those who desire a more minute detail, are referred to the appropriate works.

The grand objects held in view by the Spanish government in encouraging and patronizing projects of conquest in America, were of a nature exclusively and intensely *selfish ;* it was hoped, that by means of the treasures expected to be procured in the new world, the King of Spain, then openly aspiring to *absolute Despotism* as well as *universal Empire,* would be able greatly to strengthen his authority over his own subjects, and both extend and consolidate the ascendancy of Spain among the powers of Europe. The plan of *colonization* adopted, therefore, was framed upon principles judged most likely to forward the objects mentioned. All grants of territory in America were made with a cautious reserve of *one fifth* of all the *gold* and *silver* which might be thence obtained. Regulations were devised for the purpose of confining the operations of the colonists to the business of *mining* exclusively. Discouragement, and even prohibition, was laid upon the raising of any agricultural product in the colonies which was already successfully grown in Spain, with a view to shielding the population of the mother country against the injurious effects of a *competition* with the colonists, in articles adapted to the soil and climate of America.   A commercial system was set on foot which denied to the colonies all *direct* interchange of commodities with other nations of the world save Spain herself; and all commercial operations whatever, were confined strictly to Spanish bottoms.   The trade, even between colony and colony, was, if not absolutely interdicted, so grievously trammelled with restrictions, as to be almost impracticable. Every vessel leaving the colonies, freighted with articles of colonial growth or manufacture, was constrained, under the heaviest penalties, to proceed to Spain in the first place, and withheld from the privilege of touching, for an instant, at intermediate ports of other nations.   Such were the leading features of the *colonial policy of Spain.*   It will be at once perceived, that, independently of the deleterious operation of such a system upon the agricultural and commercial interests of the colonies, (with which I have nothing to do;) and, aside from its influence in checking the tide of emigration flowing into the colonies, (upon which no remark will be offered;) the unavoidable effect of regulations such as have been described was *to shut up the colonial settlements as to all information* of any kind whatever, save what might chance to be received from Spain herself;—to bring about a complete *stagnation of mind in the colonies,* and to obstruct even the desire of improvement in their social condition.   This state of things will be regarded as particularly deplorable, when it is remembered, that at the period under review, the whole civilized world, except Spain herself, Portugal, and a portion of Italy, was at last emergent from the hideous mental eclipse of the dark ages, and that *Science,* aroused from her long sleep, and re-animated with more even than her ancient energy, was plainly to be seen refixing her lamps along the whole moral horizon, in token of that surpassing resplendency of knowledge which has illumined and glorified these latter days of the world, as with radiance from the throne of God. Spain, Priest-ridden, Inquisition-cursed, Truth-murdering Spain, still sternly refused to permit the beauteous Aurora of Regeneration to penetrate within those borders of hers, where blood-nursed and fire-wielding *Superstition* yet sat grimly but gorgeously enthroned, and where *dishumanized* millions trembled beneath the terrible waving of her Hell-derived Sceptre. It was, therefore, wholly impossible that from Spain, had the Colonists been willing to receive instruction from any quarter, they could have received the *kind* of instruction fitted to impart dignity to their aspirations, and elevation to their aims. Indeed, under such circumstances, it would not be extravagant to declare, that Prometheus himself would have turned hopeless from the task of dispersing the darkness which was fast thickening over the beautiful hills and valleys of the new-found Ausonia of the Western Hemisphere.

It is possible, that such as are inclined to confide strongly in the reforming efficacy of well-ordered civic institutions, may indulge the supposition, that had the early Spanish settlers brought with them to Mexico a system of Jurisprudence similar, or not inferior, in wisdom, to that which is known as the common law of England; — had they been permitted to live under the wholesome and enlightening influence of the *Right of Trial by Jury;* — had they been habitually called to the high task of choosing their own Legislative functionaries, and allowed at pleasure to convene in primary assemblies for the purpose of free consultation upon questions of public moment; — at some remote period of their history, in spite of the numerous difficulties which encumbered them, they might possibly have realized something like a plan of free government, and have become not wholly unworthy to enjoy its benefits.   But, under the circumstances which actually supervened, the disqualifying action of which was so long continued, such a consummation was as impossible in the nature of things, as the accomplishment of the wildest vision ever conjured up in the fancy of Eutopian dreamer.   For, instead of a judicious and matured system of Juridical polity, the population of Mexico, since the commencement of Spanish rule, have been destitute of any code of laws whatever having a regular and uniform operation.   The Judicial tribunals established by the Spanish government were nothing more than clumsily contrived machines of Despotism, set on foot for the purpose of giving additional energy to the tyrannical mandates of the Crown; and, from the Supreme Court of Audience, down to the pettiest Alcade, the dispensers of what was misnamed Justice, were notoriously controlled in their decisions by the grossest bribery and the most abominable chicanery. All civil officers, of whatever grade or quality, derived the power which they exercised directly or indirectly from the Spanish Crown, and were in no sense responsible to the body of the colonists.   There was no public station which could not be purchased with money, and that by the most profligate wretch to be found, provided always he was a *native Spaniard ; for this was an indispensable qualification for office.*   The general population were in all respects as complete slaves as ever were the Copts of Egypt, or the modern inhabitants of Greece.   Learning was not only not patronised by government, but the establishment of schools for its propagation was prohibited under severe penalties. The whole country swarmed with Catholic Priests, who, being of *gregarious* habitudes, came over by scores in every vessel which came across the Atlantic.   Every Catholic university in Europe annually sent forth a greater or smaller number of these " saints in lawn," *nominally* to sow the seeds of spiritual regeneration in the wilderness,—*actually*, to gather the temporal *loaves and fishes* with which the New

World was represented as abounding. A majority of these same Priests were the most dissolute of human kind, and were no otherwise distinguishable from the common mass of colonial population, save by their superior debauchery. The King of Spain had become the acknowledged Head of the Catholic Church in all the Spanish colonies in America, and in that capacity, made large profit by the sale of Ecclesiastic benefices. Every Second Year, the famous Bull of Crusado was hawked about through all the colonial settlements; by means of which *absolution for past* offences, and *indulgence* touching those desired by the faithful to be committed *in future*, were transferred to all willing purchasers. Early in the history of the colony of New Spain, the Holy Office had been introduced, and all the worst effects which had accompanied its operations in the mother country had been abundantly realized.

Such is an imperfect, but certainly not a distorted or overdrawn description of the state of things in Mexico during the whole period that the country remained under Spanish control. In this condition, with slight and transient exceptions only for the better, did affairs remain up to the seizure of Spain by Napoleon Buonaparte early in the present century, and the *forced abdication* of the pusillanimous Ferdinand VII. in favour of Joseph Buonaparte; which event now suddenly raised certain questions in all the Spanish colonies, which were found quite difficult of solution. These questions were as follows: Would it be most politic tamely to submit to the new Ruler assigned them, in conformity with the example of Spain herself, and thereby become a mere appanage of Imperial France? Or, shunning this disgrace, should the colonists continue a profitless allegiance to a dethroned monarch, until some turn in the wheel of Fortune might perchance restore that monarch to the throne? Or, should they boldly embrace the opportunity, so unexpectedly presented, of setting up for themselves, as a single or as many *independent* States? And well might these same questions prove troublesome to

8 *

such a population as now existed throughout the Spanish Colonies; for among that population there were no tokens anywhere apparent as yet of a distinctive *public sentiment ;* scarcely a twentieth part of the inhabitants were at all acquainted with the Alphabet, and even the better-informed enjoyed no regular means of interchanging opinions with each other relative to the crisis upon which they had been thrust in a manner so unlooked-for. Popular meetings, for the discussion and decision of political questions, had never been even heard of in Mexico ; the power of the Newspaper Press, as a scatterer of intelligence, and a stimulant to concentrated popular action, had never been felt, and was imperfectly if at all comprehended. Scenes of confusion and violence soon ensued, such as no age or country ever before exhibited ; which finally eventuated, more by good luck than otherwise, in the establishment of what has been flatteringly termed the Mexican *Republic ;* which, in truth, has never more deserved an appellation so honourable, than did the Buccaneers who were once the terror of the South American Coast, or the Pirates of Algiers, of Tunis, and Tripoli, who so long Hectored it successfully over the Mediterranean trade of all civilized nations, even in our own times.

It may be profitable to ascertain the views of enlightened friends of freedom elsewhere than in Mexico, touching the moral capabilities of the Mexicans of the nineteenth century ; and in the United States especially, and in other countries perhaps, the judgment of Thomas Jefferson on the subject will be held entitled to more than common respect. As late as the year 1817, this distinguished gentleman, writing to the Marquis De La Fayette, used the following strong and decided language : " I wish I could give better hopes of our Southern brethren. The achievement of their independence of Spain is no longer a question. But it is a very serious one, *what will then become of them ?* Ignorance, and bigotry, like other insanities, are incapable of self-government. They will fall under *military despo-*

tisms, and become the murderous tools of the ambition of their respective Buonapartes ; and whether this will be for their greater happiness, the rule of one only has taught you to judge. No one, I hope, can doubt my wish to see them and all mankind exercising self-government, and capable of exercising it. But the question is, not what we *wish*, but what is *practicable?* As their sincere friend and brother, then, I do believe the best thing for them, would be for themselves to come to an accord with Spain, under the guarantee of France, Russia, Holland, and the United States, allowing to Spain a nominal supremacy, with authority only to keep the peace among them, leaving them otherwise all the powers of self-government, until their experience in them, their emancipation from their poverty, and advancement in information, shall prepare them for complete independence. I exclude England from this confederacy, because her selfish principles render her incapable of honourable patronage, or disinterested co-operation : unless, indeed, what seems now probable, a revolution should restore her to an honest government, one which will permit the world to live in peace." The history of Mexico, as well as of most of the republics, so to style them, of South America, has furnished conclusive proofs of the soundness and accuracy of Mr. Jefferson's views concerning them, as herein expressed ; and the prophetic language indulged by the American sage, a little more than twenty years since, has been most signally verified in Mexico, where the unhappy people have more than once succumbed " under military despotism," and have " become the murderous tools of the ambition " not of one, but several successive unprincipled imitators of Buonaparte. And at the present moment, as in due time will appear, the Mexican population are as evidently deficient in all those high faculties of soul and understanding, which can alone confer the sublime capability of *self-government*, as they have ever been at any former period of their wretched history.

Almost as much has been said already relative to Mexico and Mexican concerns, as was originally designed by the author, and perhaps more than has been altogether agreeable to some of my readers. It is hoped, though, that the importance of all that has been offered on this head will be appreciated in the sequel, and discovered to be materially contributory to the main object of the work.

There is certainly nothing in the wars, or series of wars, which began their course in Mexico, in 1808, and that cannot be asserted even yet to have found their termination, which would prove at all interesting to the *judicious* student of historic narrative. Who, for instance, could feel much interest in such details as the following:

Of the two factions arrayed against each other, in the year 1808, one of them, consisting chiefly of persons of European birth, espoused the pretensions of Joseph Buonaparte; whilst the other, embracing most of the Creoles, or native Americans, adhered to the cause of Ferdinand VII. A Junta is convoked by the Spanish vice-roy, Iturrigaray, in the capital, for the purpose of framing a provisional government. That same vice-roy is forcibly seized in his palace, and transported with his family to Spain, at the instance of the European, or Buonaparte faction, under an apprehension of the rise of a hostile Creole influence. A general insurrection of the Creole population is the consequence; at the head of a wretched mob of whom, amounting to some twenty thousand persons, a madcap priest, *Hidalgo* by name, proclaims a general *destruction of the Guachapins*, or European Spaniards, which he carries into effect, as far as he is able, in a most ferocious and sanguinary manner; storms the city of Guanaxuato, where he obtains *plunder to the amount of five millions of dollars* —the Spaniards, with all who are found adhering to them, being basely murdered by the Indians under his command. This band of *robbers* increase rapidly in number, and assume the title of *Patriots*. Hidalgo has been able to give to each of his soldiers *five hundred dollars in gold and silver ;* the intelligence of which fact spreading through the country, he soon finds himself surrounded by one hundred and ten thousand undisciplined brigands, and takes his way to the neighbourhood of the capital. These brigands are all of them armed simply with *clubs,* except about one thousand of them, who have got possession of muskets. Great alarm is excited by this movement among the European authorities at Mexico, who resort to spiritual weapons of defence, alone, in the first instance. *Excommunication* is thundered forth against Hidalgo and his insurrectionary host, by ecclesiastical potentates at the capital, who are interested in upholding the existing government, and keeping down the Creole population. Hidalgo's one hundred and ten thousand are greatly alarmed in turn by this spiritual artillery, and begin to abandon their leader, who is forced to make a precipitate and confused retreat. The fugitives are rapidly pursued by two thousand regular soldiers, in the pay of the government, which last are supplied with artillery. Hidalgo's huge army is signally defeated by the forces of Calleja, amounting only to six thousand men, though the warrior-priest yet has under his command more than a hundred thousand Creoles ; which disaster occurs at a place called *Aculco.* Calleja enters into Guanaxuato as a conqueror, and threatens that he will " purge the city of its rebellious population." He faithfully executes this threat, by dragging thousands of men, women, and children, to the great square of the city, and having their *throats cut* — a method of destruction avowedly resorted to in order to avoid the unprofitable consumption of *powder and ball.* The whole course of Calleja, through the cities, towns, and villages, of the adjacent country, is marked with similar outrages, for the perpetration of which he is highly commended in Spain, and is shortly afterwards elevated to the Spanish peerage, as *Count Calderon.*

Calleja pursues Hidalgo still farther ; the latter having

yet eighty thousand Creole soldiers under his command. A battle is fought at the bridge of Calderon, between the opposing armies, in which Hidalgo is completely routed, and compelled, with a few of his officers and a hundred or two soldiers, to fly in the direction of San Luis Potosi,—designing to seek refuge, ultimately, in the province of Texas. But Hidalgo does not reach Texas, for he is intercepted by a body of soldiers sent for the purpose by the Governor of the Internal Provinces, and being betrayed by *Bustamente*, one of the officers of his own staff, is transported to Chihuahua, in the Intendency of Durango, where he is publicly shot, on the 27th of July, 1811. All these transactions are passed by, as unworthy of comment, and of as little importance to the general welfare of mankind as would be the encounter of two menageries of wild beasts suddenly let loose upon each other by rival proprietors. There was no *principle* involved in the furious strife then waging. There was no struggle going on for *Liberty*, or even for *National Independence*. Both the contending parties were avowed devotees to *monarchy ;* both paid servile homage to a corrupt priesthood. The objects held in view, on the one side, were, *Plunder and Destruction to the Guachapins ;* on the other, *Plunder and Destruction to the Creoles.*

Such was the state of things in 1811 : I trace, in a manner almost as summary, the stream of events up to the year 1824, when the Mexican *Federation* was organized. During the same year, 1811, the remnant of the army formerly commanded by Hidalgo, falls under the command of an individual named *Rayon* — a lawyer by profession — and is very soon entirely dispersed. A desultory and unsparing warfare, meanwhile, is proceeding between small bodies of the opposing factions, in different parts of the country, who reciprocally deal out death and devastation on all sides. No attempt at the formation of government is yet made. About this period, *Morelos*, another Priest, doffs the ministerial robes, and commences his career as a military chieftain, at the head of 7000 men. He overruns rapidly the whole Western and Southern portions of New Spain. Associated with Morelos, is still another Priest, *Matamoras*, who evinces more talent for conducting military movements than any of the sacred brotherhood who had adopted the profession of arms. During the whole of the year 1813, Callejo, who commands still for the government, is unable to make head against the army of Morelos, which has become a vast multitude. Morelos convokes a *Congress ;*—strange name for an assembly such as this turns out to be ! Thus, a *pageant* of government at last appears ; but it is indeed only a pageant ; and, after fluttering for a moment in the view of men, it will shortly disappear for ever.

Meanwhile, *Toledo* has invaded the Northern Intendencies, and is defeated — of which something more will be said hereafter, and certain chivalrous Anglo-Americans, associated with Toledo, will be then introduced to the reader. Let us return now to Matamoras, who has been attacked by the army of the government, under *Iturbide*, and signally routed ; he has been still more unfortunate, for falling into the hands of Iturbide, as a prisoner, he has been put to death. A short time after this, Morelos is himself surprised whilst at the head of a small body of cavalry, taken prisoner, conveyed into the camp of the government army, and handed over to the Holy Office, in his capacity of Priest, by whom he is tried upon a charge of *heresy*, and convicted ; after which, he is handed back to the military authorities, who try him, as a subject of Ferdinand VII., on an accusation of *treason ;* of which offence being convicted also, he is sentenced to death ; which death is inflicted by *shooting in the back*. This occurs in the autumn of 1815.

The *Congress* which has been referred to, does not long survive Morelos, its author ; for the members of that Congress, who had attended, during the life of Morelos, upon all the movements of his army, after his decease, pursuing their route to *Tehuacan*, and venturing to issue certain Legislative Decrees from that place, Don Manuel Mien Y. Teran, commander-in-chief in that quarter, suspecting certain members of the body of being unfriendly to his interests, despatches a chosen band of soldiers to the hall of congressional session, arrests most of the members, and finally dismisses all of them, respectively, to their proper places of abode.

After this dissolution of Congress, the military commanders in the different provinces, no longer considering themselves subject to any superior authority, openly assume the character of *Independent Chiefs* in their respective jurisdictions—all avowing deadly hostility to Teran. During this whole period, the *Independents*, as they style themselves, but to speak more accurately, the *Creole faction*, profess a zealous devotion to King Ferdinand, and claim constantly to be an integral portion of the Spanish monarchy. In the meanwhile, several other chiefs, besides those who have been named, have been operating in various parts of the Viceroyalty, and distracting the movements of the government very seriously. Don Guadalupe Victoria has secured the strong-holds in the province of Vera Cruz: Osourno is spreading terror and confusion in the province of Mexico; whilst Dr. Coss, another Priest in armour, the Rayons, Bustamente, Liceaga, and other officers, now occupy great part of the provinces of Guanaxuato, Valladolid, Zacatecas, and Guadalaxara. Small bands of *Guerrillas*, acknowledging no superior, are constantly in motion and ravaging the whole country.

This state of affairs continues, with unimportant exceptions, up to the Autumn of 1816, when the celebrated Don Xavier Mina arrives, with three vessels, at the island of Galveston, in the Province of Texas, intending to proceed to some point on the coast of New Spain, in the neighbourhood of Vera Cruz, and if practicable, effect a junction with the forces of Victoria and give efficient aid to the cause of the Patriots. After remaining at Galveston some weeks to refit, he sets sail; and not having been able to establish a communication with Victoria, nor knowing where precisely to find him, he lands his little body of soldiers, composed almost entirely of natives of the United States, and amounting altogether to not quite *three hundred men*, in the vicinage of the Town of Soto la Marina on the river Santander, in the colony of that name, and proceeds to take possession of the town, which he occupies without opposition. And here I am strongly tempted to diverge from the course of narrative marked out, and dwell for a moment upon the heroic achievements of these three hundred Anglo-American soldiers; but I forbear, in consideration of the full justice which they have long since received in a work* specially devoted to the celebration of their deeds; a work which all would do well to peruse who desire to comprehend perfectly the vast superiority of soldiers whose bosoms are inspired with the true love of freedom, and who have been reared under the influence of free institutions, over wretches, in human shape, who have been so long accustomed to the chains of bondage that they listen to their clanking, as if the sweet harmony of musical sounds were vibrating upon the enraptured ear. To pursue the stream of narrative. Nothing important grows out of the enterprise of Mina; he is successful in numerous undertakings: the royalist forces are never known *to stand a regular charge of musquetry* made by his valiant soldiers; they fly before him wherever he appears; on one occasion, he defeats a body of **1700** men; but his numbers are too inconsiderable to accomplish any decisive movement. In a few months, we see him surprised at an obscure hacienda, when but few of his troops are about him, and subjected to the same ignominious death which has already befallen so many of the Patriot commanders and soldiers. This re-

---

* Robinson's Memoirs of the Mexican Revolution.

nowned commander is publicly shot in cold blood. The infamous and execrable Padres Torres, another sword-bearing Priest, is now in command of the chief army of the Patriots. He is cruel, crafty, vindictive,—a perfect fiend incarnate, sparing neither Patriot nor Royalist who falls into his hands for whom he happens to have conceived an aversion, or whom he suspects of hostility to him or his designs. He puts the whole population under contribution for the supply of his avarice. Padres Torres is at length, with much difficulty, displaced. In the mean time, the Royalist forces have reconquered nearly all the provinces. In the month of July 1819, the Patriot interests are almost in a hopeless condition; hardly a soldier is to be found in the open field against the government. In 1820, accounts reach Mexico of the revolution which has occurred in Spain. Ferdinand VII. has been compelled to swear to the new constitution. The Mexican Viceroy receives *public* orders from the Spanish government to *proclaim the new constitution;* he receives *secret* orders, at the same time, not to do so, and raises a body of soldiers to suppress any attempt on the part of others to proclaim it. Gen. Armigo, who is suspected by the Viceroy of a partiality for the new constitution, is dismissed from the command of the military, and *Iturbide*, already somewhat distinguished as a Royalist commander, is appointed in his place. This is the same Iturbide whom we have lately seen defeating Matamoros, and whom we shall presently behold as Emperor of Mexico. Iturbide is directed to escort a half million of dollars for embarkation at Acapulco: he seizes the money at a place called *Iguala*, and commences what is called the second Mexican revolution, by proclaiming a new form of government into which the principle of National Independence is to be incorporated. Iturbide is known in this transaction to be a mere instrument in the hands of the Ecclesiastics, who have become alarmed by the action of the new Spanish government, which they suppose to be unfriendly to their interests as a corporate class, hence they instigate Iturbide, and agree to give him a pecuniary reward, if he will make a Revolution in which their class is to be shielded from existing dangers. Thus inspired, Iturbide proceeds to bring about a conjunction between his own forces and those of Guerero, the Patriot commander, and proposes the plan of government just mentioned, the main features of which *Plan of Iguala* are: *National Independence*—a limited *monarchy*—the Imperial crown of Mexico first to be offered to Ferdinand—in the event of his refusing it, then to be tendered to the younger Princes of his family; if all of them refuse it, the *Representative Government* of New Spain to name the Emperor. A Junta and Regency are provided for in this same plan, and an army is proposed to be raised, to be denominated " The Army of the Three Guarantees—1. Religion in its existing pure form; 2. *Independence;* and 3. Union of Americans and Spaniards." The *Plan of Iguala* proves unsatisfactory to the Creole population, in consequence of its pledging them in behalf of the *House of Bourbon.* The Army of the Three Guarantees marches upon the Capital. Gen. O'Donojou arrives from Spain, at Vera Cruz, empowered to supersede Apodaco, the former Viceroy. Surprised by the revolution which he sees in progress, and having neither troops nor money to support his authority as Viceroy, O'Donojou enters into negotiations with Iturbide, and issues a proclamation declaring his cordial approval of all that has occurred. A conference takes place between Iturbide and O'Donojou, the result of which is a full recognition of the Plan of Iguala by the latter.

On the 27th of September, Iturbide and O'Donojou enter Mexico as associates in authority. A Junta is organized, and Iturbide is appointed Admiral and Generalissimo, with a yearly salary of $120,000. O'Donojou dies. Iturbide proposes to the Junta a Constitution, which is rejected; another is adopted, according to the provisions of which a

Congress is shortly to be convened in the Capitol. Congress convenes.   Iturbide takes the earliest opportunity of quarrelling with Congress, which is divided into three parties : 1, *Bourbonites*, approving the Plan of Iguala ; 2, *Republicans ;* and 3, *Imperialists*, in favour of elevating Iturbide to the crown.   On the first joint meeting of the Congress and Regency, Iturbide *attempts to occupy the President's chair ;* is opposed in his effort, and his struggle with the Congress commences.   The soldiers, who have been previously gained, suddenly proclaim *Iturbide Emperor.* After much wrangling with the Cortes, on various points, he dissolves them, and appoints a Junta, to be named by himself.   This Junta, under his direction, decree a forced loan of $2,500,000, in support of the Imperial Government. About this time, the Spanish garrison in San Juan de Ullua, makes an unsuccessful attack upon the works which flank the city of Vera Cruz.   After some correspondence with the Governor of the Castle, Iturbide resolves to have a personal interview with him, hoping to induce him to accept of terms mutually advantageous.   He sets out on his expedition ; is received with manifestations of *universal loyalty* along his whole progress, and is magnificently entertained at Puebla.   In a few days he reaches Xalapa.   His negotiation with the Spanish Governor of the Castle proves abortive.   Whilst sojourning at Xalapa, an incident occurs which brings on a new Revolution.   *Santana*, the Governor of Vera Cruz, who commanded the forces which stormed the city when it was captured from the Spaniards, and who having long enjoyed an independent command, cannot brook a superior, engages in a violent quarrel with Echavarri, the Commander in Chief of the Southern division of the Mexican army.   Echavarri prefers charges against him to the Emperor.   Santana, confident of the friendship of his imperial master, to whose fortunes he has heretofore zealously adhered, when summoned to appear before Iturbide, attends with promptitude.   Santana is disappointed in the conduct of the Emperor towards him, by whom he is basely treated. He suddenly leaves Xalapa, and, riding day and night, reaches Vera Cruz before the news of his disgrace has arrived. He instantly assembles his regiment, and delivers to them a glowing harangue in denunciation of the government of Iturbide. They agree to support him in opposition to the Emperor. The military in all the neighbouring towns second the movements of Santana, who proclaims a *Republican Government,* and addresses a letter to Iturbide, demanding his *abdication* of the throne, in language in the highest degree reproachful and insulting. Iturbide makes preparations to resist this demand; and despatches Echavarri against the rebels, as he styles them. Guadalupe Victoria leaves his retreat in the mountains, where he has been long secreted, joins Santana, and is constituted Commander in Chief of the Republican forces. On the first of February 1823, Echavarri and the officers commanding the Imperial Army, agree upon terms of union and co-operation with Santana and Victoria, and send a joint demand to Iturbide in favour of a Republic. The defection of Echavarri is immediately succeeded by a similar movement in all the Provinces. Iturbide endeavours to negotiate with the officers in command of the Republican forces. They demand more money from him than he can conveniently pay. In order to relieve his fiscal distresses, Iturbide issues four millions of *paper money*, which is made a legal tender to the amount of one third of its nominal value, in payment of debts. This paper immediately *depreciates*, and occasions great discontent among its holders, and the people generally. Iturbide heightens the excitement against himself, by calling upon the Padres Provinciales for a contribution of *Church Plate.* Driven to despair, he calls together the members of the old Congress, then in the Capital, and tenders his resignation. The members of Congress assembled, being few in number, refuse to act. He then addresses a letter to

9 *

the Congress in which he tenders his abdication, offers a shabby apology for his *usurpation*, and proposes to retire from the country. This letter is referred to a committee of Congress, who, declining to recognize his *abdication*, from a fear of impliedly admitting him once to have had constitutional authority, in a very curious epistle, recommend that he shall be permitted to depart the country, and be allowed a yearly income of $25,000 for the maintenance of his family and suite. Iturbide is escorted to Antigua, and takes his departure in an English vessel, chartered to convey him to Leghorn. On the 27th of March, the Republican army enters the Capital. The old Congress is convoked; a provisional government established, and an Executive, composed of three members, appointed. Measures are taken to convene a new Congress, which body assembles in the Capital towards the close of the year 1823, and frames the *project* of a Constitution subsequently adopted, with slight alterations; by which the Mexican nation is declared " a Representative, *Popular*, and *Federal Republic.*" This is the much-contested Constitution of 1824, (that being the year in which it was finally adopted,) under which the *Anglo-American population now in Texas, settled themselves in that delightful region.* By this Constitution, the States of Mexico, originally sixteen in number, (with a power secured to Congress of increasing their number by the admission of new States, or the modification of the old ones, as might seem expedient,) are declared to be " Free, Sovereign, and Independent," in all that relates to the administration of their internal concerns. It is in behalf of this *Freedom, Sovereignty*, and *Independence*, the destruction of which was openly attempted by the usurper Santana, in the year 1834, that the descendants of heroic and freedom-loving ancestors in Texas, nobly resolved to imperil " their lives, their fortunes, and their sacred honours." How they have prospered in this magnanimous strife for *principle*, will be hereafter disclosed.

CHAPTER VI.

View of the Reformation in England, from its original introduction to the Revolution in 1648. Its influence upon the character and history of the British colonists in America, both before the year last-named and after. Causes which concurred to give ascendancy to the principles of the Reformation in that part of North America settled from Great Britain, and which must yet give them a still wider diffusion.

WHILST the events which have heretofore attracted our notice were moving forward in Mexico, for the most part with a sluggish and irregular action, and certain demoralizing influences were operating with a benumbing if not a deadly potency, in the Southernmost portions of North America, a train of occurrences was proceeding in another quarter of the same continent, of a nature entirely different, which have resulted already in the establishment of civil and religious liberty, and in the formation of political and social institutions which are the wonder and delight of all who survey them, and are destined " to change the condition of man all over the globe." *

The religious reformation commenced by Luther in the year 1520, has already been alluded to, and some commendation has been bestowed upon himself and his co-labourers, on account of the aid contributed by them to the emancipation of mind from the thraldom of the dark ages. Something has been said also of the manner in which the sanative and recuperative influences of the Reformation were shut out from Spain ; and of the disadvantages thereby imposed both upon the people of that country, and those who emigrated from Spain, and settled themselves in different parts of North and South America. Let us now turn our attention to England ; where, as is conceded by all writers who have explored this subject, the Reformation displayed greater power, and ultimately assumed

* Thomas Jefferson.

more of the *phasis* of *Political Revolution* than in any of the states of the European Continent. And here I take leave to advertise the reader, that in most of the views which will be submitted in this chapter, I lay no claim to originality of thought ; and, as will presently be ascertained, wherever I can bring to my aid, in the discussion about to be presented, writers of *established reputation*, both for *ability* and *disinterestedness*, I shall, for various reasons, prefer using their language, to the declaration of my own crude notions, in phraseology less elegant. It is, perhaps, too late now for anything absolutely *new* to be written on this subject, and a perspicuous *condensation* of leading facts, often discussed by others, is all that will be now attempted, or is deemed necessary.

For the superior efficiency exercised by the Reformation in England, many reasons have been assigned, among which are the following : 1. In England, contrary to all examples on the European Continent, the Regal power, instead of warring against the *spirit* of the Reformation, encouraged and cherished it. Henry the Eighth, indeed, may be said to have thrown himself at the *head* of the *regenerative* movement, and to have facilitated its onward progress to a certain point, with all the authority of the crown. He aspired to absolute rule among his own subjects ; and plainly perceiving that he would not be able to realize his desire in this respect, whilst the Ecclesiastical machinery of the Catholic Church interposed, at so many vital points, the supremacy of the Pope of Rome between himself and the great body of English population, he very soon felt inclined to batter down that machinery. Another motive operated with this prince, and had, perhaps, still more influence upon his conduct. His profusion had long since dissipated the enormous treasures left by his father, and he stood in need of the wealth of the church to sustain the courtly magnificence which he affected. There was, besides the considerations mentioned, a third one, which must be acknowledged to have materially quickened, as well as invigorated, the hostile action of Henry. The Pope of Rome had not shown that accommodating spirit which he desired, in regard to his noted nuptial caprices; and had proved equally impracticable as to the manner of settling the succession to his crown, upon his own decease. Therefore was it that this selfish and headstrong monarch fiercely threw the gauntlet of defiance at the feet of his Holiness, the Pope, seized the banner of Reform in his own royal hands, and resolved to lead forward his subjects in the war against Papal Supremacy. He undoubtedly did not intend to do more than crush the Ecclesiastical authority which the Roman Pontiff claimed a right to exercise in England, and to draw to himself, as the Head of the Church, the power and patronage which were now held by foreign and hostile hands. The consequences which actually ensued from his acts, were far from being either expected or desired by him; for perhaps a greater enemy has never lived than was Henry to the invaluable rights of the popular mass, and to the general spread of knowledge in the world. But he imparted an impetus, notwithstanding, to the ball of Reformation, which was felt long after the termination of his reign, and became the unwitting author of results which will be felt and gloried in by all coming generations.

2. England was a more favourable theatre for the work of Reformation, in several respects, than any state of Europe. As early as the year 1215, a coalition of the great barons had wrested, sword in hand, the Magna Charta from the hands of King John. This Charter had been renewed and confirmed, from time to time, by almost every succeeding monarch; besides which, new statutes had been occasionally adopted, re-asserting and extending its enactments. The important rights acknowledged, and held at least in a state of nominal preservation by this Charter, placed the people of England in a much higher attitude in regard to *recognized*

civic freedom, than any people then existing. *Trial by Jury*, which has probably done more than any single agent which can be now specified, in cherishing the spirit of individual independence, and fitting men for the task of self-government, by familiarizing them with important legal principles, and calling them to participate in the high task of their judicial enforcement, had doubtless existed among the Saxons at a very early period; but it was under Magna Charta that it received a sort of *constitutional* sanction, and reached a point of efficiency never before attained. The House of Commons too had now sprung up, and taken its place, so to speak, among the sovereign institutions of the country. "Under the Plantagenets," says a writer from whose pages I delight to quote, " it had taken deep root, and become firmly established; not that at this time it played any great part, or had even much influence in the government; it scarcely, indeed, interfered in this, except when called to do so by the King, and then only with hesitation and regret; afraìd rather of bringing itself into trouble and danger, than zealous of augmenting its power and authority. But the case was different when it was called upon to defend *private rights*,—the houses and property of the citizens, or in short the rights and privileges of individuals; this duty the House of Commons performed with wonderful energy and perseverance, putting forward and establishing those principles which have become the basis of the English Constitution. Under the Tudors the House of Commons, or rather the Parliament altogether, put on a new character. It no longer defended individual liberty so well as under the Plantagenets. Arbitrary detentions, and violations of private rights, which became much more frequent, were often passed by in silence. But, as a counterbalance for this, the Parliament interfered to a much greater extent than formerly in the general affairs of government. Henry VIII., in order to change the religion of his country, and to fix the succession, required some public support, some *public instrument*, and he had recourse to Parliament, and especially to the House of Commons, for this purpose. This, which under the Plantagenets, had only been a *means of resistance*, a guarantee of private rights, became now, under the Tudors, an instrument of government, of general policy; so that at the end of the sixteenth century, notwithstanding it had been the tool, and submitted to the will of nearly all sorts of tyrannies, its importance had greatly increased; the foundation of its power was laid, the foundation of that power upon which truly *rests representative* government."

3. It has been supposed by several writers of note, that the Reformation was considerably facilitated in England by *Commerce*, which began to expand itself strikingly about this period; members of the mercantile class suddenly accumulated large fortunes; territorial wealth, baronial possessions, rapidly shifted hands; vast landed estates, which for centuries had continued in the same families, were now divided out among the gentry, composed of the lesser nobility, and persons who had become enriched by trade. All the industrious classes exhibited a great increase in point of wealth, and began to claim an influence proportionate to this increase. The House of Commons, which represented, very imperfectly to be sure, but still represented *the body of the people*, at the beginning of the seventeenth century, greatly surpassed in wealth the House of Lords, or High Nobility.

4. Upon the decease of Henry VIII., during whose reign the Reformation had advanced rapidly in its career, there was a short intermission in the vigour which had marked its movements in the outset. Mary had succeeded to the throne upon the demise of her brother Edward VI., whose short reign is hardly necessary to be noticed in connection with this subject. She was a bigoted and zealous Catholic; and was moreover married to the notorious Philip II. of Spain, distinguished for his cruel enforcement of the Inquisition. Now, therefore, as was to be expected, the

power of the Crown was turned against the Reformation ; and various efforts were made, by the persecution of obsti- nate dissenters from the Catholic faith, and otherwise, to restore Papal Supremacy in England, and all its debasing concomitants. But, happily for the world, Mary did not live long enough to execute all her schemes in favour of Catholicism ; and when, in a few years, the great Elizabeth mounted the throne, we find the work of Reformation, com- menced under the auspices of her father, going forward with a celerity altogether astonishing. Elizabeth was as fond of *prerogative* as her father himself, and had no idea of permitting a religious supremacy to exist in favour of a foreign Potentate—the Pope of Rome, which must inevita- bly diminish her own authority over the minds, and hearts, and fortunes of her subjects. She at once became a zeal- ous Patroness of the Reformation ; contributing both money and arms most liberally for its promotion, in France as well as in Holland. She became a member of the great Protestant league, whose objects were, 1. To crush the power of the Pope of Rome, and 2. To defeat the preten- sions of the Spanish monarch, the same Philip II., just men- tioned, to the Dictatorship of Europe.

5. The revival of *classical learning*, which had now al- most become complete in England, and one or two other countries on the continent ; the revolution which was taking place in all the departments of useful science under the auspices of Bacon and Descartes ; the wonderfully increased activity of the human mind about this time manifested in England ; furnished ground for the hope that the struggle with the powers of moral darkness would soon draw to a close, and in due season, all men, everywhere, would stand forth, " redeemed, regenerated, and disenthralled by the irresistible genius of universal emancipation."

There is one feature in the English Reformation alto- gether peculiar. It has been remarked that the original ob- ject of Henry VIII., as equally of Elizabeth, was to carry forward the Reformation for the exclusive benefit of the crown. No advantage to the people at large was either intended or thought of. And now, when the church had been plundered of its wealth, and the whole mass of Ecclesiastical authority and patronage had been appropriated, Royalty was ascertained to be quite willing that the machine of Reformation should become stationary. But the people, whose understandings had been healthily put in action, and who were sensible that there were many evils yet existing both in Church and State, were of a temper and inclination quite different; they demanded a thorough and sweeping reform of all abuses, the destruction of all institutions and establishments, for the preservation of which satisfactory reasons could not be adduced, and which experience had ascertained to constitute impediments to the full enjoyment of civil and religious freedom. The people had become now as averse to Bishops, appointed by the Crown, as they had been originally to a Pope, appointed by a conclave of Cardinals, and upon grounds equally substantial. They craved entire freedom in regard to matters of conscience, and a right to inquire boldly and independently in reference to affairs of state. They were inclined to complain of much in the existing organization of the high departments of government — the Executive, the Legislative, and the Judiciary, and especially of the last. Nothing, in fact, could now satisfy them but a complete *political revolution.*

There was little in the demeanour of King James I., or his unhappy successor, to allay the ferment every day increasing in the popular mind; on the contrary, they continued to assert the doctrine of Kingly Prerogative in all its latitude, and sometimes in a manner specially offensive to a people who had become alive to their own rights, and who began seriously to counsel together in regard to the means proper to be used for their successful assertion. Now, finally came on, in the natal land of Bacon, of Milton, of Sidney, in the land whence what we now call ANGLO-AMERICANISM has derived its origin, that great contest between the principle of *absolute monarchy*, on the one hand, and *popular freedom* on the other, and which, after much moral travail and much shedding of blood, eventuated in the establishment of the famous *commonwealth*, by the Treaty of Newport, signed in 1648.   The various factions which sprung up thereafter upon the ruins of Royalty—all terminating in the usurpation of Oliver Cromwell, are of necessity entitled to no description here.   We have no need to look back upon those fierce convulsions out of which that usurpation arose as an inevitable and natural consequence.   Anglo-Americans have little to do with the abandonment by Cromwell of his original Republican principles, and all that tyrannous conduct of his so unlike his early *professions*.   Still less have they to do with the subsequent renunciation of those same principles of Republicanism by the whole British people, and their willing submission for almost two centuries past, to that Aristocratico-Monarchical system which their Fathers once swore to have cast aside from them and their posterity for ever.   Sufficient for us is it, in this glancing survey which we have taken of the gradual rise of free principles in England, under the guiding and inspiring influence of Religious' Reformation, to have been able to find out something of the high sentiments and lofty faculties of our own noble Progenitors, who came across the billowy tempest-tost ocean to these then wild shores of North America, for the express purpose of carrying forward Religious and Civil Reformation—(*obstructed* in England)—as far, along the highways of moral glory, as the sun of Reason should deign to guide their steps ; and who, dying, have bequeathed to us, their descendants of the present age, and to all coming Anglo-American generations, still to bear onward and aloft the great Ark of our Social, Political, and Religious Covenant, until the whole world shall confess that the Jehovah of all Truth reigneth in Heaven.

And now let *one* speak in reference to the first American colonists, whose voice has been already heard on the subject in two continents, and who being himself no Anglo-American, the civilized world will believe. M. De Tocqueville, in his " Democracy in America," (which is, by the bye, not precisely what would be called a *democratic book*) says: " The emigrants who came at different periods to occupy the territory now covered by the American Union, differed from each other in many respects ; their aim was not the same, and they governed themselves on different principles. These men had, however, certain features in common, and they were all placed in an analogous situation. The tie of language is perhaps the strongest and the most durable that can unite mankind. All the emigrants spoke the same tongue ; they were all off-sets from the same people. Born in a country which had been agitated for centuries by the struggles of faction, and in which all parties had been obliged, in their turn, to place themselves under the protection of the laws, their political education had been perfected in this rude school, and they were more conversant with the notions of right, and the principles of true freedom, than the greater part of their European contemporaries. At the period of the first emigrations, the *Parish* system, that fruitful germ of free institutions, was deeply rooted in the habits of the English ; and with it, the doctrine of the sovereignty of the people had been introduced, even into the bosom of the monarchy of the House of Tudor.

" The religious quarrels which have agitated the Christian world were then rife. England had plunged into the new order of things with headlong vehemence. The character of its inhabitants, which had always been sedate and reflecting, became argumentative and austere. General information had been increased by intellectual debate, and the mind had received a deeper cultivation. Whilst religion was the topic of debate, the morals of the people were reformed. All those national features are more or less dis-coverable in the physiognomy of those adventurers who came to seek a new home on the opposite shores of the At-lantic."

M. De Tocqueville again says: " All these European colonies contained the elements, if not the developement, of a *complete democracy*. Two causes led to this result. It may safely be advanced, that on leaving the mother coun-try, the emigrants had in general no notions of superiority over one another. The happy and the powerful do not go into exile, and there are no surer guarantees of equality among men, than poverty and misfortune. It happened, however, on several occasions, that persons of rank were driven to America by political and religious quarrels. Laws were made to establish a gradation of ranks ; but it was soon found that the soil of America was entirely op-posed to a territorial aristocracy. To bring that refractory land into cultivation, the constant and *interested* exertions of the owner were necessary ; and when the ground was prepared, its produce was found to be insufficient to enrich a master and a farmer at the same time. The land was naturally broken up into small portions, which the proprie-tor cultivated for himself. Land is the basis of an aristo-cracy, which clings to the soil that supports it ; for it is not by privileges alone, nor by birth, but by landed property, handed down from generation to generation, that an aris-tocracy is constituted. A nation may present immense for-tunes and extreme wretchedness ; but unless those fortunes are territorial, there is no aristocracy, but simply the classes of the rich and the poor.

" All the British colonies had then a great degree of similarity at the epoch of their settlement. All of them, from their first beginning, seemed destined to witness the growth, not of the aristocratic liberty of the mother country, but of that freedom of the middle and lower orders, of which the history of the world had as yet furnished no complete ex-ample."

The same accomplished writer, speaking of the colonists of New England in particular, says: "The settlers who established themselves on the shores of New England all belonged to the more independent classes of their native country. Their union on the soil of America at once presented the singular phenomenon of a society containing neither lords nor common people; neither rich nor poor. These men possessed, in proportion to their number, a *greater mass of intelligence than is to be found in any European nation of our own time.* All, without a single exception, had received a good education, and many of them were known in Europe for their talents and their acquirements. The other colonies had been founded by adventurers without family; the colonists of New England brought with them the best elements of order and morality—they landed in the desert with their wives and children. But what most especially distinguished them, was the aim of their undertaking. They had not been obliged by necessity to leave their country; the moral position thus abandoned was one to be regretted, and their means of subsistence were certain. Nor did they cross the Atlantic to improve their situation or to increase their wealth; the call which summoned them from their homes was purely intellectual; and in facing the inevitable sufferings of exile, their object was the triumph of an idea.

"The emigrants, or, as they deservedly styled themselves, the Pilgrims, belonged to that English sect, the austerity of whose principles had acquired for them the name of Puritans. Puritanism was not merely a religious doctrine, but it corresponded in many respects to the most absolute democratic and republican theories. It was this tendency which had aroused its most dangerous adversaries. Persecuted by the government of the mother country, and disgusted by the habits of a society opposed to the rigour of its own principles, the Puritans went forth to seek some rude and unfrequented part of the world, where they could live

10 *

according to their own opinions, and worship God in freedom."

The same writer observes, that it is " difficult to detect the link which connected the emigrants with the land of their forefathers, in studying the earliest historical and legislative records of New England. They perpetually exercised the rights of sovereignty; they named their magistrates, concluded peace or declared war, made public regulations, and enacted laws, as if their allegiance was due only to God."

In reference to the character of the connection existing between Great Britain and her American colonies, anterior to the Revolution which severed that connection entirely, Mr. Jefferson, writing in Paris about the year 1786, in answer to questions addressed to him by Monsieur de Meusnier, who was preparing an article to be inserted in the *Encyclopédie Methodique*, asserts that " the settlement of the colonies was not made by public authority, or at the public expense of England; but by the exertions and at the expense of individuals. Hence it happened, that their constitutions were not formed systematically, but according to the circumstances which happened to exist in each. Hence, too, the principles of the political connection between the old and new countries were never settled. That it would have been advantageous to have settled them, is certain; and, particularly, to have provided a body which should decide, in the last resort, all cases wherein both parties were interested. But it is not certain that that right would have been given, or ought to have been given to the Parliament; much less, that it resulted to the Parliament, without having been given to it expressly. Why was it necessary, that there should have been a body to preside in the last resort? Because it would have been for the good of both parties. But this reason shows, it ought not to have been the Parliament, since that would have exercised it for the good of one party only."

Whilst upon this subject of the political relations exist-

ing between Great Britain and her American Colonies, generally, I embrace the opportunity of citing from the distinguished statesman just quoted, the following extract from
the instructions proposed by him, in the year 1774, to be
given to the Representatives of Virginia, in the first Con-
federative Congress which assembled. It is known that
these instructions, offered in the form of a Resolution,
were not adopted, as being considered too harsh towards
the mother country, at that juncture, but were published a
short time after in London, at the instance of English
friends of the Colonies, (including the celebrated Edmund
Burke) under the title of " A Summary View of the Rights
of British America." The Resolution alluded to, after a
long and highly appropriate preamble, reminds King George
III., that " Our ancestors were the free inhabitants of
the British dominions in Europe, and possessed a right,
which nature has given to all men, of departing from the
country in which *chance*, not *choice*, has placed them, of
going in quest of new habitations, and of there establishing
new societies, under such laws and regulations as to them
shall seem most likely to promote public happiness : that
their Saxon ancestors had, under this universal law, in like
manner, left their native wilds and woods in the North of
Europe, had possessed themselves of the island of Britain,
then less charged with inhabitants, and had established
there that system of laws which has so long been the glory
and protection of that country. Nor was any claim of
superiority or *dependence* asserted over them by that mother country from which they had migrated : and were
such a claim made, it is believed his majesty's subjects in
Great Britain, have too firm a feeling of the rights derived
to them from their ancestors, to bow down the sovereignty
of their State before such visionary pretensions. And it is
thought that no circumstance has occurred to distinguish,
materially, the British from the Saxon emigration. America was conquered, and her settlements made and firmly

established, *at the expense of individuals,* and not of the British public. Their own blood was spilt in acquiring lands for their settlement, their own fortunes expended in making that settlement effectual. For *themselves* they *fought,* for *themselves* they *conquered,* and for *themselves* they have *a right to hold.*"

Such were the views entertained upon this subject in America, generally, in the year 1774; such were the views doubtless entertained in all the British Colonies uniformly before that period; and such were the views which good sense and expanded principles of moral equity would in any age of the world have ratified.

I shall conclude this sketch of the British Colonial population, with a few more extracts from works, which, from the high character of their authors, will receive, and have received, much more respect and confidence in the reading world, than any loose suggestions which it would be in my power to originate. M. De Tocqueville says : " The general principles which are the ground-work of modern Constitutions — principles which were imperfectly known in Europe, and not completely triumphant even in Great Britain, in the seventeenth century — were all recognised and determined by the laws of New England : *the intervention of the people in public affairs, the free voting of taxes, the responsibility of authorities, personal liberty, and trial by jury,* were all positively established without discussion. From these fruitful principles, *consequences* have been derived and applications have been made, *such as no nation in Europe has yet ventured to attempt.* In Connecticut, the electoral body consisted, from its origin, of the whole number of citizens ; and this is readily to be understood, when we recollect that this people enjoyed an almost perfect equality of fortune, and a still greater uniformity of capacity. In Connecticut, at this period, all the executive functionaries were elected, including the governor of the State. The citizens, above the age of sixteen, were obliged to bear arms; they formed a national militia, which appointed its own officers; and was to hold itself at all times in readiness to march for the defence of the country.

"In the laws of Connecticut, as well as in those of New England, we find the germ and gradual developement of that *Township independence*, which is the life and mainspring of American liberty at the present day. The political existence of the majority of the nations in Europe commenced in the superior ranks of society, and was gradually and always imperfectly communicated to the different members of the social body. In America, on the contrary, it may be said that the Township was organized before the County, the County before the State, the State before the Union.

"In New England, townships were completed and definitely constituted, as early as 1650. The independence of the township was the nucleus round which the local interests, passions, rights, and duties, collected and clung. It gave scope to the activity of a real political life, most thoroughly democratic and republican. The colonies still recognised the supremacy of the mother country; monarchy was still the law of the state; but the republic was established in every township. The towns named their own magistrates of every kind, rated themselves, and levied their own taxes. In the townships of New England, the law of Representatives was not adopted, but the affairs of the community were discussed, as at Athens, in the market-place, by a general assembly of the citizens. In studying the laws which were promulgated at this first era of the American Republics, it is impossible not to be struck by the remarkable acquaintance with the science of government, and the advanced theory of legislation which they display. *The ideas these formed of the duties of society towards its members, are evidently much loftier and more comprehensive than those of the European legislators at that time:* obligations were there imposed which were elsewhere slighted. In the states of New England, from the first, the condition of the poor was provided for ; strict measures were taken for the maintenance of roads, and surveyors were appointed to attend to them ; registers were established in every parish, in which the results of public deliberations, and the births, deaths, and marriages of the citizens, were entered ; clerks were directed to keep these registers ; officers were charged with the administration of vacant inheritances, and with the arbitration of litigated landmarks ; and many others were erected whose chief functions were the maintenance of public order in the community. The law enters into a thousand useful provisions for a number of social wants which are at present very inadequately felt in France.

"But it is by the attention it pays to *Public Education,* that the original character of the American civilization is at once placed in the clearest light. "*It being,*" says the law, "*one chief project of Satan, to keep men from the knowledge of the scriptures by persuading from the use of tongues, to the end that learning may not be buried in the graves of our forefathers, in church and commonwealth, the Lord assisting our endeavours. . . .*" Then follow clauses, establishing schools in every township, and obliging the inhabitants, under heavy fines, to support them. Schools of a superior kind were founded in the same manner in the more populous districts. The municipal authorities were bound to enforce the sending of children to school by their parents ; they were empowered to inflict fines upon all who refused compliance ; and in case of continued resistance, society assumed the place of the parent, took possession of the child, and deprived the father of those natural rights which he used to so bad a purpose."

The writer just cited, running a comparison between the population of Europe during the seventeenth century, and that of the British colonies in America, observes : " Never were the notions of right more completely confounded than in the midst of the splendour and literature of Europe; never was there less political activity among the people; never were the principles of true freedom less widely circulated; and, at that very time, those principles which were scorned, or unknown, by the nations of Europe, were proclaimed in the deserts of the new world, and were accepted as the future creed of a great people. The boldest theories of the human reason were put into practice by a community so humble, that not a statesman condescended to attend to it; and a legislation, off-hand, was produced by the imagination of the citizens. In the bosom of this obscure democracy, which had, as yet, brought forth neither generals, nor philosophers, nor authors, a man might stand up in the face of a free people, and pronounce, amidst general acclamation, the following definition of liberty: " Nor would I have you to mistake in the point of your own liberty. There is a liberty of corrupt nature, which is affected by men and beasts to do what they list; and this liberty is inconsistent with authority, impatient of all restraint; by this liberty *sumus omnes deteriores*, 'tis the grand enemy of truth and peace, and all the ordinances of God are sent against it. But there is a civil, a moral, a federal liberty, which is the proper end and object of authority; it is a liberty for that only which is *just* and *good;* for this liberty you are to stand up with the hazard of your very lives, and whatever crosses it, is not authority but a distemper thereof. This liberty is maintained in a way of *subjection to authority;* and the authority set over you will, in all administrations for your good, be quietly submitted unto by all but such as have a disposition to shake off the yoke and lose their true liberty, by their murmuring at the honour of power and authority."

Such is the *liberal* and *impartial* testimony of an enlightened foreigner in behalf of the British colonial population in North America; so superior does he view it to have been in intelligence and virtue, and in a familiar knowledge of the great principles of liberty, to the general mass of European population at the same period.   What has been here said of the colonial population of New England might have been repeated, with slight and immaterial variations, in reference to the whole body of British Colonists, North and South ; for, as De Tocqueville has before observed, in language already cited : " All the British colonies had a degree of similarity at the epoch of their settlement.   All of them, from their first beginning, seemed destined to witness the growth, not of the *aristocratic* liberty of the mother country, but of that freedom of the middle and lower orders of which the history of the world has as yet furnished no example."

Is it at all wonderful that such a population, going on to advance in numbers, in knowledge, and in virtue, from generation to generation, should have been found unwilling tamely to submit to the attempts of a tyrannical and proverbially selfish government—(not *nation*) at a subsequent period in their history, to tear from them the most precious of their rights and privileges, and to drag them back to a state of servitude worse even than that from which they had sought refuge in the wilderness of a remote region ?   Can it be regarded as at all surprising, that among *such* a people, a valiant and patriot soldiery should have been found, on the first suggestion of danger to their liberties, springing forth joyously and spontaneously, by thousands, to rescue them from destruction ?   It was in fact perfectly natural, amidst such institutions,—such a moral organization as has been described, — that these thousands of heroic soldiers should have thus presented themselves ; and it was equally natural that appropriate officers should have come forward successfully to command the armies of Freedom ; enlightened and high-souled statesmen, to guide and direct the united energies of the colonists, made *one people*, by common sufferings, and common dangers ; " forest-born" orators to rouse in the most lethargic the unconquerable spirit of resistance to Tyranny. Nor is it at all more re-markable that *written constitutions* of government should in due time be framed, which should guard and perpetuate to all ages the great principles of civil and religious liberty. And it would have been even strange, if these same written constitutions, made deliberately, and upon full and free in-terchange of opinion and sentiment, among millions of en-lightened freemen, should not have greatly improved upon the colonial models before possessed, and have evinced the capability, now displayed to the view of an admiring world, of pushing forward still farther the triumphs of *Reason*, and *Virtue*, and genuine *Liberty*, over *Bigotry*, and *Vice*, and the principles of monarchical and aristocratical Des-potism.

Surely it would not have required a large amount of pro-phetic sagacity, fifty years ago, to have predicted, that if ever a struggle should occur between the Anglo-American population of North America, or rather of the United States, and that enervated and degraded mongrel race, who have been described in the preceding chapters of this work, precisely such results as have taken place in Texas, in the progress of the war carried on there for Independence and Liberty, would be seen to arise. The mind of one who would not have anticipated such results, could not have form-ed any acquaintance with the brightest pages of ancient his-toric lore ; nor have read, with soul on fire, of the imperish-able glories of Marathon, and Platæa, and Salamis. Perhaps as little astuteness is necessary now to foresee that the pe-riod is not far remote, when Anglo-American heroes, and statesmen, and moralists,—the descendants of those British colonists of whom we have been just reading, whose early settlements only dotted, here and there, for a few miles, the bleak and barren Atlantic coast of North America, will be seen, with the consent of good men and true of all nations, to bear "forward and aloft, over the land and over the sea," that very Banner of Moral Regeneration spoken of in

the first page of this work, until even, " amidst the murmurs
of the Pacific sea," and over the beautiful plains and valleys of
Eastern Mexico, a voice shall be heard saying : " *There is
no God, but the God of Truth, and Justice, and Brotherly
Kindness ; and his favourites are the Spreaders of Knowledge, the Practisers of Virtue, and the heroic yet merci-
ful Chastisers of wicked men and nations.*"

CHAPTER VII.

View of the relations between Spain and the United States at the close
  of the American Revolution.   Unfriendly feeling between the two
  countries.   Progress of that unfriendly feeling, with some explanation of the causes of the same.   The Miranda expedition.   Burr's
  project ; *What was it ?*

At the termination of the War of Independence, the people of the United States found themselves in an attitude both
unpleasant and perilous in regard to the bordering dominions of two of the great powers of Europe, Great Britain and
Spain. The Northern Posts, agreed by the treaty of peace
with Great Britain to be surrendered, were still unjustly
and arrogantly detained. Indemnity for spoliations committed on private property during the war, and which the
British Government had contracted to pay, was, upon various pretexts, for a long time withheld ; whilst British in-
cendiaries, with the evident sanction of their own Government, were assiduously engaged in stimulating the savage
tribes proximate to the Canadian frontier, to the massacre
of unoffending American settlers. To the South and West,
the Spanish Government was patronizing a course of
treacherous annoyment, prosecuted in various modes,
which it was evident could not be much longer tolerated
by a high-spirited people, however inclined to peace and

true amity. Unfortunately, the boundary lines between the territorial possessions of Spain and the United States had never yet been definitely settled, and the negotiations which had been opened at Madrid, for this and other purposes, seemed to be moving on with but faint prospect of ultimate success, and with no indications of a disposition to do justice on the part of the Spanish Government. In the meantime, the navigation of the Mississippi river had been most ungraciously obstructed, and this grand high-way of Western trade had been suddenly closed to all American commerce whatsoever. This transaction had become a source of continually increasing irritation to the inhabitants of the great Mississippi Valley. At the same period, the Creek and Cherokee tribes of Indians were threatening serious hostilities, and no doubt existed that their malevolence had been secretly instigated by Spanish machinations. Popular ferment, growing out of this state of things, finally reached such a height in many parts of the country, West of the Alleghany Mountains, that public assemblages of the citizens were held, at which resolutions were adopted denouncing in the strongest language the Administration of which General Washington was the head, for supposed inattention and indifference to Western interests. At Lexington, Kentucky, especially, a public meeting took place, at which a Committee was appointed to hold correspondence with the whole aggrieved section of the Union, with a view to uniting popular feeling on this subject, and maturing suitable means of redress and safety. A remonstrance was despatched to the Government, in which (says the distinguished author of the " Life of Washington,") the Western citizens " claimed much credit for their moderation in having thus long, out of regard to their Government, and affection for their fellow-citizens on the Atlantic, abstained from the use of those means which they proposed for the assertion of what they termed a natural and inalienable right ; and seemed to indicate the opinion that this forbearance could not be long continued."

About this time, a plan was set on foot by Mr. Genet, the minister from the French Republic to the United States, for an invasion of the Spanish dominions in North America, from the States adjacent to them ; which indeed progressed almost to the point of maturity and execution, and was only defeated finally by the seasonable interposition of the American government, and the efficient instrumentality of an armed force.   The inflamed condition of public feeling in the Western States at this crisis, may be inferred from a noted transaction which then occurred.   Four Frenchmen had been sent out from Philadelphia by Mr. Genet to the state of Kentucky, to organize and take command of the expedition then preparing for an attack upon the City of New Orleans, under the superintendence of a citizen of the United States, who had received a commission appointing him Commander in Chief of the Army expected to be immediately raised for this purpose.   The Secretary of State (Mr. Jefferson) was instructed to make these particulars known to the Governor of Kentucky, and to request that he would employ his Executive authority to arrest the proposed expedition.   The reply of the Governor to the letter of the Secretary of State, contains the following striking declarations : " I have great doubts, even if they do attempt to carry their plan into execution, (provided they manage their business with prudence) whether there is any legal authority to restrain or punish them, at least before they have actually accomplished it.   For if it is lawful for any one citizen of the State to leave it, it is equally so for any number of them to do it.   It is also lawful to carry with them any quantity of provisions, arms, and ammunition; and if the act is lawful in itself, there is nothing but the particular intention with which it is done which can make it unlawful.   But I know of no law which inflicts a punishment on *intention* only : or any criterion by which to decide what would be sufficient evidence of that intention, if it was a proper subject for legal censure.   I shall, upon all occasions, be averse to the exercise of any power which I do not consider myself as clearly and explicitly invested with; much less would I assume power to exercise it against men whom I consider as friends and brethren, in favour of a man whom I view as an enemy and a tyrant. I shall also feel but little inclination to take an active part in punishing or restraining any of my fellow-citizens for a supposed intrusion only, to gratify or remove the fears of the minister of a prince who openly withholds from us an inalienable right, and who secretly instigates against us a most savage and cruel enemy."

The extract cited may be doubtless received as embodying the views and sentiments of a large portion of the citizens of the most populous State west of the Mountains; and though the war against Spain for which the valorous sons of Kentucky were then ready, was prevented in the manner already stated, and its prevention has supplied no just ground for the application of censure to the administration of General Washington; yet is it unquestionably true, that feelings of hostility grew out of the aggressions practised by Spain at that period, which have lost little of their efficiency in the Valley of the Mississippi up to the present moment.

It was not before the year 1795, that Spain, encumbered by the war in which she was then engaged on the European Continent, finally consented to do full justice to the United States, upon the several grounds of complaint insisted on. But, although the Treaty then finally effected with that power was as comprehensive in its provisions as could in reason be claimed; yet the continued dominion of a nation so little to be relied on, over the finest portion of North America, or perhaps the world, and the danger of future encroachment to which the people of the Western States would yet plainly remain exposed, especially in connexion with the navigation of the Mississippi, kept up a feeling of uneasiness among the whole people of the West,

11*

which all discerning men perceived would eventually **result** in something like war between the two nations.

The views of leading American statesmen **at an early** period in the history of the United States, as a nation, in reference to the future supplantation of the Spaniards in North, and perhaps South America, by the Anglo-American family, constitute a curious and not unpleasing subject of inquiry at the present time.

In the year 1786, before the Federal Constitution **had** been adopted, Mr. Jefferson writes to A. Stewart, Esq., **as** follows : " I learn from an expression in your letter, that the people of Kentucky think of separating, not only from Virginia, (in which they are right,) but also from the Confederacy. I own I should think this a most calamitous event, and such a one as every good citizen should set himself against. Our present federal limits are not too **large** for good government, nor will the increase of votes in Congress produce an ill effect. On the contrary, it will drown the little divisions still existing there. Our Confederacy must be viewed as the nest, from which all America, North and South, is to be peopled. We should take care, too, not to think it for the interest of that great Continent, *to press too soon upon the Spaniards.* Those countries cannot be in better hands. My fear is that they are too feeble to hold them till our population can be sufficiently advanced to gain it from them, *piece by piece. The navigation of the Mississippi we must have.* This is all we are, as yet, ready to receive. I have made acquaintance with a very sensible and candid gentleman, here, who was in South America, during the revolt that took place there, while our Revolution was going on. He says, that these disturbances, (of which we heard hardly anything,) cost, on both sides, an hundred thousand lives."

It is a fact, not perhaps generally known, that most of the personages who have been conspicuous upon the political arena in the United States, turned their attention, very early, to the condition of the Spanish Provinces in America ; and, speculating upon the character of the government, as well as upon the oppressed condition of the people, anticipated civil disturbances of a serious nature, and possibly Revolution. All of them, too, seem to have adopted nearly the same opinion as to the inability of the Spanish Colonists to free themselves without foreign aid, and in reference to their incapacity for self-government, in the absence of instructors from the United States, competent to initiate them in the rudiments of political freedom. The Biographer of Aaron Burr tells us, that " as early as the year 1796, when John Jay was Governor, Col. Burr had various conversations with him on the subject of these provinces. In these conversations, Col. Burr expressed his views in reference to South America, which he said he could revolutionize and take possession of. Governor Jay replied, that the boldness of the project would contribute to its success ; expressing his opinion that it was not impracticable. From this period until 1805, Mr. Burr's mind seemed to have been constantly engaged in reflecting on the feasibility of the measure, and the proper period for carrying it into effect."

About the year 1797–8, the celebrated Gen. Miranda visited the United States. He is said to have consulted with Gen. Hamilton, Gen. Knox, Mr. Jefferson, and other distinguished citizens, without regard to party. " Miranda's plan," says the author of the " Memoirs of Aaron Burr," (who was, probably, from his intimacy with Col. Burr, correctly informed,) was, " that the United States should furnish ten thousand troops, and, in that event, the British government agreed to supply the necessary funds, and ships to carry on an expedition. As soon as Miranda had completed his arrangements with the British ministry," continues Mr. Davis, " he addressed a letter to Gen. Alexander Hamilton, dated April 6th, 1798, in which he says :—

" ' This, my dear and respectable friend, will be handed

to you by my countryman, Don ——————, who is charged with despatches of the highest importance to the President of the United States.   He will tell you, *confidentially*, all that you wish to know on this subject.   It appears that the moment of our emancipation approaches, and the establishment of Liberty, on all the Continent of the New World, is confided by Providence to us.   The only danger I see, is the introduction of French principles, which would poison our Liberty in its cradle, and would finish by destroying yours.'   So far did these arrangements advance," asserts Mr. Davis, "that Miranda wrote to Gen. Hamilton, under date of the 19th of October, 1798 :

"' Your wishes are, in some sort, already accomplished, seeing that it has been agreed here, on one side, not to employ, in the operations on land, English troops ; seeing that the auxiliary land forces are to be exclusively American, while the naval force shall be purely English.   Every thing is smooth, and we wait only for the fiat of your illustrious President to depart like lightning.'   On the same day, Gen. Miranda wrote to Gen. Knox as follows :

"' I cannot express to you, my dear General, with what pleasure I heard of your nomination in the continental army of the United States of America.   It would appear that your wishes are at length *accomplished*, and that every possible circumstance is united, at this moment, in our favour. Would to God that Providence would endow us with sufficient wisdom to make the most advantageous use of these circumstances.'

"At this time, (continues the Biographer of Col. Burr,) Mr. Adams, Senior, was President of the United States, and declined entering into the arrangement.   It is believed that no reply was made to the letter addressed to the President. Two questions here present themselves to the inquiring mind : Was there any connection between this plan of Miranda for the invasion of Mexico, and the raising of an army in 1798, under the pretext of an attack upon this country by

France? Was the policy adopted by President Adams on that occasion any way connected with that embittered warfare which subsequently ensued between Mr. Adams and Mr. Hamilton?" These questions are left undetermined by Mr. Davis, who has not even given his readers the benefit of his own opinion; though it is easy to see the inclination of his judgment. I confess that the letters of Miranda, both to Hamilton and Knox, but especially the one addressed to the latter, seem to me to indicate very strongly the existence of such a connection as that suggested between the plan of Miranda for invading Mexico, and the army raised under the auspices of Col. Hamilton in 1798. For, in addition to the fact, (mentioned in a note by Mr. Davis,) that this Army was raised " *nominally*, for the purpose of repelling a French invasion, at a moment when France had not a ship of war on the ocean, and when British squadrons were hovering on her coast ;" I do not perceive how it is possible, except upon the supposition of such a *connection*, to attach a sensible interpretation to the language of Miranda to General Knox, who, after complimenting him upon his appointment to a station of high authority in that very army, says : " It would appear that your wishes are at length accomplished, and that every possible circumstance is now united in our favour." When it is considered that Miranda was devoted, heart and soul, at that moment, to the Mexican expedition, and yet declares that the bestowal of high military command upon General Knox, with whom he had been in frequent consultation in reference to his scheme of invasion, would have the double effect of gratifying his (General Knox's) wishes, and uniting every possible circumstance in favour of that scheme, it is impossible to resist the conclusion that the army then raising in the United States was expected to be employed, to some extent, in the furtherance of Miranda's views.

But there is other evidence showing that such an inference is not wholly unworthy of respect. General Wilkinson in the first volume of his Memoirs, declares as follows : "In the Spring of 1797, the equivocal conduct of the Spanish authorities of Louisiana in relation to the Treaty of Limits, &c., induced me to reinforce our military posts on the Mississippi ; and for this service I selected Captain Isaac Guion, an officer of tried confidence and approved intelligence, who had served with General Montgomery before Quebec, and possessed great energy of character. The discussions which ensued, and the pretexts urged by the Spaniards for delaying the line of demarcation, conspiring with other circumstances which had come to the knowledge of the American Government, produced suspicions of a meditated infraction of the Treaty on the part of Spain ; in consequence of which I was ordered from Pittsburg in the Spring of 1798, to descend the waters to our western frontier, with a respectable force ; having by order of the executive previously addressed a harsh and firm remonstrance to the Spanish Governor Gayoso, on the subject, which, it would seem, produced the desired effect ; for, on my arrival in the low country, I found the commissioners were proceeding amicably on a survey of the line of limits.   *   *   *   *   *   *   *   I found our advanced post at Natchez, which I immediately removed, and sat down at Loftus Heights with my whole force, that being the most southern tenable position within our limits, on the banks of the Mississippi, about six miles north of the 31st degree of North latitude.   Whilst engaged at this point, preparing quarters for the troops, and erecting batteries to command the river, I received the following letter from Major General Hamilton."   Here follows a letter, in which General Hamilton announces that, in consequence of General Washington's "having for the present declined actual command," the control of the army had been transferred to himself and General Pinckney ; goes somewhat into detail on several points, and then urges upon General Wilkinson that he should visit New York without delay, for the purpose of conferring with his superior officers, with a view "to the formation of a more perfect plan for present and eventual arrangements." Then occurs the following paragraph : " It must rest with you to dispose of the command of the troops at the different stations, during your absence, and to give the proper instructions in conformity with those which have been received from the Secretary of War. On this head only one remark will be made : the confidence in your judgment has probably led to the reposing in your discretion powers too *delicate* to be entrusted to an officer less tried ; capable perhaps of being so read as to commit prematurely the peace of the United States. Discretions of this tendency ought not to be transferred, beyond what may be indispensable for defensive security. Care must be taken that the nation be not embroiled, but in consequence of a *deliberate policy in the government.*"

Now, here is a plain avowal that it might possibly become the " deliberate policy of the government," to get " embroiled." With what power ? With Spain, of course, for with no other power could war have been brought on by the movements of General Wilkinson, or his subordinate officers, in the South-west. How was the *embroilment* to occur as a measure of *deliberate policy ?* Evidently by *invasion of the Spanish territories ;—the very plan of Miranda.*

This view of the matter is still further sustained by the following statement of " heads for conversation," which General Hamilton furnished to General Wilkinson on his arrival in New York, as preliminary to the grand conference between them :

" OBJECTS.

" 1st. The disposition of our western inhabitants towards the United States and foreign powers.

" 2d. The disposition of the Indians in the same aspects.

" 3d. The disposition of the *Spaniards* in our vicinity ; their *strength* in *number*, and *fortifications.*

" 4th. The best expedients for correcting and controlling hostile tendencies in any or all these quarters, including,

" 5th. The best defensive disposition of the Western army, embracing the country of Tennessee and the Northern and Western lakes, and having an eye to economy and discipline.

" 6th. The best mode (*in the event of a rupture with Spain*) of *attacking the two Floridas;* the troops, artillery, &c., requisite.

" 7th. The best plan for supplying the Western army with provisions, transportation of forage, &c.

" 8th. The best arrangement of command, so as to unite facility of communication with the sea-board, and the proper combination of all the parts under the General commanding the Western army."

It is matter of history, that whatever plan had been at that time devised for an attack upon the Floridas, and, eventually, for invading Mexico, was defeated by the sudden reduction of the army; but it is certain that General Wilkinson's views, once turned towards Mexico, were never withdrawn, during his period of command in the Southwest. For, independent of his obvious connection with the project of Burr, some years afterwards, in aid of which he despatched an agent three several times to the City of Mexico, to obtain information of the interjacent country, as ancillary to a military invasion from the United States, and other acts of his of the same tendency, hereafter to be spoken of; we find him, as late as 1812, in an address to the Secretary of War, relative to the most proper means of defence to be adopted for the security of New Orleans against the forces of Great Britain, wandering copiously into Mexican details—" Still harping on my daughter." Of which the following extracts will furnish curious evidence :—" But, while preparing for the defence of New Orleans, we should not be inattentive to the Mexican provinces ; for it is a fact, derived from good authority, that Great Britain has appointed three commissioners, to co-operate with the same number from the Spanish regency, expressly to effect a reconciliation, and restore the former relations between the provinces and the parent state. Whatever may be the effect of these negotiations, it is the obvious policy of Great Britain, to acquire some direct or indirect control over the people of South America, and more particularly those of the Mexican provinces ; and it appears to be our interest and our policy, to take measures to counteract those views, as it may be fairly inferred, that the Mexicans must become our enemies or our friends ; enemies, should the British intrigues prevail, and the ancient government be re-established ; — friends, should the natives be enabled to assert and establish their independence.

"In this state of things, it might be presumptuous in a subordinate agent of the government, to obtrude his ideas on a subject of such complication and magnitude ; yet it is too manifest to escape notice, that some concert should be effected with the native chiefs of the Internal provinces, and that this government should be prepared to furnish them succours of small-arms, light artillery, ammunition, equipments, and field equipage, with experienced officers to instruct them, and select corps from the different branches of service, as a *nucleus* for the revolutionists to rally round, and skeletons for them to form by. It would seem that no time should be lost in carrying this project into execution ; and, preparatory thereto, a couple of light-armed vessels should explore the coast of the gulf west of the Mississippi to Grand River, and ascertain the entrance into El Espirito Santo Bay, where La Salle landed. I have been informed, four or five fathoms water may be carried into that Bay, and that it is completely land-locked. The position is certainly the most convenient for maritime intercourse with the inhabitants of the province of Texas, to be found east of Grand River ; it receives the river St. Antonio or Medina, which is navigable for batteaux eighteen leagues, to the town of La Bahia,* situated on the right bank of the same, twenty-five leagues from St. Antonio, the capital of Texas, to the neighbourhood of which, navigation may be found for perogues, during the high waters of the country."

Whilst upon the subject of Miranda's expedition, (which, having been designed to operate against the Spanish power in Mexico, falls properly under survey in such a work as the present) it may not be unseasonable to show the attitude assumed by the administration of Mr. Jefferson towards the hostile plan of Miranda, when submitted in a form somewhat different from the original one, and having in view an expedition against the South American provinces.   Mr. Jefferson, in writing to Don Valentine De Foronda, then minister from Spain to the United States, says : " Your predecessor,† soured on a question of etiquette against the Administration of this country, wished to impute wrong to them in all their actions, even where he did not believe it himself.   In this spirit, he wished it to be believed that we were in unjustifiable co-operation in Miranda's expedition. I solemnly, and on my personal truth and honour, declare to you that this was entirely without foundation, and that there was neither co-operation nor connivance on our part. He informed us he was about to attempt the liberation of his native country from bondage, and intimated a hope of our aid or connivance at least.   He was at once informed, that though we had great cause of complaint against Spain, and even of war, yet whenever we should think proper to act as her enemy, it should be openly and aboveboard, and that our hostility should never be exercised by such petty means.   We had no suspicion that he intended to engage men here, but merely to purchase military stores.   Against this there was no law, nor consequently any authority for us to interpose obstacles.   On the other hand, we deemed it

---

* Now Goliad.   † Marquis of Yrujo.

improper to betray his voluntary communication to the agents of Spain. Although his measures were many days in preparation at New York, we had never the least intimation or suspicion of his engaging men in his enterprise, until he was gone; and I presume the secresy of his proceedings kept them equally unknown to the Marquis of Yrujo at Philadelphia, and the Spanish Consul at New York, since neither of them gave us any information of the enlistment of men, until it was too late for any measures taken at Washington to prevent their departure."

Upon which letter, it may be here observed, that whatever course Mr. Jefferson, as the Executive Chief of a Nation at peace with Spain, might have felt himself bound to adopt in regard to Miranda's operations, had they been made known to him in a satisfactory manner, with a view to the preservation of amicable relations between the United States and Spain; it cannot be doubted, that his sympathies as a private citizen, and as a friend to freedom, were deeply enlisted in favour of Miranda's scheme of emancipation, and that any interposition for its defeat would have been to him, as well as to the citizens of the United States generally, a duty altogether disagreeable. A considerable number of young Americans are known to have accompanied the Liberating General in the expedition referred to, belonging to the best families in New York and other states; among whom may be here named, the honourable David G. Burnet, the first President, and the present *Vice President of the Texan Republic — who attended upon Miranda, as will be hereafter narrated, as one of his aids and as private secretary, and who then gave clear proofs of those high virtues and capabilities which have been since made conspicuously manifest on a new but congenial theatre.

In order to place the conduct of Mr. Jefferson in a clear point of light in reference to his feelings towards the cause

* In consequence of the lamented indisposition of President Lamar, Vice President Burnet is at this time officiating as President.

of Independence and Liberty in the Spanish Provinces of North and South America, and to show conclusively that he, in common with the great body of his countrymen, was sincerely solicitous that the people of those provinces gene- rally, whether under Spanish or Portuguese rule, should accomplish their emancipation, it is only necessary to read a letter addressed by him to the honourable John Jay, at so early a period as the year 1789. Being at the time engaged in a journey of observation through the south of France and Italy, he writes to Judge Jay: "My journey into this part of the country, has procured me information which I take the liberty of communicating to Congress. In October last, I received a letter dated Montpelier, October 2d, 1786, announcing to me that the writer was a foreigner, who had a matter of very great consequence to communi- cate to me, and desired I would indicate the channel through which it might safely pass. I did so. I received, soon after, a letter in the following words, omitting only the formal parts. (*A translation of it is here given.*)

"'I am a native of Brazil. You are not ignorant of the frightful slavery under which our country groans. This continually becomes more insupportable since the epoch of your glorious Independence; for the cruel Portuguese omit nothing which can render our condition more wretched, from an apprehension that we may follow your example. The conviction that these usurpers against the laws of na- ture and humanity only meditate new oppressions, has de- cided us to follow the guiding light which you have held out to us, to break our chains, to revive our almost expiring liberty, which is nearly overwhelmed by that force which is the sole foundation of the authority that Europeans exer- cise over America. But it is necessary that some power should extend assistance to the Brazilians, since Spain would certainly unite herself with Portugal; and, in spite of our advantages for defence, we could not make it effec- tual, or, at least it would be imprudent to hazard the attempt, without some assurance of success. In this state of affairs, Sir, we can, with propriety, look only to the United States, not only because we are following her example, but, moreover, because nature, in making us the inhabitants of the same Continent, has in some sort united us in the bonds of a common patriotism. On our part, we are prepared to furnish the necessary supplies of money, and at all times, to acknowledge the debt of gratitude due to our benefactors. I have thus, Sir, laid before you a summary of my views. It is in discharge of this commission that I have come to France, since I could not effect it in America, without exciting suspicion. It now remains for you to decide whether those views can be accomplished. Should you desire to consult your nation on them, it is in my power to give you all the information you may require.' "

" As, by this time, I had been advised to try the waters of Aix, I wrote to the gentleman of my design, and that I would go off my road as far as Nismes, under the pretext of seeing the antiquities of that place, if he would meet me there. He met me, and the following is the sum of the information I received from him." Here follows a long and specific statement of the precise condition of Brazil in every material respect, which it would be useless now to exhibit. Mr. Jefferson's reply is contained in the following paragraph :

" I took care to impress on him, through the whole of our conversation, that I had neither instructions nor authority to say a word to any body on the subject, and that I could only give him my own ideas, as a *single individual:* which were, that we were not in a condition, *at present,* to meddle *nationally* in any war ; that we wished particularly to cultivate the friendship of Portugal, with whom we had an advantageous commerce. That yet, a successful revolution in Brazil could not be uninteresting to us. That prospects of lucre might possibly draw numbers of individuals to their aid, and purer motives our officers, among

12 *

whom were many excellent. That our citizens being free to leave their own country individually, without the consent of their government, are equally free to go to any other."

In the same letter, Mr. Jefferson details the particulars of a conversation held by him with a Mexican, in which he evinces a similar solicitude to behold the progress of free principles, but in which there is a still greater caution manifested in reference to committing the government which he represented in a manner that might prove embarrassing to it. His words are as follows: " A little before I received the first letter of the Brazilian, a gentleman informed me there was a Mexican in Paris, who wished to have some conversation with me. He accordingly called on me. The substance of the information I drew from him was as follows. He is himself a native of Mexico, where his relations, principally, are. He left it at about seventeen years of age, and seems now to be about thirty-three or four. He classes and characterizes the inhabitants of that country as follows. 1. The natives of Old Spain, possessed of most of the offices of government, and firmly attached to it. 2. The Clergy, equally attached to the government. 3. The natives of Mexico, generally disposed to revolt, but without instruction, without energy, and much under the dominion of their priests. 4. The slaves, mulatto and black : the former enterprising and intelligent, the latter brave, and of very important weight, into whatever scale they throw themselves ; but he thinks they will side with their masters. 5. The conquered Indians, cowardly, not likely to take any side, nor important which they take. 6. The free Indians, brave and formidable, should they interfere, but not likely to do so, as being at a great distance. I asked him the numbers of these several classes, but he could not give them. The first, he thought very inconsiderable ; that the second formed the body of the freemen ; the third equal to the two first ; the fourth to all the preceding : and as to the fifth, he could form no idea of their proportion. Indeed, it appeared to me that his conjectures as to the others were upon loose grounds. He said he knew from good information, there were three hundred thousand inhabitants in the city of Mexico. I was still more cautious with him than with the Brazilian, mentioning it as my opinion (unauthorized to say a word on the subject, otherwise) that a successful revolution was still at a distance from them; that I feared they must begin by enlightening the minds of their people; that as to us, if Spain should give us advantageous terms of commerce, and remove other difficulties, it was not probable that we should relinquish present and certain advantages, though smaller, for uncertain and future ones, however great. I was led into this caution by observing, that this gentleman was intimate at the Spanish Ambassador's, and that he was then at Paris, employed by Spain to settle her boundaries with France, on the Pyrenees. He had much the air of candour; but this can be borrowed; so that I was unable to decide about him in my own mind."

In the same letter, Mr. Jefferson, alluding to the troubles which had, a few years before, occurred in Peru, says:—" The truth was, that the insurrections were so general, that the event was long on the poise. Had Commodore Johnson, then expected on that coast, touched and landed two thousand men, the dominion of Spain in that country would have been at an end. They only wanted a point of union, which this body would have constituted. Not having this, they acted without concert, and were at length subdued separately. This conflagration was quenched in blood: two hundred thousand souls on both sides perished; but the remaining matter is very capable of combustion. I have this information from a person who was on the spot at the time, and whose good faith, understanding, and means of information, leave no doubt of the facts. He observed, however, that the numbers above supposed to have perished, were on such conjecture only as he could collect."

Mr. Jefferson concludes his statement, on this interesting subject, thus :—" I trouble Congress with these details, because, however distant we may be, both in condition and dispositions, from taking an *active* part in any commotions in that country, nature has placed it too *near us* to make its movements altogether indifferent to our interests or to our curiosity."

Such was the language held by prominent statesmen in the United States, before the close of the last century ; and among the body of the people it has been seen that similar opinions were entertained, and a sensibility, if not more ardent, at least more open in its manifestations, was everywhere cherished. Up to the treaty of 1795, already referred to, and afterwards, likewise, with little or no change, three leading sentiments prevailed in the United States with great force and unanimity : 1. Contempt mingled with abhorrence for Spain and her institutions, civil and religious. 2. A generous and painful solicitude for the unfortunate millions she held in bondage : and 3. A jealousy, active and unintermitting, towards the Spanish Government and people, on account of the power which they possessed of disturbing the peace and retarding the growth of the United States, as well by obstructing the navigation of the Mississippi, as by distressing the Southern and remote Western settlements with continual Indian incursions.

The first year of Mr. Jefferson's administration, the year 1801, was productive of new and serious grounds of complaint against the Spanish government. It will be recollected that Spain, in conjunction with France, was then at war with Great Britain. The whole Mediterranean Sea was beset with Barbary corsairs ; in consequence of which, American vessels entering that sea were compelled to touch at Gibraltar, a place in the occupancy of Great Britain, for the purpose of obtaining convoy against these ferocious pirates. A large number of them were seized upon by Spanish cruisers, carried into the port of Algeziras, and subjected to condemnation ; and their crews were either thrown into prison, or made to feel other injuries and indignities of a character not to be borne with patience. Numerous memorials, from merchants in Philadelphia, New York, Boston, and other cities, interested in the Mediterranean trade, were from time to time presented to the government on the subject, replete with details calculated to engender strong excitement throughout the whole Republic. To all the remonstrances and applications for redress which were then made to the government of the United States, the Spanish government, relying upon the protection of France, manifested the utmost indifference, not to say contempt.

Agressions upon American trade, of a character equally offensive, occurred about the same period on this side of the Atlantic. Various merchant vessels engaged in *authorized* trade with the Spanish Cities of the New World, were captured by armed cruisers of Spain, upon different pretences, all of which turned out, upon investigation, to be altogether frivolous and unsubstantial. These grievances chiefly arose along the coast of the Island of Cuba. From the list of commercial wrongs done to the citizens of the United States, under Spanish direction and authority, too numerous for special citation here, a single instance may be selected for special mention. The American Consul, at St. Jago de Cuba, was surprised at midnight in his own dwelling, by a Spanish armed force, robbed of his official papers, and thrown into a filthy prison ; where he was detained for several months, without even any allegation of misconduct on the part of the Spanish government.

In the meantime, affairs were rapidly approaching a crisis in the South-Western part of the United States. On the 22d of December, 1802, Mr. Jefferson, as President, communicated to Congress intelligence of some occurrences which had then recently taken place, of a nature highly portentous, in the neighbourhood of New Orleans, and at other points of the territorial district at that time in the occupancy of Spain. In order to take an accurate view of the state of affairs then existing, it is necessary to bear in mind the fact, that, some time before, the Spanish government had ceded to France the whole country then called Louisiana, but had not yet relinquished actual possession of the same. By the Treaty of *friendship, limits,* and *navigation,* of 1795, it had been solemnly agreed, that his Catholic Majesty would permit the citizens of the United States, for the space of three years from the date thereof, " to deposit their merchandises and effects in the port of New Orleans, and to export them from thence, without paying any other duty, than a fair price for the hire of the stores;" and the King of Spain furthermore bound himself " either to continue this permission, (if he found, during the three years specified, that it was not prejudicial to the interests of Spain,) or, if he should not continue it, then to assign to said citizens of the United States, on another part of the banks of the Mississippi, an *equivalent establishment.*" On the 16th of October, 1802, Juan Ventura Morales, the Spanish Intendant of the Province of Louisiana, issued a decree, which, in violation of said Treaty of 1795, prohibited the bringing in or depositing American merchandise within the limits of the City of New Orleans, and this decree was issued without assigning the " *equivalent establishment,*" mentioned in the Treaty, elsewhere upon the banks of the Mississippi. Among the documents then submitted by the President of the United States to Congress, was one from William E. Hulings, some time before appointed Vice Consul of the United States at New Orleans, two from William C. C. Claiborne, Governor of the Mississippi territory, and a third from James Garrard, the Governor of Kentucky. Mr. Hulings announces to the Governor of the Mississippi territory the fact, that the decree of the Spanish Intendant, already described, had been posted up in the City of New Orleans, on the 18th of October; states that " the port of

New Orleans is shut against foreign Commerce, and not against foreign Commerce only, but against the *American deposit* in this city. No mention is made," he says, " of any other place appointed for a deposit." Governor Claiborne's letters, one to the Spanish Intendant, and the other to Mr. Madison, testify high indignation at the faithless conduct of the Spanish government ; and he says to the Secretary of State : " This late act of the Spanish government at Orleans, has excited considerable agitation at Natchez and its vicinity. It has inflicted a severe wound on the agricultural and commercial interests of this territory, and will prove no less injurious to the whole Western Country." The Governor of Kentucky, in his communication to the President of the United States, under date November 30th, 1802, says : " The citizens of this State are very much alarmed and agitated ; as this measure of the Spanish government will, if not altered, at one blow cut up the present and future prosperity of their best interests by the roots. To you, Sir," he continues, " they naturally turn their eyes, and on your attention to this important subject, their best hopes are fixed."

The *right of deposit*, a deprivation of which Mr. Jefferson says, in his annual Message of October 17th, 1803, had " produced extraordinary agitation in the public mind," by the timely and energetic interposition of the general government, was restored before much injury to the citizens of the United States had ensued. " Previously, however, to this period, (says the President in the Message just alluded to,) we had not been unaware of the danger to which our peace would be perpetually exposed, whilst so important a key to the commerce of the western country remained under foreign power. Difficulties, too, were presenting themselves as to the navigation of other streams which, arising within our territories, pass through those adjacent. Propositions had therefore been authorised for obtaining, on fair conditions, the sovereignty of New Orleans, and of other possessions in that quarter interesting to our quiet, to such an extent as was deemed practicable, and the provisional appropriation of two millions of dollars, to be applied and accounted for by the President of the United States, intended as a part of the price, was considered as conveying the sanction of Congress to the acquisition proposed.   The enlightened Government of France saw, with just discernment, the importance to both nations, of such liberal arrangements as might best and permanently promote the peace, interests, and friendship of both; and the property and sovereignty of all Louisiana, which has been restored to them, has, on certain conditions, been transferred to the United States by instruments bearing date the 30th of April last.   When these shall have received the constitutional sanction of the Senate, they will, without delay, be communicated to the representatives for the exercise of their functions, as to those conditions, which are within the powers vested by the constitution in Congress.   Whilst the property and sovereignty of the Mississippi and its waters secure an independent outlet for the produce of the Western States, and an uncontrolled navigation throughout their whole course, free from collision with other powers, and the dangers to our peace from that source, the fertility of the country, its climate and extent, promise in due season proper aids to our treasury, and ample provision to our posterity, and a wide spread for the blessings of freedom and equal laws."

It might have been reasonably expected that after the judicious purchase of Lousiana from the French Government by the United States, all further trouble from Spain and her citizens would thenceforth cease.   But it seems this was far from being the case.   Spain publicly protested against the acquisition of this country by the United States; and, denying that such acquisition was at all compatible with the terms of cession to France, urged warm objections against the validity of the title obtained from the French Emperor.   The establishment by Congress of a district and port of entry on the waters of Mobile bay, was complained of by the Government of Spain as a flagrant offence, and every symptom of opposition was evinced to any part of the ceded country coming under the dominion of the United States. On the 15th of May, 1804, the Spanish Minister at Philadelphia announced the determination of his government to sanction the act of cession, and pretended in his communication to the Government of the United States on that subject, that special sentiments of amity on the part of his Catholic Majesty towards the American Republic had been a ruling motive with him in finally acquiescing in the act of transfer. Yet we find Mr. Jefferson, in his annual message of December 3d, 1805, using the following language : " With Spain our negotiations for a settlement of differences have not had a satisfactory issue. Spoliations during the former war, for which she had formerly acknowledged herself responsible, have been refused to be compensated but on conditions affecting other claims in no wise connected with them. Yet the same practices are renewed in the present war, and are already of great amount. On the Mobile, our commerce passing through that river, continues to be obstructed by arbitrary duties and vexatious searches. Propositions for adjusting amicably the boundaries of Louisiana have not been acceded to. While, however, the right is unsettled, we have avoided changing the state of things, by taking new posts, or strengthening ourselves in the disputed territories, in the hope that the other power would not, by a contrary conduct, oblige us to meet the example, and endanger conflicts of authority, the issue of which may not be easily controlled. *But in this hope we have now reason to lose our confidence.* Inroads have been recently made into the territories of Orleans and the Mississippi. Our citizens have been seized, and their property plundered in the very ports of the former, which had been actually delivered up by Spain ; and this by the regular officers and soldiers of that government. I have, therefore, found it necessary at length to give orders to our troops on that frontier, to be in readiness to protect our citizens, **and** to repel by arms any similar aggressions in future."

It had become now evident to the people of the United States that *a war with Spain could scarcely be avoided*, and might indeed almost be considered as commenced. But in a few months the signs of an approaching conflict became still more distinct; for we find Mr. Jefferson addressing Congress on the 6th of December 1805, in this language: " The depredations which had been committed on the commerce of the United States during a preceding war, by persons under the authority of Spain, are sufficiently known to all; these made it a duty to require from that government indemnifications for our injured citizens. A convention was accordingly entered into between the minister of the United States at Madrid and the minister of that government for foreign affairs, by which it was agreed, that spoliations committed by Spanish subjects and carried into the ports of Spain should be paid for by that nation, and that those committed by French subjects and carried into Spanish ports should remain for further discussion. Before this convention was returned to Spain with our ratification, the transfer of Louisiana by France to the United States took place, an event as unexpected as disagreeable to Spain. From that moment she seemed to change her conduct and dispositions towards us : it was first manifested by her protest against the right of France to alienate Louisiana to us, which, however, was soon retracted, and the right confirmed. Her high offence was manifested at the act of Congress establishing a collection district on the Mobile, although, by an authentic declaration, immediately made, it was expressly confined to our acknowledged limits; and she now refused to ratify the convention signed by her own minister under the eye of his sovereign, unless we would consent to an alteration of its terms, which would have affected our claims against her for spoliations by French subjects carried into Spanish ports.

"To obtain justice, as well as to restore friendship, I thought a special minister advisable, and accordingly appointed James Monroe minister plenipotentiary and extraordinary, to repair to Madrid, and, in conjunction with our minister resident there, to endeavour to procure a ratification of the former convention, and to come to an understanding with Spain as to the boundaries of Louisiana. It appeared at once, that her policy was to reserve herself for events, and in the mean time keep our differences in an undetermined state; this will be evident from the papers now communicated to you. After nearly five months of fruitless endeavours to bring them to some definite and satisfactory result, our ministers ended the conferences without having been able to obtain indemnity for spoliations of any description, or any satisfaction as to the boundaries of Louisiana, other than a declaration that we had no right eastward of the Iberville; and that our line to the west was such a one as would have left us but a string of land on that bank of the river Mississippi. Our injured citizens were thus left without any prospect of retribution from the wrong-doer, and, as to boundary, each party was to take its own course. That which they have chosen to pursue will appear from the documents now communicated. They authorise the inference, that *it is their intention to advance on our possessions until they shall be repressed by an opposing force.* Considering that Congress alone is constitutionally vested with the power of changing our condition from *peace* to *war*, I have thought it my duty to await their authority for preparations which their means admitted of to commence the War *with advantage.*"

The leading circumstances are now before the reader out of which arose the celebrated project of Colonel Burr, about which so much wild conjecture has been indulged in the United States, and in reference to which, it is acknowledged that so little has been yet authentically ascertained. This has been heretofore a topic of some *delicacy*, and men hardly dared, from the dread of odium, to speak out their opinions with perfect independence. If it was his design to divide the Federal Union, to make war upon any part of the United States, no language of condemnation too harsh could be applied to it. If he simply intended an expedition into the Spanish territories, a little in advance of his countrymen—all of whom expected to be, in a short time, conflicting in war with Spain—perhaps the time which has passed away since the year 1807, may enable many so far to relieve their minds from prejudice, as to pronounce very differently concerning it. It would be, certainly, rather unfortunate, if the world should be always left in doubt concerning this project; and I am not certain that the national honour, both of the United States and Texas, is not somewhat concerned in clearing away the fog which has so long hung round it. Two Presidents* of the United States have been charged at one time very formally with being associates of Colonel Burr, and, so far as I am informed, neither of them has denied the fact of such connection having once existed; and several personages now in Texas, one† of whom, at least, is in high station there, have long openly acknowledged that they were united with him, and are not at all inclined to censure what he did, or intended to do, at this juncture. It is in the point of view just suggested, that some remarks will be offered in the next chap-

---

* General Jackson and General Harrison are the persons alluded to; Blennerhasset's Journal, published several years since, asserts, positively, that they were both *Burrites.* If so, and the fact could be certified, much would be gained; for there are few in the United States, or elsewhere, it is presumed, however opposed in political sentiments to either the one or the other of these distinguished statesmen, that would doubt the inflexible honour and lofty patriotism of either of them, or would believe, for an instant, that the Hero of New Orleans or the Hero of Tippecanoe could have been guilty of enlisting in a project which they did not *know* to be free from the stain of *treason* or *corruption* of any sort.

† Dr. Branch T. Archer, Secretary of War in Texas; of whom many honourable things will be said hereafter.

ter, and some evidence adduced which may possibly enable the reader to make up his mind about this perplexing affair, and decide favourably, or otherwise, relative to this first effort of Anglo-Americans *to advance to the far South-West.*

CHAPTER VIII.

View of Aaron Burr's project for opening all Spanish America to the Anglo-Americans and their institutions; with some remarks upon his conduct and character, not elsewhere to be found.

FEW individuals have at any time flourished whose character and conduct have seemed to be so imperfectly understood by their cotemporaries, or who have been fated to suffer such lasting and extensive detriment from misrepresentation and prejudice, as the personage, in regard to the leading event in whose public career, some remarks are about to be offered. The eminent intellectual powers of *Aaron Burr* have been at all times acknowledged,* by his bitterest enemies. "The dignity and elegance" of his manners, "the light and beauty of his conversation, and the seductive power of his address," were felt and admitted by all who approached him. The brilliant services which he rendered to his country, during her struggle for Liberty and Independence, have never been denied. —The faithful and efficient support which he gave to Republican principles, up to the portentous winter of 1800–1, (when a concurrence of circumstances, more than any misconduct of his own, threw him into conflict with Thomas Jefferson for the Presidential station,) has been at one period a favourite theme of applause with his own party, and of

* See Wirt's speech on his trial.

13*

revilement among those politically opposed to him. After the Presidential struggle alluded to, he found himself no longer possessed of the confidence and esteem of the great leader of the Republican party ; who, as well as his particular friends and associates, had become for ever estranged from him.   The unfortunate encounter between himself and General Hamilton upon the duelling-field, which terminated in the death of that distinguished party chieftain, raised up against Colonel Burr a countless host of fierce and implacable foes, whose rancour was so vehement and merciless that even his life was not for some time secure against their malice.   All who had enjoyed the confidence of this great Magnus Apollo of Federalism, and had expected at some future period to be rewarded for their fidelity to his person and principles,—all who had looked to HIM for the recuscitation of their now prostrate political cause, and who saw in his death the extinction of all present hope of its resurrection in future, were ready to shed the blood of the man who had presumed to assail the object of their idolatrous admiration ; although he had done so in *necessary* vindication of his own character against malevolent assaults *acknowledged* to have been made upon it.   At this moment, Colonel Burr was beset with the unanimous denunciations of the newspaper press, from Maine to Georgia : Federal editors accused him of *outrageous murder*, and demanded that the death of General Hamilton should be expiated by him upon the scaffold ; the editors of the Republican party would not defend a man who they believed had proved himself a *traitor* to their cause, and most of them accordingly joined heartily in the thundering chorus of denunciation then resounding through the land.   In the mean time, Colonel Burr remained completely passive, with an *indiscreet* contempt for the efforts which were making to undo his reputation ; he responded to no allegation, however vitally affecting his good name ; he stooped not to a disproof of charges however plausibly arrayed against him. The consequence was easy to be foreseen : the continuous pattering even of the gentle rain-drops of heaven will in time wear away the surface of the hardest rock ; and the fame of a man, who had but lately been enthusiastically elevated by the suffrages of millions of enlightened freemen to the second office in their gift, the high duties of which he was even then performing, if not with unsuspected fidelity, at least with a stately and imposing magnificence rarely equalled,—was seen to tumble piecemeal into ruin, beneath the well-directed and *unparried* missiles of steady and persevering revilement. It is not my province to pourtray the characteristics of Colonel Burr in all their mystic amplitude, or to vindicate his private morals from aspersions which appear to have received the deliberate sanction of his own chosen Biographer. Still less is it my duty, or inclination, in the observations about to be indulged, to utter a single word in decrial of that great and good man, under the influence of whose potent genius, the flattering prospects of Colonel Burr as a military chieftain were so completely blasted. Yet it may be permitted to one, who has ever looked upon *Thomas Jefferson* as a man to whom the cause of *free principles* owes more of its success and present glory than to any other individual whatever, to declare the conviction which he has long entertained, that even this profound sage was most obviously imposed upon by *false* statements in reference to the true character and objects of Colonel Burr in the grand scheme of conquest which he attempted to carry into execution in the year 1806 ; and that after all, it is most evident that Aaron Burr did not deserve to be considered *a traitor to his country.*.

Let us explore the prominent facts of this extraordinary case, with a sober attention, and if it be possible, (after the lapse of thirty-five years,) with unprejudiced minds. A war had been brewing between the United States and Spain for many years ; and recent occurrences had transpired of such a nature as induced the President of the United States to recommend to Congress, almost in so many words, a regular declaration of hostilities. A violent ferment pervaded the whole Republic, and a wish was almost unanimously expressed that the expected conflict of arms should not be longer postponed. The Western and Southern States, as has been seen, had become so vehemently excited that it seemed impossible even for the arm of government much longer to hold the dark cloud of war in a state of suspension. Spain was preparing to invade the territory of the United States at two points; her myrmidon soldiers were already gathering in menacing array upon the Eastern and Western frontiers of Louisiana.

What more natural, under such circumstances, than for an old soldier like Col. Burr, conscious of his own high ability for military command, and an enthusiastic devotee to the renown of arms as he was,—who had in youth rushed impetuously from his collegiate exercises to the snow-clad heights of Montreal, to battle at the side of the illustrious Montgomery for his country's freedom—what more natural, I repeat, than for such a man, disappointed in his pursuit of honour along the slippery pathways of political strife, whilst yet in the prime of his mental and bodily faculties, and glowing with all the fervour of his earlier days, to seek the renewal of a fame which time and ill accidents had contrived to despoil of a portion of its primeval lustre, by throwing himself at the head of the grand military movement in contemplation among his countrymen, and volunteering to lead forward the generous Crusade apparently about to be prosecuted against a bigoted, tyrannical, and perfidious nation; a nation from which the American people had received so many evidences of fraudful hostility, and the Anglo-American race such multiplied tokens of peculiar and unappeasable hatred? What more consistent than that a *warrior statesman*, who had been ever since the year 1796, maturing a scheme for revolutionizing all South America—and redeeming millions of human beings from the bondage of centuries, should embrace the fair opportunity now presented of carrying this magnificent scheme of emancipation into triumphant execution? Surely nothing but the most conclusive proof could authorize the belief, or even justify the faintest suspicion, that an individual who had given so many and such shining evidences of devotion to the principles of civil liberty, and of affectionate attachment to his native country—as Col. Burr had unquestionably done, had now become all at once so basely unmindful of his own high example, as well as so meanly regardless of the lofty precepts of classic history, as, *Catiline-like*, to plot a diabolical conspiracy against the institutions of freedom which adorned the land of his birth, and impiously to plunge the dagger of treason into the vitals of a Republic over whose interests he had so lately in part presided. Whatever surmises may at one time have gained currency touching Col. Burr's conduct at this juncture, — however highly popular excitement may have been enkindled against him at a former period, it must now be conceded that the most diligent and laborious research would be in vain instituted in pursuit of evidence calculated seriously to criminate either himself or the patriotic men associated with him.

As little justice as *discretion* would be displayed in reprobating the conduct of Mr. Jefferson at this crisis, and charging him with the ungenerous persecution of a political rival, because he thought proper to use means of extraordinary energy for the purpose of arresting the movements of Colonel Burr, and subjecting his acts to judicial investigation. Doubtless the Federal Executive of that day proceeded upon information received by him through channels apparently authentic, and on which he confidently relied. The suspicions which Mr. Jefferson had conceived relative to the supposed evil designs of Colonel Burr, seem strongly justified by statements made to him at the time by General Wilkinson and others ; and occupying the attitude which he did as Executive Chief of the nation, he was bound to use the utmost vigilance and energy of which he was capable.

It is due to *Truth* to acknowledge now, in the year 1841, that the celebrated judicial scrutiny instituted in Richmond before Chief Justice Marshall, at the instance of the government, developed no testimony in the least degree calculated to sustain the charge of *Treason*. For though several of the witnesses brought forward on that occasion did evidently *strain hard* to make out such a case as would take away the life of Colonel Burr; yet did these very witnesses, on cross-examination, involve themselves in such palpable contradictions, and such glaring absurdities, that no virtue-swayed juror in the world would have been willing, on their *testimony alone*, to award a verdict of *guilty* against the accused. Extraordinary professional ability of every kind was displayed by the learned and eloquent barristers who represented the government in that trial; all authorized facilities were supplied by the upright and accomplished Judge who presided at it; in order to afford to the government a fair opportunity, if it could do so, of making good the accusation of Treason; and yet was no evidence adduced which could be considered as going beyond the maintenance of a charge, the truth of which was not even denied, viz: " *A Preparation of the means of a Military Expedition against Mexico, a territory of the King of Spain, with whom the United States were at peace;*" and although this must be acknowledged an offence against the *strict* law of the land, and as such was punishable as a *misdemeanour ;* yet, in the light of a liberal and long-sighted morality, looking beyond the present moment to remote consequences, even this illegal transaction will be apt to receive more respect than condemnation with many now living. At any rate, it is precisely what has been done in all civilized countries, in all ages; it is what has been done by citizens of the United States of approved standing, both in the case of Texas and the Texans, and in aid of the heroic Papineau in Canada ; with this difference only, that in the two latter instances there was neither war, nor prospect of war, between the United

States and the Republic of Mexico, in the one case, and between the United States and Great Britain in the other.

This is not the proper place for a minute examination of the testimony brought forward against Colonel Burr when the trial alluded to at Richmond was going on; it is presumed that few who may read these pages are unacquainted with its precise nature and extent. But before this branch of the subject is dismissed, it will be perhaps not unprofitable to present the statement of Commodore Truxtun, to whose evidence much importance was attached at the period of the trial, by the counsel who represented the government. This venerable personage spoke on the occasion referred to, as follows: " Colonel Burr told me, (sometime in July, 1806,) that he contemplated an expedition to Mexico, in the event of a war with Spain, which he thought inevitable. He asked me if the Havana could be easily taken in the event of a war. I told him that it would require the co-operation of a naval force. Mr. Burr observed to me that *that* might be obtained. He asked me if I had any personal knowledge of Carthagena and La Vera Cruz, and what would be the best mode of attacking them by sea and land. I gave him my opinion freely. Mr. Burr then asked me if I would take command of a naval expedition. I asked him if the executive of the United States were to be concerned in the project. He answered *emphatically* that he was not. I asked that question, because the executive had been charged with a knowledge of Miranda's expedition. I told Mr. Burr that I would have nothing to do with it; that Miranda's expedition had been intimated to me, but I declined to have anything to do with such affairs. He observed to me, that in the event of a war, he intended to establish an independent government in Mexico; that Wilkinson, the army, and many officers of the navy, would join. I told Mr. Burr that I could not see how any officer of the United States could join. He said that General Wilkinson had projected the expedition, and he had matured it; that many greater men than Wilkinson would join, and that thousands to the Westward would join. I told Colonel Burr that there would be no war. He said, however, that if he was disappointed as to the event of a war, he was about to complete a contract for a large quantity of land on the Washita; that he intended to invite his friends to settle it; that in one year he would have a thousand families of respectable and fashionable people, and some of them of considerable property; that it was a fine country, and that they would have charming society, and that in two years, he would have double the number of settlers; and, being on the frontier, he would be ready to move whenever a war took place." Commodore Truxtun, when cross-examined, said in addition, "that he was very intimate with Colonel Burr; that in their conversation there appeared to be no reserve; that he never heard Colonel Burr speak of a division of the Union; that Burr said his Mexican expedition would be beneficial to the United States; that so far from doubting Burr's intention to settle the Washita lands, he was astonished at hearing that he had different views, which accounts were contained in Newspapers from the Western country."

The accusation of Treason against Col. Burr, must be admitted to be strongly negatived by the fact, that he had succeeded in enlisting in his scheme, (whatever was its true nature,) a large number of as patriotic men as any in the nation; to all of whom, it is understood, he made a free disclosure of his objects. Many of those personages, who have been long recognized by the public as his allies, have subsequently signalized their devotion to their country, by the most unequivocal evidences, both in the battle-field and in civic station. It cannot be presumed that they would have remained associated with a man whom they believed to be guilty of *high treason;* and more especially can it not be supposed, that they would have maintained friendly and respectful communication with such a miscre-

ant, up almost to the period of his decease, as some of
these individals are well known to have done. It is much
more reasonable to conclude, that they all occupied very
much the attitude of the venerable Ex-President of the
United States, General Andrew Jackson, in reference to
whose connection with Col. Burr, the following publication
was made, more than three years ago, in a work * generally
read on both sides of the Atlantic, without any contradic-
tion to the statement being offered, from any quarter, so
far as is known or believed : " During the year 1806, Col.
Burr was at the house of General Andrew Jackson. Repeated and detailed conversations were held between them
in relation to the expedition. Subsequently, General Jackson addressed a letter to Col. Burr, in which he alluded to
rumours that were afloat of his having hostile designs
against the United States ; adding, that if this were true,
he would hold no communication on the subject ; but, if
untrue, and *his intentions were to proceed to Mexico, he
would join and accompany him with his whole division.*"
  General Adair, of Kentucky, a gentleman whose veracity
and lofty honour are so well known, that his statement on
any subject ought to be held conclusive, declares, in a letter written by him in 1807, as follows : " So far as I know
or believe of the intentions of Col. Burr, (and my enemies
will agree that I am not ignorant on this subject,) they
were to prepare and lead an expedition into Mexico, predi-
cated on a war between the two governments ; without a
war, he knew he could do nothing. On this war taking
place, he calculated with certainty, as well from the policy
of the measure at the time, as from the positive assurances
of Wilkinson, who seemed to have the power to force it in
his own hands. This continued to be the object of Col.
Burr, until he heard of the venal and shameful bargain of
Wilkinson at the Sabine river ; this information he received soon after the attempt to arrest him in Frankfort."
  But there remains evidence which will possibly prove

---

* Davis's Memoirs of Aaron Burr.

more availing with many than any yet mentioned ; it is that of Mr. Jefferson himself; who, however prejudiced against Col. Burr, and deceived by the statements of false witnesses, writes, notwithstanding, early in the year 1807, to Mr. Bowdoin, a gentleman then occupying a high station abroad, as follows : " No better proof of the good faith of the United States could have been given, than the vigour with which they have acted, and the expense incurred in suppressing the *enterprise meditated lately by Burr on Mexico.* Although *at first* he proposed a separation of the Western Country, and on that ground received aid and encouragement from Yrujo, according to the usual spirit of his government toward us, yet he very early saw that the fidelity of the Western Country was not to be shaken, and *turned himself entirely towards Mexico.* And so popular is an enterprise on that country in this, that we had only to lie still, and he would have been in the City of Mexico in six weeks." Here Mr. Jefferson himself plainly admits, that if Col. Burr ever had such an object in view, as the separation of the Western from the Eastern States, he *very early* abandoned it. *How* early would be *very* early ? Col. Burr, it is known, was engaged in this project for several years anterior to his first visit to the Western Country, in the Spring of the year 1805. It was not until the Autumn of 1806, that he met first with the individual who subsequently became his prime associate in the enterprise, the celebrated Herman Blennerhasset. It was not until the succeeding winter, that the *levying of troops* on the Ohio river was alleged to have taken place. Nothing can be clearer than the proposition, that if Burr, *very early* in the course of his operations, abandoned the notion which Mr. Jefferson imagines him at first to have entertained, of attacking the government of the United States, and "turned himself entirely towards Mexico," no important part of his proceedings in the Western Country that has yet encountered the public eye, can be considered otherwise than as appertaining to the intended expedition to Mexico. This view of the affair, taken in connexion with what has been already said, must inevitably relieve this famous project of all the odium at one time attached to it. It will be noticed, that when Mr. Jefferson speaks of Burr's original purpose being hostile to the United States, he evidently does so *loosely*, and upon mere impression; not at all upon *testimony* such as would be requisite to enforce conviction upon any unprejudiced mind.

It is not a little amusing, at this distance from the period under examination, to observe, that whilst Mr. Jefferson testified such decided unwillingness to permit Col. Burr to carry on his scheme of conquest against Mexico, and could not consent to *lie still* even for the short space of *six weeks*, without interposing for the rescue of the renowned Capital of Montezuma from the grasp of Burr and his enterprising *followers*, he was still far from being in a good humour with the Spanish government, and was not altogether unambitious, either, of gilding his administration with the acquisition of this magnificent city. For, in the letter just referred to, he says : " Never did a nation act with more perfidy or injustice than Spain has constantly practised against us : and if we have kept our hands off of her till now, it has been purely out of respect to France, and from the value we set on the friendship of France. We expect, therefore, from the friendship of the Emperor, that he will either compel Spain to do us justice, or abandon her to us. *We ask but one month to be in the city of Mexico*." It has been already mentioned, that this letter to Mr. Bowdoin was written early in the year 1807 : the trial of Burr took place in the latter part of the summer of the same year. I cannot refrain from suggesting, that, instead of looking to the Emperor of France for justice against Spain, and depending upon the *friendship* of Napoleon for indemnity on account of the long list of wrongs committed upon the citizens of the United States by the Spanish government, it would have been decidedly better policy and equally consistent with Anglo-

American dignity, to have lain still, for six weeks, whilst
Burr, the Avenger, rushed at the head of his chivalrous followers to Mexico, and compelled the enemies of his country
and countrymen to pay down full recompense for all grievances remaining unredressed.   Had Mr. Jefferson been able
to reconcile this course with his own views of propriety,
Burr, the *Conspirator*, would never have been heard of,
and, in his place, Aaron Burr, *the Liberator of Mexico and
all South America*, might have filled a page in the history
of the world now divided among numerous chieftains of far
inferior merit.   Those who have candidly examined the
career of Col. Burr as a politician in the United States —
have coolly and dispassionately explored his peculiar frame
of intellect — and have looked without prejudice into his correspondence with different personages whilst in a state of
voluntary exile from his native country — still zealously and
perseveringly urging forward his well-digested project for
the emancipation of the Spanish provinces in North and
South America, — will require no arguments to convince
them, that, had he not been obstructed in the outset of his
labours, he would not only have been able speedily to
achieve all of conquest over Spanish power of which he was
ambitious, but that his military successes would have been
faithfully consecrated to the cause of civil and religious liberty.   This presumption, so reasonable upon the basis just
suggested, is powerfully fortified by awarding due weight
and consideration to the illustrious attributes of many of
those individuals in the United States whom he had selected
as his co-operators ; whose high character would have afforded to the civilized world a sure guarantee against any
unworthy use of the authority which, by their aid and co-
operation, Col. Burr might have acquired by arms.   In
connection with this view, the important fact should not be
overlooked, that whilst abroad, and especially during his
sojourn in England, his familiar associates were all men
who had been long celebrated for virtue and for wisdom,

and who were distinguished above all others of their age and nation for enlarged and *liberal principles.*

Among these, it is sufficient to mention *Jeremy Bentham* and *Sir Samuel Romilly*—two men whose fame will endure, and grow every day more resplendent, whilst profound learning, bold and independent intellectual research, devotion to free institutions, and disinterested love for human kind, shall be prized among the children of men. It is of Jeremy Bentham, that Lord Brougham spoke, more than twenty years ago, in the following terms, in the discussion of a question in the British Parliament, whereupon he differed with him in opinion :—" From this charge of inconsistency there was one great authority who was exempt—he meant Mr. Bentham. He had the greatest respect for that gentleman. There existed not a more honest or ingenuous mind than he possessed. He knew no man who had passed a more honourable and useful life. Removed from the turmoil of active life, voluntarily abandoning both the emolument and the power which it held out to dazzle ambitious and worldly minds ; he had passed his days in the investigation of important truths, and had reached a truly venerable, although he hoped not an extreme old age. To him he meant not to impute either inadequate information, or insufficient industry, or defective sagacity." It was in defence of the same individual, that Sir Francis Burdett spoke in the same debate, thus :—" The learned gentleman, whilst he professed himself friendly to Reform, had at the same time attempted to render ridiculous, the ablest advocate which Reform had ever found — the illustrious and unrivalled Bentham. It was in vain, however, for the learned gentleman to attempt, by stale jokes and misapplied sarcasms, to underrate the efforts of a mind the most comprehensive, informed, accurate, acute, and philosophical, that had, perhaps, in any time or in any country, been applied to the subject of *legislation*, and which, fortunately for mankind, had been brought to bear upon *Reform*, the most important

14 *

of all political subjects. The *abilities* of Bentham, the learned gentleman could not dispute, his *disinterestedness* he could not deny, his *benevolence* he could not but admire, and his unremitted labours he would do well to respect, and not attempt to disparage."

Sir Samuel Romilly, in the debate of which the preceding extracts constitute a portion (and which arose upon certain resolutions for Parliamentary Reform, drawn up by Mr. Bentham himself,) is spoken of by Lord Brougham, as " looking up to Mr. Bentham with the almost filial reverence of a pupil for his tutor ;" and in his masterly speech, " On the State of the Law," delivered in the House of Commons, in the year 1828, Lord Brougham introduces the name of Sir Samuel Romilly, then dead, as one, " never to be pronounced by any without veneration ;" and bestows high and deserved commendation upon him, on account of his successful labours as a member of the British Parliament, in the important work of *Juridical Reform*. It would ill become one wholly unknown to the learned world, and whose dispraise or commendation would be necessarily exceedingly limited in its influence, to offer anything additional, in illustration either of the extraordinary intellectual powers or amiable social qualities of Jeremy Bentham and Sir Samuel Romilly. Especially is this unnecessary at present, since a gentleman,* better qualified, doubtless, for the task, in all respects, than any other individual now living, has recently communicated, to the reading public, a masterly Biographical sketch of each of these great champions of Reform, embodying therewith, a profound and perspicuous analysis of their mental attributes, in volumes which, from the deserved popularity of their author, have been read with delight and admiration on both sides of the Atlantic. *Noscitur a sociis*, is a received maxim both in law and in social life ; and the fact that Colonel Burr counselled habitually with such men as have

---

* Lord Brougham.

been mentioned, in regard to all the particulars of his *Revolutionary project*, will be acknowledged by liberal minds everywhere, to administer most persuasive proof, as to the purity of the motives by which he was actuated, and the entire worthiness of his objects.

At the period of Col. Burr's visit to England, immediately upon the termination of his trial in Richmond, Mr. Bentham had thrown out several of his incomparable volumes upon Juridical Reform. They had been received among his own countrymen with less favour than their uncommon merit authorized him to expect. He was still, and for many years thereafter, urging upon the British Parliament and people his unanswerable views on the subject, and exposing the manifold abuses which had crept into the common law system of England, and which then needed expurgation. But his hope of doing good in his day and generation, was, from the first, directed chiefly to the people of the United States ; and, subsequently, in various modes, through the President of the United States, Mr. Madison, and several leading governors of the respective States of the Union, he is known to have pressed his plans of legal reformation upon the public mind in this country, with a power and persuasive eloquence worthy of greater success than he was able to realize. In his celebrated Address to the people of the United States, in 1817, the anxiety which this great Chieftain of Reform felt, to rescue a free people to whose welfare he was devoted, from the Aristocratic manacles of the common law, and to induce them to adopt a juridical system at the same time adapted to their peculiar frame of government, and worthy of an age of increased and increasing illumination, is most strikingly manifested. In the following extracts from that address, his enthusiastic solicitude to have the theatre of the *New World* opened to him may be discerned : " Bad enough is it, in any country, to any sort of people, on each occasion, to have to hunt for the rule of action, in the breath of no one knows what in-

dividual, with or without a lawyer's gown upon his back:
an individual of whom this much only is known, viz. that,
even if he had—which he never can have—the *inclination*,
—he would not have the *power*—he would not have the
means—the means in any shape—to make it fit for use.
But in your land of freedom, and good government, to *you*
and *your* legislators, freely deputed agents and servants of
a free and self-governed people—thus to be perpetually on
the hunt for law—thus to rake for it in every sink of corruption—thus blindly to keep on importing a succession of
deaf and dumb matter from a country of slaves, what is
this but treason against your constitution?

" Yes, my friends, if you love one another—if you love
each one of you his own security, shut your ports against
our common law, as you would shut them against the
plague.   Leave us to be ruled — us who love to be thus
ruled—leave us to be ruled by that tissue of imposture.   *
   *   *   *   *   *   *   *   *   *

" The yoke of English monarchy — the yoke of English
Aristocracy—the yoke of English Prelacy—all these galling yokes, you have happily broken off.   Remains the yoke
of English *Eithersides*—exalted into Judges : the common
law, that tissue of imposture to which you still yield your
necks—to be pinched and galled, under the hands of one
class among you, for whom, while they are comforted, all
others are tormented.   Day by day it continues,—and so
long as you continue to crouch under it, will continue,—to
be more and more bulky—more and more afflictive—the
pressure of this yoke.   Will you repel—will you suffer to
be repelled—the hand that offers,—the only hand that ever
did offer—to relieve you from it?   *   *   *   *
" Let but *one* of your *twenty* States give acceptance to a
body of laws endowed with all these *qualities*,*—by that

---

* Mr. Bentham has previously described the *qualities* of the legal
system proposed by him.

one, sooner or later, will it be forced upon the others : forced upon them *all*, though by the gentlest of all pressures. "In America thus will Reason spread her conquests. As for that quarter of the world, from which shame is banished—in which, in the name of Christ, the *subsistence* of the *subject many* is, with such indefatigable devotion, made a constant sacrifice to the *luxury* of the *ruling few*—in which all men are governed, by those who, feeling themselves, are determined to keep themselves their enemies ; — in which that which calls itself *government* is but a system of *regulated pillage ;* in *that* quarter of the world, by no such Utopian conquest, will *its tranquillity*, and that sort of *order* which calls itself *good order*, be disturbed.

"On the ground of *Constitutional* Law, the system of law you have already—you, who on *that* ground have so nobly shaken off the yoke of *English* law—the system you have already, is, as to all essentials, a model for all nations. Accept then my services ; so shall it be on the ground of *Penal* law, so shall it be on the ground of *Civil* law : accept my services, at one lift you shall ease your backs of that degrading yoke * * * * * Yes, my friends, these labours of mine—labours which of themselves are nothing—dreams of an obscure individual—let them but be accepted by *you*—you shall be a *people of Conquerors.* Conquerors ! and with what arms ? with the sword ? No : but with the pen. By what means ? violence and destruction ? No : but reason and beneficence. As this, your dominion, spreads, not tears and curses, but smiles and blessings will attend your conquest in its course. Where the fear of his sword ends, there ends the empire of the military *Conqueror*. To the Conquest to which *you* are here invited, no ultimate limits can be assigned, other than those which bound the habitable globe. To *force* new laws upon a *reluctant* and abhorring people, is, in addition to unpunishable depredation—the object and effect of *vulgar conquest :* to behold your laws not only accepted but *sought after*—sought after by an admiring people, will be yours. * * * * * * * *

"*Stranger!* (say you) *why thus pressing?* pressing and for *labour without hire?* Friends, (say I,) *your* comfort will be *mine*. Your *Conquests*—the conquests I have been thus planning for you—these, indeed, I cannot live to see. But of your *comfort*—your internal comfort—the increase of comfort I have been speaking of—of this scene, to the eye of a sanguine and self-flattering imagination, a sort of *Pisgah* view is not impossible. My last hour cannot be far distant; this is the preparation I am making for it; by prospects such as these, if by anything, will it be sweetened."

There can be no doubt that the arrival of Colonel Burr in London, and the unfoldment of his project for revolutionizing the Spanish Provinces in North and South America, were hailed by Mr. Bentham as omens highly propitious to his own warmly cherished plans of Reform. He saw in the success of Colonel Burr, a whole continent at once thrown open for the establishment of those sublime moral conquests upon which he dwells so eloquently in the extracts just cited. With the eye of a "self-flattering imagination," as he elegantly styles it, he beheld the progress of a moral dominion, whose course would be signalized not by "tears and curses, but by smiles and blessings." It was not in the heart of Jeremy Bentham, or of Jeremy Bentham's friend and disciple, Aaron Burr, "to *force* new laws upon a reluctant and abhorring people"—"the object and effect of vulgar conquest:" it was not the contemptible "empire of the military conqueror alone," of which *such* men could be ambitious; but the spread of knowledge and virtue, the diffusion of free principles, and the perpetuation of Liberty and happiness through all the endless successions of posterity, and in all countries under the sun.

It cannot appear at all strange, therefore, under the views now presented, that Colonel Burr should have been

welcomed to London by this great Philosopher and Philanthropist, with a warm cordiality, and that an intimacy
and friendship should at once have sprung up between
them, which was to continue during life. Colonel Burr, in
a letter addressed to one of his correspondents, from the
summer residence of Mr. Bentham, near London, on the
27th of August, 1808, thus writes: "He (Mr. Bentham,)
received me with something more than hospitality. After
assigning to me my apartment, he led me immediately into
what he calls his 'work-shop,' (a spacious room, fitted up
with great convenience for his purposes,) showed me his
papers, and gave me an unqualified privilege to read anything and at any time. It was impossible to have given
me a more flattering mark of confidence. We pass about
six hours a day in our separate rooms, and the residue together—hitherto without *ennui*. Mr. Bentham loses nothing
by being seen and known. I have daily more reason to
admire the amazing extent and acuteness of his mind; but
I am more agreeably surprised to find that he is frank and
social in his temper, cheerful even to playfulness; qualities extremely rare in men habituated to intense intellectual
labour."

On the next day we find Col. Burr writing to Mr. D. M.
Randolph, in reference to one of the works of Mr. Bentham, which had recently issued from the press, thus:
" Since writing to you this morning, I have laid my hands
on the work in question, and herewith enclose it to be
shown to the Marquis. It will give a better idea of the
nature of the work than the perusal of any detached part.
The reputation and known ability of the author, are a sufficient guarantee for the execution. You may leave it
with the Marquis, if he shall appear to desire it, from a
wish to promote the publication; but you must be very careful to stipulate for the return of this sheet; to be returned
Tuesday morning. Mr. Dumont,* a literary man of some

* Author of Recollections of Mirabeau.

note, has been for some time employed in making, and has now completed, an abridgement of the work, having selected such parts only as, in his opinion, might be *immediately* useful to the Spanish Cortes."

Of the same work he thus writes, on the 1st of September, 1808, to Jeremy Bentham himself, after an interview with the minister of Spain, then resident at the British Court, undertaken with a view to propitiate him in its favour, and procure its introduction into Spain. "There is no longer a hope of the patronage, nor even of the good will of the *Don* for any political improvement in *Political Tactics.* The horrors of *innovation* have invaded him. The Cortes must, and ought to, and will, proceed in its own way, and according to its ancient usage. The attempt to instruct it by the example of foreign assemblies, especially of any so tainted with democratic infection as those of France at one time, and those of England at all times, would be odious and alarming," &c., &c.

"It is a task, one would think, of no great difficulty, to discriminate between the forms which preserve decorum and dignity, and facilitate the attainment of an end, and those changes in *principle* which may impair or extend the power, or vary the objects of an institution. If similar apprehensions, and they would be equally rational, should obstruct these improvements in *Military Tactics,* God help the Patriots of Spain! The truth is, my friend has an *interest,* a deep and imperious personal interest, in the perpetuation of abuse. How would you reason against fifty thousand dollars per annum? Only by holding out the prospect of one hundred thousand, which I fear neither you nor I can do, just at this time. *Commissares* will, nevertheless, it is hoped, be free from the influence, if not wholly from the prejudices, of this new patriot."

In another letter to Mr. Bentham, of September 2d, of the same year, he says: "I am resolved that *Panopticon* *

---

* A celebrated work of Bentham's.

shall be known in America. It will appear incredible to you that I should never even have heard of it till I read the sketch contained in Dumont's work, about three years ago."

In writing to his daughter, seven days later, he says: " I hasten to make you acquainted with Jeremy Bentham, author of a work entitled ' Principles of Morals and Legislation,' (edited in French by Dumont,) and of many other works of less labour and research. You will well recollect to have heard me place this man *second to no one,* ancient or modern, in profound thinking, in logical and analytic reasoning. * * * * Mr. Bentham's countenance has all the character of intense thought which you would expect to find; but it is impossible to find a physiognomy more strongly marked with ingenuousness and Philanthropy. He is about sixty, but cheerful even to playfulness. * * * * By this time you will begin to wonder whether we ever talk of *you.* Not a little, as you will see. In a letter of the 3d instant, he writes: ' Make up, if you can have room, for *my* dear Theodosia, a packet of all my *combustibles* that you can find, viz: *Panopticon, Ward-Labour Bill, Pelham's Letters and Plea for the Constitution, Poor Management, Judicial Establishment, Political Tactics and Emancipation.'* * * Thus you see you are to possess his works by his own special gift. * * * * * * * * I am very much charmed with Panopticon; and as the State of South Carolina is just now about to erect her Penitentiary, it would undoubtedly adopt his system if seasonable knowledge was given of it," &c., &c.

It would be easy to multiply testimonials of this kind, all going to show the close intimacy and reciprocal esteem existing between Col. Burr and Jeremy Bentham, and corroborating the vindicatory reasoning, in support of which the extracts given have been brought forward. But I content myself with a single additional extract, from a letter addressed to his son-in-law, Mr. Alston, under date of November 10th, 1808. Speaking of his daughter, who had been urged to join him in London, he says : " In case of any accident to me, she will find a *father* in that venerable sage and philosopher, Jeremy Bentham, of whose literary works you have so often heard me speak with enthusiastic admiration. He is, indeed, the most perfect model that I have seen or imagined, of moral and intellectual excellence. He is the most intimate friend I have in this country, and my constant associate. I live in his house, and compose a part of his family."

I shall not pursue the rambles of Colonel Burr through Europe, or dwell upon the scenes of his subsequent life ; but return, for a moment, to the period when his scheme of invading the dominions of Spain was yet in its infancy, for the purpose of illustrating, if such a thing be now possible, the interesting point of its *origination*, and examining, also, some of the facts connected with its attempted execution. It has been seen, that Colonel Burr's statement to Commodore Truxtun, as that gentleman proved on the trial at Richmond, was, that General Wilkinson was the *projector* of the plan of invasion, and that he (Colonel Burr) was its maturer only. To this account of the matter, Colonel Burr himself always adhered during his life ; and the published journal of Blennerhasset is fully corroborative of it likewise. Some circumstances, not heretofore, so far as known to me, particularly looked into, place this statement almost beyond reasonable question. Colonel Burr and General Wilkinson had been long known to each other, and considerable familiarity and friendship existed between them as early as the year 1799, at least. In that year, it has been mentioned that General Wilkinson visited the city of New York, at the command of General Hamilton, to aid in concerting measures connected with the movements of the grand army just set on foot by the government. He states in his Memoirs, that when the first interview between General Hamilton and himself on this subject had terminated, he, Wilkinson, observed: "Well, sir, having fatigued you with my *prattle*, I now propose to visit an *old friend* whom I have not seen for several years. I know you are twain in politics, but I hope there is no disagreement between you, which might render the renewal of my acquaintance with him indecorous to my superior officer. He asked me if it was *Lamb*, meaning Colonel Lamb; I replied in the negative, and named Colonel Burr. "Little Burr," said he; "Oh no, we have always been opposed in politics, but always on good terms. We set out in the practice of law at the same time, and took opposite political directions; Burr beckoned me to follow him, and I advised him to come with me; we could not agree, but I fancy he now begins to think he was wrong and I right." This visit to his "old friend," Colonel Burr, was doubtless made by General Wilkinson; the particulars which occurred between the parties have never been made known; but, from the *communicative* character of General Wilkinson, and his morbid passion for *ostentatious display*, there can be little question that he made known fully to Colonel Burr the object of his journey to New York, and the prominent facts embodied in the report a few days after made by him to General Hamilton. This report, it has been already seen, related mainly to the practicability of successfully invading the Spanish dominions from the Southwestern part of the United States, and abounded in details evincing the advantages likely to arise from such a plan of operations. General Wilkinson was then ardently desirous of being associated with an expedition into the Spanish territories, and urged such an expedition most zealously upon the government at this precise period. Every argument was used in the report referred to, to induce the government to *strengthen the army* under his command in the Southwest, and he almost avows his object to be *forcibly to seize upon the city of New Orleans* as soon as he should be supplied with adequate means. I cite a short extract from the report, in confirmation of what has been here asserted.

" The quantum and disposition of our force on the Mississippi and the Southern frontier, are subjects which, in the existing state of things, have claim to *prompt deliberation* and *decisive action ;* the present calm in that quarter may prove a deceitful one, and if the storm should take us unprepared, sad scenes may ensue. The handful of men now on that station, would make but feeble resistance even against the enthusiastic yeomanry of Louisiana, once put in motion. It appears rational and necessary that we should determine, either to defend the country or abandon it ; in the first case .the means should be correspondent, and in the last case the troops now there should be withdrawn ; for in the present state of hands, the game on our part may be soon a desperate one. The imbecility of the Spanish Government on the Mississippi, is as manifest as the ardour of the gallant Louisianians is obvious. A single individual of hardy enterprise presenting himself with Directorial* credentials, and hoisting the national standard at New Orleans, might depose the Spanish administration in one hour, and have the population of the country at his disposal for any *chivalrous enterprise.* Under such circumstances, will it be indecorous should I express my apprehension that we repose in false security, and that if we are not aroused, the *dismemberment of the Union* may be put to hazard.

" Whoever consults the passions and interests of the human breast, and is acquainted with the geography of the country, will discover that the nation which holds the arbitrary control of the Mississippi, must eventually direct the *politics*† *of the Western Americans ;* and it is equally

---

* The Directory of France is here alluded to. Does not the dullest mind perceive in this little sentence the germ of the grand plot of *dismemberment*, afterwards falsely charged against Colonel Burr ? Is it not evident that even now some "chivalrous enterprise" was fermenting in the mind of Wilkinson against the fair Spanish province of Mexico ?

† How adroitly does this wily Reynard play upon the existing prejudices of the Administration of the Elder Adams against the French Republic !

obvious to all, who are acquainted with the habits and relative interests of the citizens, and Indians of the United States, that the latter can never cease to be the enemies of the former, and will continue ever ready to strike for vengeance, whenever opportunity may favour. The Indians who inhabit the tract of country bounded by the Tombigbee on the east, the Tennessee on the north, the Mississippi on the west, and the Mexican gulf on the south, can muster at least 4500 fighting men; I speak from good information. We will suppose this force armed against us, and 1000 regular troops and 500 *chasseurs* posted at the Walnut Hills,* (the first spot below the Chickasaw bluffs,† which is not inundated during the floods of the river) with ten stout galleys, bearing twelve and twenty-four-pounders, well-built and well-manned. At a point so remote, with the impediments which intervene, the casualties to which we shall be subject, the delays which are unavoidable, and the disaffection we may have to encounter among our own people, whose population is so much scattered; who can calculate the time, the toil, the blood, and treasure which may be found necessary to drive the usurpers out of the national territory? Or if the power in possession be hardy and enterprising, who can ascertain the practicability of the attempt? In my own judgment, the event would be at least problematical, because the resources of the invader would be more convenient, and his intercourse more prompt and facile than our own could be. Before we dismiss this subject, it may be necessary to take into view, that we dare not move out of the Ohio, until we have built a river navy of decided superiority; for it may be received as a truth, that an expedition, after four days' sail down the Mississippi, must succeed, surrender, or perish; as we can find no retreat for an army through deep, difficult, extensive, and trackless wilds; for instance, an army driven on shore near

---

* Near the present city of Vicksburg.
† The site of the city of Memphis, in the state of Tennessee.
15 *

the river St. Francis, with an enemy in front, will find itself
at least four hundred miles removed from succour, and
without transport must fall a prey to hostile savages, or
starve.   Reverting to the question of *abandonment* or *defence*, which has been suggested for the sake of argument
and elucidation, let us contemplate the unmeasured range
of the Mississippi, let us view its countless tributary waters, which bathe the most extensive tract of luxuriant soil
in the universe; let us reflect that the most valuable portion
of this soil is ours, of right, and that on the maintenance
of this right must depend the national union: under such
well-founded reflections and the impressions consequent, I
flatter myself we shall not hesitate, and that a determination may ensue, no longer to hazard such precious and important interests ; for the safety, the subordination, and
prosperity of our western possessions, the most cheap and
conducive plan would be the *capture of New Orleans;** but
as this step is *at present* unwarrantable, we must turn our
thoughts to the defensive protection of the settlements, and
in this view it will naturally occur, as a general principle,
that the means to be opposed must bear a due proportion
to the force which may possibly be employed against us.
But in the present state of things, I deem three regiments†
of infantry, three companies of light artillery, two troops
of cavalry, and our two galleys, competent to the defence
of the country, against any force which could have been
brought into action from Louisiana, when I left that province in June last, provided we receive a reasonable supply
of artillery and ordnance stores."

Such were the notions, wishes, and expectations of General Wilkinson, at the moment of his seeking an interview
with his " old friend," Colonel Burr, already alluded to.

---

* Here the scheme of invasion plainly peeps out.
† See how solicitous he is to get such a military force assembled under his command, as may, finally, enable him to prosecute the same
" chivalrous enterprise," before alluded to.

It is difficult to resist the conviction, that even then, in 1799, something like a proposition was made to Col. Burr by General Wilkinson, to unite with him in a "chivalrous enterprise" against the Spanish province of Mexico.

From that time, up to a short period before the arrest of Colonel Burr upon the charge of *high treason*, their intimacy and friendship remained unbroken, and a constant and confidential correspondence was maintained between them. In March, 1802, Colonel Burr writes to his daughter :—"*Mrs. Wilkinson is much obliged to you for your friendship to the General, which she says she never can forget;*" a circumstance only material, as going to show particular relations of amity continuing between Colonel Burr and General Wilkinson, and the desire felt by Colonel Burr to keep the General's friendship towards him from cooling off. In 1804, he writes to Charles Biddle of Philadelphia, thus :—"Your letter of the 28th of February, covering a newspaper, was received last evening. It cannot yet be settled whether there will be commissioners to run the boundary line with Spain ; but I will mention the thing to the Smiths, who still profess a friendship for General Wilkinson. My direct interference otherwise would probably not be useful to him. Please put the endorsed for *Truxtun* in the post-office. One of his friends here (not a man in power, for he has, I believe, no such friend) thinks he will certainly be called into service, and he states to me pretty plausible grounds for the opinion." The exertions of Colonel Burr at this time, at the instance of Wilkinson, to procure his appointment as commissioner to run the Spanish line spoken of, evinces, demonstrably, not only the continuance of kind feelings between them, but their actual conjunction in March, 1804, in the enterprise against Mexico. The co-incident mention of *Commodore Truxtun's* name, in the same letter, in reference to his being called into service, in connection with his testimony subsequently given on the trial of Burr, goes far to prove the existence of a plan of operations against Mexico at that moment, in which Burr and Wilkinson expected, or, at least hoped, the Commodore would participate.   And this is not the *first* time that Truxtun's name is thus introduced ; for, in February, 1802, writing to his son-in-law, Mr. Alston, Colonel Burr says :—" It has for months past been asserted that Spain has ceded Louisiana and the Floridas to France ; and it may, I believe, be assumed as a fact.   How do you account for the apathy of the public on this subject ?   To me the arrangement appears to be pregnant with evil to the United States.   I wish you to think of it, and endeavour to excite attention to it through the newspapers.   If you publish anything, send me the papers which contain it.

" *Truxtun* is going out to the Mediterranean with three large and one small frigate."

Whether the expedition to Mexico had been *originated* by Wilkinson and fully *matured* by Burr as early as 1802, or not, it is certain that the attention of the latter had been specially directed to the City of New Orleans in the month of February, 1803 ; for during that month, we find him receiving a letter from Charles* Biddle, of Philadelphia, (already named as the particular friend of General Wilkinson, and who was still more the devoted friend of Commodore Truxtun) in which the following striking paragraph occurs : " The business of New Orleans is much talked of here.   In my opinion, and it is the opinion of many others, we should immediately *take possession* and then treat about it.   We have no business to make excuses for the Spanish government, by saying that they gave no orders to treat us in that manner.   For my own part, I do not fear a war with France and Spain.   We could do more injury to them than they could do us.   If we were at war with them, and Great Britain did not join us, we should have our ports filled

---

* The father of Commodore Biddle and the celebrated Nicholas Biddle.

with their seamen, and the coasts of France and Spain would soon swarm with our cruisers!

In March, 1804, when Colonel Burr is setting out upon his first visit to the Western States, we find him still holding General Wilkinson in sight and referring to him in a letter to his daughter as having been appointed Governor of Louisiana. Speaking of General Wilkinson and Dr. Brown in the letter just named, (the latter of whom had been recently appointed Secretary to the government of Louisiana) he says: " Wilkinson and Brown will suit most admirably as *eaters* and *laughers*, and, I believe, *in all other particulars*." On the 29th of March, he says, in a letter to his son-in-law: " For ten or twelve days I shall be on my way westward. My address, till further orders, is at Cincinnati, Ohio, to the care of the Hon. John Smith. The objects of this journey, not mere curiosity, or *pour passer le tems*, may lead me to *Orleans*, and perhaps further." On the 30th of April, 1805, he arrives in Pittsburg, and proceeds on his tour of exploration. He encounters General Wilkinson, not until the 6th of June of the same year, at a place called Massac on the Ohio river, whereupon, (he says in a letter to his daughter,) " The General and his officers fitted me out with an elegant barge, sails, colours, and ten oars, with a serjeant and ten able, faithful hands."

Thus far the ancient friendship between General Wilkinson and Colonel Burr remains undisturbed, and the tokens of a perfect understanding between them in regard to the plan of invading Mexico, are plainly traceable. Many individuals are now living, in the States of Louisiana and Mississippi, who well know that for a long time afterwards, up to the moment when Wilkinson made his treacherous and deceptive revelations to the government against his confiding chief, he honoured that chief, both publicly and privately, with conclusive and multiplied evidences of deferential homage and enthusiastic attachment. What may have been the precise motives which instigated the abandonment of the Mexican project by General Wilkinson, it is, at this period of time, difficult to determine. Most probably though, he was chiefly influenced by the fear that he would himself be overshadowed by the majestic genius of Burr, and that he might not be permitted to reap such large advantages from the conquest projected, as he had at first anticipated. Perhaps General Eaton was more than half right, when he said, as a witness on the trial of Burr, that " he knew General Wilkinson well, and he would not act as Lieutenant to any man in existence."   Whatever may be the truth on the subject, it is certain, that his failure to execute his engagements with Colonel Burr *alone* defeated the grand scheme of conquest; and it seems now to be conclusively established, that at the very time he was volunteering testimony against Colonel Burr in Richmond, in support of the charge of *High Treason*, and vehemently asserting that his principal object had been to bring about a *dismemberment* of the American Confederacy, he was secretly despatching an emissary,* (whom he notices in his Memoirs, as " a dear and honoured friend") to the City of Mexico, for the purpose of urging upon the Spanish government of the Vice-Royalty then existing, the payment to himself of the enormous sum of *Two hundred thousand dollars*, for baffling the designs of Colonel Burr upon the American dominions of his Catholic Majesty.   Such complicated treachery it is difficult to conceive, especially in an individual who had for many years maintained a high standing among his countrymen ; yet the documentary testimony† recently laid before the public by the Biographer of Colonel Burr, leaves no room for rational doubt as to the delinquency of General Wilkinson in the premises.

It does not fall within the scope of this work to trace the meandering course of Colonel Burr through the Western and South-Western States of the Union, or to narrate all

---

* Captain Walter Burling.
† See Memoirs of Aaron Burr, 2d vol. page 400.

the vicissitudes that marked his career along the banks of the Ohio and Mississippi rivers. It is to be hoped that some writer better suited to the task, will collect and transmit to posterity the rich and romantic memorials which yet survive ; which memorials I know to be conveniently obtainable, and would prove worthy the pen of an Irving, a Cooper, or a Paulding. It is sufficient here to have noticed, in a cursory manner, the first grand movement of the Anglo-American race towards the far South-West. In doing so, I trust to be pardoned by the generous reader, for having said something in vindication of a distinguished soldier and statesman, for whom, since the death of his accomplished daughter, the world seems to have been without sympathy ; who has so far, heretofore, received no vindication save such as was calculated to tarnish his fame ; and is yet viewed by thousands only as a *Lucius Catiline*, guilty of plotting the downfall of his own country. For thirty years and more, has the character of Colonel Burr been the subject of continued denunciation, or insidious praise, more damning than the language of open censure. Florid declamation early seized on all his movements in connexion with the Expedition to Mexico as a favourite theme for display ; and the school-going youth of nearly three generations, have been diligently trained to the recitation of gorgeous speeches illustrative of his supposed designs and attributes. Perhaps the best commentary upon the whole business will be to lay before the reader in conclusion of this chapter, an address delivered on the 12th day of January, 1807, to the Legislature, Council, and House of Representatives of the Mississippi Territory. The gentleman* who pronounced it, is now

---

* General Cowles Meade, a very excellent person remarkable for his elegant hospitality, and fine conversational powers, whose charming residence is distant not a mile from the town of Clinton. He is familiarly mentioned in Mississippi as the *Captor of Burr ;* and justly enough, since it is absolutely true that Burr surrendered to an armed force under his command, near Cole's Creek, in Mississippi ; and was conducted to the town of Washington, a few miles from the city of

eight miles distant from the writer, rejoicing equally in the comforts of an ample fortune, and in the renown of by-gone days ; and perhaps reciting, at this moment, to some delighted hearer, the wondrous *Capture of Aaron Burr, the Conspirator*. The Address will be found throughout to breathe a spirit of *romantic patriotism*, and may possibly also be viewed by some as furnishing evidence of that hallucinating excitement which distinguished the tempestuous period of its fulmination.

Washington, (Miss.) January 12th, 1807.

WAR ADDRESS OF GOVERNOR MEADE.

Gentlemen of the Legislative Council, and House of Representatives :

In consequence of communications received from the general government, I am now convinced, that the cloud which has so long been anticipated, begins to assume a settled aspect of offence. Charged with belligerent countenance, it slowly presses upon us, and presages an explosion dangerous to domestic safety, and insulting to national dignity. These circumstances bid us convert the pen of legislation into the *weapon of war*, and suspend the eloquence of debate for the clangour of military array. You, who blend the civil and the military characters, must relinquish, for the moment, the functions of the one, for the *prerogatives* of the latter. The station which you leave, though honourable

---

Natchez ; where he underwent a judicial investigation, which has not been at all noticed by his Biographer—was acquitted, and proceeded towards the Alabama River ; where he was apprehended anew, under circumstances known to the whole public. Those at all curious about particulars, are referred to the celebrated Ex-Senator of the United States, George Poindexter ; who, on the occasion of the capture at Cole's Creek, officiated as a sort of Diplomatic agent between Governor Meade and the great Conspirator, and was afterwards professionally connected with the trial in Washington. I have heard from the lips of Mr. Poindexter, a full account of both affairs ; than which nothing can be imagined more ludicrous.

and important, is exchanged for one where your patriotism may be as effectually displayed, and where you may acquire new claims to the confidence of your country. How long this cloud will hang over your heads, is uncertain : but it is deemed unsafe, that you should be sitting here in the pacific operations of Legislation, while our country's honour calls us to the field. From you, gentlemen, who wear the garb of civic rule, we expect that aid which the good and the patriotic may afford, by *example*. Your respective standings in your counties, and among your fellow-citizens, are such as will give weight and influence to your opinions and your example. In remanding you to your homes, you are not suspended in your duties. No : you are transferred to a theatre where your services may be more important and beneficial to our common country."

CHAPTER IX.

Return of Colonel Burr to the United States in 1812. Expedition of Magee into Texas during that year. Magee takes Nacogdoches and Goliad. His small force is besieged in Goliad for a whole winter. They turn out in the spring and defeat General Salcedo. Death of Magee. Capture of the town of San Antonio by the Patriot forces. Dreadful massacre there. Defeat of Toledo. Kemper, Ross, Perry, and other valiant Anglo-Americans introduced to the reader. La Fitte, the Pirate of the Gulf.

It was in the year 1812, that Colonel Burr left Europe, and returned to his native country ; content, for the remainder of his days, to be a quiet observer of great affairs, without participating in their management, and relinquishing to other adventurers more fortunate than himself, the accomplishment of those noble designs which had so long absorbed all the feelings of his soul, and kept in action all the energies of his gigantic intellect. In the mean time, the cause to which he had so generously devoted himself, was far from languishing; it was steadily advancing in the hearts and understandings of men on both sides of the Atlantic. The striking events of the French Revolution, followed up by the magnificent career of Napoleon Buonaparte, had exercised a wonderful influence in dispelling the mists of *legitimacy* which had so long overhung institutions respected alone on account of their *ancientness*, which ancientness had given them a hold upon the respect of mankind due to the products of enlightened reason only. The insurrection of Aranjuez, which had occurred in 1808, succeeded by the abdication of Charles IV., had taken away from the Royal authority, some portion of that stupid veneration which had been antecedently accorded to it by all classes of the Spanish Colonists in America. " An absolute monarch, (says an English writer,*) compelled to bow before the will of a tumultuous populace, insulted by his subjects, and deserted by his guards, in the very heart of his Kingdom, was a sight that could not but diminish those feelings of religious awe, with which any thing like opposition to the will of the sovereign had been previously contemplated!" " The subsequent invasion of the Peninsula by Napoleon, (continues the same writer) the captivity of the Monarch, and the abdication of the old dynasty at Bayonne, contributed to destroy whatever remained of the *prestige* which had before attached to the name of Spain, and created an impression only the more strong, because to the mass of the people in America, she was still the Spain of the sixteenth century, in whose dominions the sun never set, and whose arms were the terror of the world. This belief had long been the tutelary angel of the Mother country: with it she lost her moral force, (the only force capable of compelling the obedience of seventeen millions of Transatlantic subjects,) and, from that moment, the loss of the Colonies themselves became inevitable. It was in vain to struggle against nature, or to at-

---

* Ward's Mexico.

tempt to subdue the new spirit, which within two years after the invasion of the Peninsula, began to appear among all classes of the Creoles. Its progress was both rapid and irresistible ; and, without any previous concert amongst the parties themselves, without the possibility of foreign interference, a mighty revolution broke out at once, in almost every part of the New World."

Thus the Spanish Colonists, both in North and South America, had risen up in hostile array against their tyrants, and were struggling fiercely for Independence, if not for freedom. The sympathies of the civilized world were becoming deeply enlisted in their favour, partly from particular hatred of Spain, partly from more generous considerations. In England, the colloquial eloquence of Col. Burr had won for the cause of Colonial emancipation the aid of several of the most powerful minds of the age, who had already rendered efficient service in the removal of prejudice entertained originally by many in that country towards the Revolutionists in Spanish America. As late as January 1812, a few months only anterior to Col. Burr's leaving England for the last time and setting out on his return to the United States, we find the illustrious Jeremy Bentham, (of whom already as much has been said as the reader would probably endure in a work like the present) earnestly occupied in furthering the project of Colonial emancipation, which he knew Col. Burr still to have so much at heart, by bringing about a friendly understanding between himself and the Patriot General Miranda ;* who was at that time in

* It is believed that this is the same individual who will be found mentioned in M. Thiers's History of the French Revolution as associated with the celebrated Dumoriez in the invasion of Belgium in 1792. He is thus introduced to the reader's attention by the historian : "Labourdonnaye, who had entered Antwerp on the 18th, was organizing clubs, alienating the Belgians, by the encouragement which he gave to popular agitators, and meanwhile neglecting to act vigorously in the siege of the castle. Dumoriez, unable to put up any longer with a Lieutenant, who attended so much to clubs and so little to war, sent as his suc-

England soliciting aid from the government and people of that country. At the instance of this untiring friend to human liberty, a letter was addressed by Mr. J. Mills, to General Miranda, in which that confidential associate of Mr. Bentham writes as follows : " Our friend (Mr. Bentham,) whose mind is alive to everything conducive to the prosperity of you or your country, in the great cause in which you are engaged, reflecting upon the return of this gentleman (Col. Burr) to his own country, where he once had great power and might possibly have again—reflecting that his partisans and power lay chiefly in that part of his own country which is nearest to your's, and that his talents, and the chapter of accidents, of so much importance in human affairs, might, if nothing else did, give him an influence that might be exerted to much good effect towards South America, in the present critical state, thought the present opportunity ought not to be lost of doing what he could to secure to you the good offices of Col. Burr. He communicated to me his idea, which was to write to the Colonel, in fear he might not have an opportunity of seeing him ; and, if there were any grounds of dislike towards you in his mind, to show him that they were neither reasonable nor prudent."

In the United States, there were, at the period alluded to, thousands who stood ready to risk their lives and fortunes in the grand conflict against Spanish dominion, in any form, and to any extent, warranted by a proper respect to the government and laws of their own country. This assertion is fully justified by details already submitted ; but there are

cessor Miranda, a Peruvian of extraordinary bravery, who had come to France at the epoch of the revolution and obtained high rank through the friendship of Petion." Something has been said of the various efforts of Miranda to aid the revolutionary movements in North and South America, which the attentive reader will not fail to recollect. He will hereafter be noticed more particularly in the Biographical sketch of Vice President Burnet, to be found in another part of this work.

some additional occurrences, which had their progress in 1812, that supply "confirmation strong as holy writ," on this subject.

Some time in the year just mentioned, a band of outlaws were ascertained to have established themselves at a point proximate to the Sabine river, which separated the Province of Texas from the territory of the United States. This association of shameless brigands was fast acquiring a dishonourable celebrity by the commission of robberies, murders, and other crimes of an infamous and astounding character. In order to secure their suppression, it was judged necessary, by the officer commanding the United States' forces at New Orleans, that a body of soldiers should be sent to their vicinage, under the direction of a leader of tried fidelity and valour ; and Lieutenant Magee was despatched for this purpose, at the head of a force competent to effect the desired object. On arriving at the destined point, Lieutenant Magee lost no time in executing the orders given to him, and quickly brought to an end those scenes of marauding violence which had been previously in progress, reducing the offenders to the necessity of suing for pardon and promising better conduct in future. Whilst upon the borders of the Spanish territory, the idea suggested itself to the mind of Magee of resigning his commission in the army of the United States, where the chance of acquiring immediate distinction was not at the time particularly encouraging, raising an army of volunteers as speedily as he could, and marching over to the assistance of the patriots of Mexico, then in the midst of their revolutionary struggle. This project was no sooner framed than executed ; and, in a few weeks, we find Magee, who appears to have been a man of more than ordinary accomplishments, and in all respects admirably fitted for the task which he had undertaken, at the head of a force of more than three hundred men,* ready to march to the

---

* It is supposed that a considerable number of these newly-enlisted

16 *

attack of the town of Nacogdoches.   Associated with him was a Spaniard, whose name was Bernardo, a professed entertainer of *liberal* principles,—a man who is described as possessing a highly commanding person, most insinuating manners, and extraordinary mental accomplishments. With a view to conciliating the Spanish population, into whose midst this small body of adventurers were about to cast themselves, it was judged expedient to announce Bernardo as the ostensible commander-in-chief of the expedition; although in fact all substantial authority was reserved to Magee himself.   The contemplated assault upon Nacogdoches was made, and the place was yielded up with but little attempt on the part of its inhabitants towards defending it :—the principal reason of whose inaction is said to have been, that most of the population in Nacogdoches and its vicinage were partial to the Patriot cause ; a striking proof of which, indeed, was afforded by a prompt supply of the army of Magee with provisions, horses, and munitions of war, sufficient to enable him to prosecute his plan of invasion.   Whilst the adventurers tarried at this place, their ranks were considerably strengthened by the seasonable arrival of recruits from the United States, many of whom were young men of respectable character and of most daring valour, and who became participants in this enterprise, under the guidance of motives altogether honourable. Among these may be mentioned* Kemper, Ross, Luckett,

---

champions of freedom were the very ruffians whom Magee had just subdued ; whose principal object in uniting with him was doubtless that they might thus enjoy an opportunity of plundering upon a more extended scale.

   * The three last named of the seven individuals mentioned above are now living, and recognised as worthy citizens of the State of Mississippi, personally well known to me. With Ross I became familiarly acquainted many years ago, when a boy at school, in the town of Lexington, in the State of Virginia. Eight or ten years had then elapsed since the occurrences described above had taken place; but they were all fresh in his memory, and he delighted to detail to his friends the perilous adventures which had marked his early manhood. I saw Ross,

Perry, Robinson, Deane, and Wolforth. The whole force of the invaders, when they took up the line of march from Nacogdoches, was about five hundred men. They proceeded in a south-western direction, to the beautiful and romantic banks of the San Antonio River, and entered the town of Labahia (Goliad) amidst the rejoicings of its population, all of whom were enthusiastically devoted to the Patriot cause. But Magee did not remain long at Labahia without molestation; for General Salcedo, a royalist officer, being despatched against him, laid siege to the town, and held it in a state of close investment during the whole winter. Repeated skirmishes ensued, during this period,

---

for the last time, in the city of New Orleans, about eleven years since; when he was about setting forth upon a journey by land to the city of Mexico, with a view to urging upon the Mexican government his claims to recompense for military services rendered to the cause of the Patriots. In ten days more, the newspapers published an account of his *robbery* and *murder*, in the bosom of that delightful region where he had heroically battled for the freedom of strangers. *Kemper*, generally known as Col. Kemper, was also a Virginian, and was born in my own native county—*Fauquier*. He was a scion of a noble stock—and worthy of it. A venerable brother and other members of his family still reside in Fauquier, and hold the virtues of their distinguished kinsman in affectionate remembrance. The last time I ever saw Col. Kemper was when I was a boy of some 13 years of age. Being upon a Saturday's visit to a beloved school-fellow, now alas! no more! at the house of the celebrated William Wirt, I found Col. Kemper an honoured guest. I was far too young particularly to note the conversation which occurred between these worthies, nor do I know that there was any thing in it deserving special attention; but I well recollect having been forcibly struck with the marked and somewhat *deferential* courtesy exercised towards Col. K. by Mr. Wirt, and of having been constrained to render my full tribute of youthful admiration to the towering, Achilles-like form, and majestic aspect and demeanour of the chivalrous Texan commander. How one whose chief claim to respect arose from his honourable participation in an attempt to carry into execution, at least in part, the Liberating project of Col. Burr, happened to find favour so far as to be invited to the house of his distinguished prosecutor, is more than I can explain. Perhaps Col. Kemper and Mr. Wirt were old acquaintances, and the respect accorded him had no connection with his Texan career. But I have always looked upon the incident as a little curious, and as such it will not perhaps be held unworthy of mention.

between the besiegers and the besieged, all of which resulted
favourably to the latter; when, finally, in the opening of
the spring, the Spanish general drew off his forces and commenced a rather precipitate retreat up the country towards
San Antonio (Bexar), the capital of the province,—a place
which has since become immortal in Texan history.   The
Spanish army had no sooner commenced retrograding than
a vigorous pursuit was instituted by the Americans, who
overtaking the army of Salcedo, at Salado Creek, about
nine miles from the Capital, rushed upon it fiercely and defeated it at once with astonishing slaughter.   This victory
opened the way to San Antonio, into which place the Patriot
army marched without either delay or impediment.   Lieutenant Magee had unfortunately died, a few weeks previous
to the capture of San Antonio, at Labahia, and the duty of
commanding the Patriot army had devolved upon Colonel
Kemper, a man every way equal to the responsibility,—
Bernardo still enjoying a nominal supremacy.

Almost immediately on taking possession of San Antonio, by the *secret* order of Bernardo, and without consult-
ing any of his associates in command, a scene was displayed to view of the most shocking brutality, and which was
productive, in the sequel, of consequences signally disastrous to the Patriot cause.   There were, among the numerous prisoners in the hands of the Americans, seventeen
Spanish officers, all of whom were caused by Bernardo to
be butchered in cold blood, in accordance with the inhuman
usages then, as at present, prevailing throughout the Mexican Provinces.*   Such a deed of atrocity could not be

---

* Every man of humane sentiments, will unhesitatingly condemn this
bloody and disgraceful transaction ; and some will feel more than ordinary regret, upon learning the names and a little of the history of
the two most conspicuous of these victims of Spanish cruelty—Don
Antonio Cordero, and Don Simon de Herrara—personages honourably
mentioned in the interesting narrative of Gen. Pike, as having exercised
great kindness and hospitality towards him, whilst exploring the region
where they held command, in the year 1807.   "We then," says this

otherwise than deeply disgusting to all the Americans engaged in service, save, possibly, the most degraded of that gang of ruffians enlisted by Magee on the borders of the

accomplished American officer, "repaired to their quarters, at San Antonio, where we were received like their children. Cordero informed me, that he had discretionary orders as to the manner of my going out of the country; that he wished me to choose my time, mode, &c.; and that any sum of money which I might want, was at my service; that, in the meantime, his quarters would be my residence, and that he had caused to be erected a house immediately opposite for my men." Gen. Pike describes these two Spanish officers in the following terms: "Don Antonio Cordero was fifty years of age, about five feet ten inches in height, of fair complexion, and blue eyes. He wore his hair turned back, and every part of his dress was soldier-like. He still possessed an excellent constitution, and a body which appeared to be neither fatigued by the various campaigns he had made, nor disfigured by the numerous wounds he had received from the enemies of his King. He was one of the select officers who had been chosen by the Court of Madrid to be sent to America, for about thirty-five years, to discipline and organise the Spanish provincials, and had been employed in all the various Kingdoms and Provinces in New Spain, and through the parts which we explored. He was universally beloved and respected, and by far the most popular man in the internal provinces. He spoke the Latin and French languages well; was generous, gallant, brave, and sincerely attached to his King and country. These numerous qualifications have advanced him to the rank of Colonel of Cavalry, and Governor of the Provinces Coahuila and Texas. His usual residence was Montelovez, which he had greatly embellished; but since our taking possession of Louisiana, he had removed to San Antonio, in order to be nearer the frontier, to be able to apply the remedy to any evil which might arise from the collision of our lines.

" Don Simon de Herrara is about five feet eleven inches high, has sparkling black eyes, with dark complexion and hair. He was born in the Canary Islands; served in the Infantry in France, Spain, and Flanders; he speaks the French language well, and a little of the English. He is engaging in his conversation with his equals, polite and obliging to his inferiors; and in his actions one of the most gallant and accomplished of men. He possesses a general knowledge of mankind, from his experience in various countries and societies, and knows how to employ the genius of each of his subordinates to advantage. He had been in the United States during the Presidency of General Washington, and had been introduced to that hero, of whom he spoke in terms of exalted veneration. He is now Lieutenant-Colonel of Infantry, and Governor of the Kingdom of New Leon. His seat of govern-

Sabine. Accordingly, we find Kemper, Luckett, Ross, and many others, immediately abandoning the expedition, and returning to the United States ; notwithstanding it had

---

ment is Monterey ; and, probably, if ever a chief was adored by his people, it is Herrara. When his time expired last, he immediately repaired to Mexico, attended by three hundred of the most respectable people of his district, and carried with him the sighs, tears, and prayers of thousands, that he might be continued in his government. The Viceroy thought proper to accede to their wishes, *pro tempore*, and the King has since confirmed the nomination. When I saw him, he had been about one year absent, during which time the citizens of rank in Monterey had not suffered a marriage or baptism to take place in any of their families, waiting until their common father could be there, to consent and give joy to the occasion by his presence. What greater proof could be given of their esteem and love? In drawing a parallel between the two friends, I should say, that Cordero was a man of the greatest reading, Herrara of the greatest knowledge of the world. Cordero has lived all his life a bachelor. Herrara married an English lady in early youth, at Cadiz, who, by her suavity of manners, makes herself as much beloved and esteemed by the ladies, as her noble husband is by the men. By her he has several children, one now an officer in the royal service. The two friends agree perfectly on one point, their hatred of tyranny of every kind, and a secret determination never to see that flourishing part of the New World subject to any European lord, except him whom their honour and loyalty bind them to defend with their lives and fortunes.

"It may not be improper to state," continues Gen. Pike, " that we owe to Governor Herrara's prudence, that we are not now (1807) engaged in a war with Spain. This will be explained by the following anecdote, which he related in presence of his friend Cordero, and which was confirmed by him. When the difficulties commenced on the Sabine, the Commandant-General and the Viceroy consulted each other, and both determined to maintain what they deemed the dominions of their master inviolate. The Viceroy therefore ordered Herrara to join Cordero with 1300 men ; and both the Viceroy and General Salcedo ordered Cordero to cause our troops to be attacked, should they pass the Rio Onde. These orders were positively reiterated to Herrara, the actual commanding officer of the Spanish army on the frontiers, and gave rise to the many messages which he sent to General Wilkinson, when we were advancing with our troops ; but, finding they were not attended to, he called a Council of War on the question whether to attack or not. The Council gave it as their opinion, that they should immediately commence a predatory warfare, but avoid a

advanced so far with extraordinary and almost unequalled success. Well might they despair of acquiring laurels worthy to adorn the brow of a free-born and civilized soldier of Liberty, under auspices so demoniacal!

Shortly after the detestable act of massacre just recorded, and whilst a majority of the Americans who belonged to the Patriot Army were abandoning the country for ever, a personage arrived whose name is known in history as General Toledo. He had been formerly a member of the Spanish Cortes in Mexico, and had been subjected to banishment on account of his supposed partiality for Republican principles. Upon the departure of Kemper, Toledo took command of the Patriot forces, who numbered now at least seventeen hundred men, notwithstanding the withdrawal of many Americans, for the honourable reason already stated. But it was not an *army* of which Toledo found himself the commander, but a mob—a disorderly and undisciplined multitude, principally Indians and Mexicans, who were better fitted for almost anything that could be mentioned than a firm display of valour upon a regular battle-field. Col. Perry,* a valiant American officer, though

---

general engagement. Yet, notwithstanding the orders of the Viceroy and the commanding general, Governor Cordero, and the opinion of his officers, he had the firmness or the temerity; to enter into the agreement with General Wilkinson which at present exists relative to our boundaries on that frontier. On his return, he was received with coldness by Cordero, and they both made their communication to their superiors. "Until an answer was received," said Herrara, "I experienced the most unhappy period of my life, conscious that I had served my country faithfully, at the same time that I had violated every principle of military duty." At length the answer arrived; and what was it but the thanks of the Viceroy and Commandant General for having pointedly disobeyed their orders, with assurance that they would represent his services in exalted terms to the King! What could have produced this change of sentiment is to me unknown; but the letter was published to the army, and confidence was restored between the two chiefs and their troops."

* This gentleman is represented to me as having been a near relative of the late gallant Commodore Perry.

indignant at the massacre of prisoners which had occurred, yet eager for military glory, and hoping that a repetition of this scene would not be hazarded, still remained united with the Patriots, and had under his command a small company of Americans upon whose courage he felt he could thoroughly rely. Being upon a reconnoitring excursion one evening, a few miles from San Antonio, he was suddenly attacked by General Elisando, a Spanish officer, at the head of fifteen hundred men. Perry defended himself both with vigour and success, drove back the assailants, forced them to ignominious flight, and killed and wounded a large number of them in the pursuit. But General Aredondo arriving in the neighbourhood suddenly, in command of two thousand men, united his forces with those of Elisando, and encountering the whole body of the Patriots under Toledo, near Medina river, completely defeated them, taking numerous prisoners, killing a great many, and pursuing the retreating remnant across the country as far as the Trinity river. Here, coming up with Toledo, and the small number who had fled with him, he slaughtered nearly all of them with little or no resistance on the part of the fugitives; who left their dead* bodies on the banks of the Trinity, as permanent vestiges of the disastrous issue of the campaign in which they fell. Toledo again escaped with a few trusty friends, and succeeded in making good his passage across the Sabine : on the eastern bank of which he established an encampment, and struggled for several years to reinstate his army, but was never able afterwards to re-commence offensive operations.

The Spanish General, Bernardo, the author of this train of ills, is represented to be still living in a town on the Rio Grande, retired from all public cares, in the quiet enjoyment of a comfortable fortune, demeaning himself decently enough as a Mexican citizen. Among the Americans who fought

---

* I am told that the mouldering bones of these poor fellows are yet to be seen on the very spot where they experienced the fate of war.

under the Patriot standard after the chief command was assumed by General Toledo, may be mentioned, Judge Bullard, of Louisiana, who has since acquired wealth and distinction in the United States. He was one of Toledo's aid-de-camps in the fatal battle of Medina river; attended him on his retreat; and after the entire failure of the expedition, located himself in the town of Natchitoches as a practitioner of the law: in which vocation, his success was very soon sufficient to console him fully for all the perils and sufferings which he had encountered in his short military career.

Nothing now occurred in the Province of Texas, for several years, worthy of special notice. The termination, or rather the suspension of hostilities, between the Patriots and Royalists, which intervened at the close of what is generally called the first Revolution in Mexico, left the Northern Province of the Vice-Royalty of New Spain in a state of comparative repose; and very little change of any kind took place in the condition of the population for some time. General Pike reckoned the whole number of inhabitants in Texas, in the year 1807, at seven thousand souls; of whom, two thousand resided in San Antonio, the capital; which city he describes as consisting chiefly of " miserable mud-wall houses, covered with thatch-grass roofs. The town," he says, " is laid out on a very grand plan: to the east of it, on the other side of the river, is the station of the troops. About two, three, and four miles from San Antonio, are three missions, formerly flourishing and prosperous. These buildings, for solidity, accommodation, and even majesty, were surpassed by few that I met with in New Spain. Nacogdoches is merely a station for troops: it is situated on a small branch of the river Toyac." In describing the general population of the Province at that time, he says:— " These are principally Spanish Creoles, some French, some Americans, and a few civilized Indians and half-breeds. This Province trades with Mexico by Monterey and Montelovez, for merchandise, and with New Orleans by Natchitoches; but the latter being contraband, is liable to great damage and risks.   They give in return, specie, horses, and mules.   Taken generally, it is one of the richest, most prolific, and best watered countries in North America."

The celebrated Humboldt, speaking of the Mexican internal provinces of the east, including Texas of course, says, that, at the period of his travels, their " position, on the eastern limits of New Spain, the proximity of the United States, the frequency of communication with the colonists of Louisiana, and other circumstances, will probably soon favour the progress of civilization and prosperity in these vast and fertile regions."

There can be but little doubt in the minds of dispassionate persons, who have examined the subject, that nearly the whole of what is now known as Texas, at one time, rightfully belonged to the United States, by virtue of the Treaty of 1803 with France, which secured the annexation of Louisiana.   Such was the view of Mr. Jefferson in 1806, when he wrote to the American minister then at the court of Madrid, as follows : " With respect to our western boundary, your instructions will be your guide.   I will only add, as a comment, to them, that we are attached to the retaining of the Bay of St. Bernard, because it was the first establishment of the unfortunate La Salle, was the cradle of Louisiana, and more incontestably covered and conveyed to us by France, than any other part of that country.   This will be secured to us by taking for our western boundary the Guadalupe, and from its head around the sources of all waters eastward of it, to the high-lands, embracing the waters running into the Mississippi."   In another letter, written about the same period, he declares the title of the United States to be " good as far as the River Bravo ;" and the American ministers to Spain were unquestionably instructed to insist upon the last-named River as the boundary line of the United States to the South-West, and only to yield it in case of imperious necessity.   Although this desirable region could not be secured by negotiation, at that time, as will be seen in the sequel, it has been subsequently won back by the prowess of that heroic race, who, in Mr. Jefferson's judgment, more than thirty years ago, were justly entitled to it; and it is now in the possession of a *nation of soldiers*, who will never relinquish it to force, or permit themselves to be a second time cheated out of it by diplomatic subtilty.

About the year 1817, La Fitte, the celebrated "Pirate of the Gulf," some of whose exploits have found record in the pages of authentic history, and have also supplied rich materials for the pen of both the Poet * and Novelist, took possession of the island of Galveston, and finding there safe harborage for his vessels, selected it as a place of rendezvous

---

* This will scarcely need explanation; as most of the reading world must long since have known that the celebrated poem of *The Corsair*, by Lord Byron, was founded upon the romantic, though well authenticated story of the adventures of *La Fitte*; of whom it might indeed be said, with the noble poet,

> He left a Corsair's name to other times,
> Linked with one virtue and a thousand crimes.

The conduct of La Fitte at New Orleans, during the last war, was perhaps the single act of his boisterous life which deserves universal commendation; and has enabled a gentleman, a short time since well known as a citizen of the State where I reside, to interest the public very highly with a novel, which I am glad to hear has received considerable respect in the literary world, under the title of *The Pirate of the Gulf*. It is a little singular, (and I may mention it here, I trust, without any appearance of egotism,) that I was travelling in company with Mr. Ingraham, the author of the novel just mentioned, a little more than four years ago, from Troy to the City of New York, when the following incident occurred: The novel had just been dramatized by a lady of literary eminence, and for several successive nights, the citizens of New York had been enjoying the satisfaction of beholding the Hero of New Orleans, the Pirate of the Gulf, and other characters, striding over the stage with "all the pride, pomp, and circumstance of glorious war," at the Bowery theatre. Mr. Ingraham was now passing on rapidly to New York, expecting to receive his *benefit* that very night. But when we got to Albany, lo! the fact was announced to us, that the Bowery theatre had been consumed by fire the night before. Whether the accident was owing to too much *combustible* matter being thrown into the play, or to some other cause, I never learned; but the particulars are a little curious.

for his whole fleet. He erected a fort upon the Eastern extremity of the island, the remains of which are still visible. His whole marine force is said to have amounted to 18 or 20 vessels; * among which was an armed brig. He cruised under the flag of Venezuela, from the government of which he held a commission. Galveston was occupied by this daring corsair for several years: what has become of him since has not been ascertained; though several of his associates are supposed still to lurk in the vicinage of their former seat of empire; more than one of whom was pointed out to me last summer in the progress of an excursion which I made through the Republic of Texas.

In the winter of 1818, a party of French refugees, about one hundred in number, under the command of General Salleman, arrived at Galveston. They were well provided with arms, ammunition, and implements of husbandry, and it is said, displayed in a striking manner, the force and virtue of military discipline. It has not been ascertained that they had in view the execution of any scheme of territorial conquest by arms; nor even that they meditated hostilities at all: except such as might become necessary in defence of themselves, as settlers of a region nominally under the dominion of Spain—a nation far from friendly to their own. country: or such as might be brought on by the neighbouring savages, who were known to look with dissatisfaction at all attempts on the part of the whites to locate anywhere in their vicinity. The colonists proceeded up the Trinity river as high as the Cacasau bluffs; where they commenced the erection of a fort, and took the necessary preliminary steps towards cultivating a portion of the fertile lands around them. But provisions becoming scarce among them, and being at the same time menaced by a strong Spanish force, reported to be on its way for their destruction, they abandoned their new abodes and returned to Galveston. A short time after this occurrence, an American cutter arrived at Galveston,

---

* Who has not read Mr. Ingraham's sprightly novel?

whose captain permitted General Salleman, the leader of the colonists, to go with him to New Orleans; after which he was no more heard of. The colonists, thus abandoned, it is supposed, fell under the dominion of La Fitte, as no vestige of their independent existence, subsequently, has yet rewarded the scrutiny of the inquisitive.

CHAPTER X.

Long's early history. Appointed by the citizens of Natchez to head an expedition into Texas. Arrives at Nacogdoches and takes possession of the place. Establishes civil government. Declares the country an Independent Republic. Offers Headrights and Bounty lands. Disposition of his military forces. Journey of Mrs. Long to Nacogdoches. Long leaves for Galveston Island. Advance of the enemy. Flight of the people from the country. Long and his lady at Natchitoches. She goes to Alexandria. He returns to Texas. Meets his followers at Bolivar Point. Learns the disasters of his expedition. Leaves for New Orleans. Returns to Texas. Captures Goliad. Is assassinated in Mexico.

THE patient reader, who has deigned to accompany the author, step by step, whilst he has been feebly essaying to trace out the *moral influences*, of whose origin and varied course of operation so much has been said in the preceding pages, and who has perchance occasionally grown tired of the laborious examination of facts and principles lying somewhat out of the range of ordinary observation,—will be doubtless pleased to learn, that an opportunity is now about to be afforded him, of recreating his wearied faculties by the perusal of a chapter written in a style of composition at once elegant and fanciful, and abounding with incidents which though related, as they unquestionably are, with a due regard to the strictest historic verity, have in them, notwithstanding, much of the body and complexion of well-imagined romance. The narrative which follows, is the product of a pen already favourably known to the

17 *

literary world — the *gift of friendship*, to the author of this humble work, from one * of the most distinguished of those high-souled chieftains who successfully battled for independence, for liberty, and for martial renown, in the late Texan Revolution,—and who, since the close of his military career, has added much to his own fame by the faithful and dignified performance of high civic duties as President of the beautiful young Republic that has for the last five years sparkled brilliantly in the far south-west, as " some bright particular star" of glory.   I proceed to adorn these pages with the narrative alluded to, and beg the critical not too strenuously to object to my thus seeking the aid of Texan genius in illustration of " Texas and the Texans."

In the spring of eighteen hundred and fifteen, there dwelt near the City of Natchez, a juvenile belle of great vivacity and loveliness, whose wit and beauty were heightened by the refinement of her manners and the purity of her sentiments.   Though young in years, she was not a minor in mental accomplishments ; and attracting the admiration of all, she was wooed unwon by suitors of the highest renown.

---

* The allusion to his Excellency, General Mirabeau Lamar, is doubtless distinct enough to make a more specific declaration on the point unnecessary.   But I will here mention, what may not be wholly uninteresting, that, but for the unavoidable absorption of this gentleman in harassing political cares, he would long since, in accordance with the desire of numerous friends, have furnished to the world a History of Texas, worthy of the name, in which he could so justly have exclaimed in the language of Eneas, " *Quorum pars magna fui.*"   He had indeed collected most of the materials for such a work, and had written perhaps some fifty or sixty experimental pages, when I had the honour of being invited, as heretofore explained, to undertake a task the execution of which by one more gifted had become impracticable, at least for several years : upon which, with a liberality altogether *characteristic*, General Lamar at once handed over to me most of what he had written, together with copious memoranda supplied by others, with authority to use the whole in such form as I might deem judicious.

She was now arrived at that age when the laws of Mississippi require a parentless child to choose a guardian. Accident led to the choice which she made; and whether it was a prudent and judicious one, the reader must determine when he hears the sequel.

Tying a sun-bonnet of green silk under her fair round chin, and slinging her satchel on her arm, she was about to obey the summons of the academy bell, when she was suddenly stopped by a little negro girl, who announced in a joyous mood, that a stranger had just gone into the sick man's room. "And what is that to me?" said the youthful beauty, "do his friends not call upon him every day?" "But this is the handsomest man in the world," replied the unsophisticated servant, "and I want you to see him before you go to school." Now the handsomest man in the world was certainly a sight worth seeing, for which a belle in her teens might very well afford to lose an afternoon's recitation. Accordingly she doffed her bonnet and threw aside her books, with a determination to take a peep at this fair Adonis. Whether this was done with the usual negligence of juvenility, or whether she stole a glance at the mirror to adjust her shining ringlets, is a matter of which fame reporteth not; but it is said of her, however, that she never looked more lovely in her life, nor glowed her cheeks with a deeper crimson than when the unexpected visiter—leaving the room of his patient—entered the parlour *sans ceremonie*, without the formalities of an introduction, but with a dignity and ease that bespoke the gentleman and the man of breeding. His personal appearance came up fully to her excited expectations; and although he was not the handsomest man in the world, he nevertheless possessed a very commanding figure—tall, active and erect, with a fiery eye and a martial tread, the very hero for a tale of love and war. His name and the purpose of his visit, were mysteries soon explained. He was a surgeon in the army, and had come to administer to one of his companions in arms who was then experiencing the hospitality of the family.

It is unnecessary to tell the reader, for he has guessed already, that our youthful heroine experienced the fate of Dido. She saw and was subdued. But more fortunate than Dido, her partiality was met by a generous requital. The heart of our hero bowed to the dominion of beauty. Indeed, for him to have gazed unmoved and passionless upon a flower of such unrivalled sweetness would have argued a want of that ardour and enthusiasm which are considered essential to the character of a soldier. In a few minutes, the happy couple, mutually pleased, found themselves seated by the window, contending with each other in a game of draughts. The lady of course was victor, and won of her antagonist a pair of gloves. The payment of this debt formed a fair pretext for our hero to renew his visit on the succeeding day. " I come," said he, " to settle accounts ; for debts of honour must be punctually paid." The lady, however, declined receiving the gloves, on the ground that she had played for amusement only, with no view of exacting the forfeiture. " Then," said the gentleman, " if you will not take them as your due, you must at least accept of them as a present." To this the lady could not politely demur ; and as she put forth her snowy fingers to receive the gloves, the happy donor, in a tone betwixt jocularity and earnest, expressed a wish that the hand that gave might go with the gift. This was enough. The lady understood the hint, and was pleased to see how the wind was blowing. In a short time they were open and avowed lovers. But it is known that the course of true love never did run smooth. The friends of the lady objected to the union on the very good grounds of the youth and inexperience of the parties ; and for a good while the uncompromising character of the opposition seemed in a fair way to defeat the wishes of the sighing couple. Chance and courage however decided the matter.

We have already told that our young heroine would

shortly have to choose her guardian. The time for making this selection was now arrived; and being called upon to name the individual of her choice, she turned and pointed to her lover. An objection was made. "I will name no other," said the thwarted damsel; "you force me to choose, and he is my choice." Her friends remonstrated—she was obstinate—they scolded—she persisted—and at length when it became obvious that she really intended what she said, all further hostility ceased, and it was not many days before the delighted lover was hailed in the family in the double capacity of guardian and husband. They were married on the fourteenth day of May, eighteen hundred and fifteen, the bride being in her fourteenth year, and the bridegroom in his twentieth. And ask ye who were the parties? The lady's maiden name was Jane H. Wilkinson, the niece of General Wilkinson. She was born in Charles county, Maryland; and losing her father at an early age, removed with her mother to the state of Mississippi in eighteen hundred and eleven. The hero of the story is no other than the chivalrous General Long.*

James Long was born in Virginia, and at an early age removed to Kentucky, and thence to Tennessee. He was a merchant at fifteen; but being illy qualified for such pursuits, soon failed in business, and then acted as clerk in his father's store for two years, during which time he saved by great economy six hundred dollars, with which he educated himself, and afterward studied medicine under Dr. Holland, of Tennessee. From the shop he entered the army; was a great favourite of General Jackson, who used to call him his young lion. He was attached to the medical staff of Carroll's brigade, and distinguished himself in the battle of New

---

* General Long, I have learned, was a native of the county of Culpeper, in the Old Dominion, and was either nephew or grand-son to the celebrated General Long, who was during the Revolutionary war one of the renowned captains of Morgan. It is a little singular that Kemper and Long should have been born in adjoining counties of the same State.

Orleans.   After this memorable victory, Carroll and Coffee being ordered to Natchez, Long accompanied them in his official character; and it was whilst he was at this place in attendance upon an invalid soldier at Mr. Calvert's, that he fell under the observation of the negro girl whose favourable report of his personal appearance had led to such an unexpected and happy result.   On the third day after his marriage, having first resigned his station in the medical staff, he left Natchez on a travelling excursion; and after the lapse of two months, settled at Fort Gibson,* pursuing his profession for a short time, when at the earnest entreaties of his wife, he abandoned the practice of medicine altogether, and purchased a plantation near the Walnut Hills, in Warren county.   He subsequently owned the tract on which the city of Vicksburg is located.   He soon however disposed of his farm and commenced merchandising in Natchez, where he continued in business for two years, when he was called to other objects more congenial to his enterprising and martial feelings.   Long was by nature a soldier, and had always sighed after a proper field for the indulgence of his military spirit.

From the disastrous overthrow of the Patriot army at the battle of Medina in 1813, the revolutionary spirit in Texas had pretty well subsided.   The insurgents seemed effectually quelled, and but for the valour of Anglo-Americans, they would have long groaned under the yoke of Spanish cruelty and despotism.   The reign of tyranny, however, was not permitted to continue undisturbed.   The citizens of Natchez, with a noble enthusiasm, resolved to make one more effort in behalf of the liberties of that oppressed and bleeding province.   A meeting was accordingly held by the inhabitants of that place, and arrangements entered into for an immediate and vigorous assault upon the country.   General Adair, of Kentucky, was to have been the leader of the expedition; but from some cause unknown to us, he declined

---

* Now known as the town of Port Gibson.

the proffered honour, and the command was tendered to General Long, who, nothing intimidated by the misfortunes of his gallant predecessors, who had figured so heroically but unavailingly in the cause of Texan independence, accepted the responsibility with pride and pleasure, and entered at once upon the duties of the station with his characteristic energy and enthusiasm. His activity and zeal, as well as his acknowledged military talents, soon rendered the project quite popular. He pledged the whole of his private fortune in the enterprise; in which he was joined by some of the choicest spirits of the day. With the best wishes for his welfare, he left Natchez with about seventy-five of the most hardy and intrepid followers, on the 17th of June, 1819. As he pushed from the shore, a shot from the cannon was fired to his success. It was evident, however, that an expedition so publicly gotten up and openly conducted, could not be permitted to pass off without the notice of the government. Attempts were accordingly made by the proper authorities to arrest the leader; but the officers not being over-active and vigilant, their efforts were easily eluded, and General Long moved off in triumph with his Spartan band, awakening the spirit of war in his march, and gathering strength as he moved along. He pushed for Natchitoches, where he had means of his own, and many friends; thence to the Sabine and on to Nacogdoches, where in a short time after his arrival he was able to muster about three hundred strong.

It is certainly a matter of much regret that there are so few objects upon which the minds of human beings can harmonize and act in concert. The most laudable and exalted purposes seem fated to breed a diversity of sentiment, and that diversity to engender passion. But if there is any one point upon which a whole community might think and feel and act together with unity and pleasure, we should suppose it would be just such an expedition as that on which our hero has embarked. Yet this, like many other of the noblest efforts in the cause of freedom, was doomed to encounter the opposition of the ignorant and the malice of the vicious, notwithstanding the purity of the motives that prompted it, and the glorious ends to which it was directed. Long's designs were by many either misunderstood or misrepresented.   Even some of his own followers looked upon the project as one which was entered upon merely because of its perils, and the individual glory to which it might lead. But such a view is not only unjust to the intellect and principles of the gallant leader, but it reflects discredit upon some of the purest and most distinguished citizens of Louisiana and Mississippi.   The expedition was founded in neither private speculation nor a desire of personal aggrandizement. It was known to the intelligent portion of the people both of Natchez and New Orleans, that its sole design and intention were to get possession of the country, to rescue it from the grasp of tyranny, and, by establishing good government, order and security, to invite to its settlement by North Americans.   General Long hoped to achieve by military operations what the two Austins had the ability and address to accomplish by peaceful negotiation.   To show that no sinister or unworthy motives influenced his movements, and that his views were liberal and comprehensive, directed solely to the freedom and independence of the country, we have only to give a plain statement of his proceedings on his arrival at Nacogdoches, and let them speak for themselves.

In taking possession of this place, the first thing to which he directed his attention, was the establishment of civil government.   If power or speculation had been his object, he might have made his *will* the law, and the sword his executive; but instead of this we find a "*Supreme Council*" elected, invested with unlimited and controlling powers of legislation.   "Did this in Cæsar seem ambitious?"   The council was to be composed of twenty-one members, but from some cause unknown to the writer, eleven only were chosen, to wit: Horatio Biglow, Hamlin Cook, W. W.

Walker,* Stephen Barker, John Sibley, (of Natchitoches,) S. Davenport, John G. Burnett, J. Child,† Pedro Procello, and Jose Bernardo Guitaris. The two last mentioned were Mexicans of liberal principles, who signified their acceptance of their seats, but never attended any of the sessions. General Long himself was chosen President. The Council met on the twenty-second of June, eighteen hundred and nineteen; and on the succeeding day declared the province a free and Independent Republic. Various laws were now enacted for the organization of the country, and the raising of revenue. The public domain, as a matter of course, was the chief dependence for means. A bill was accordingly passed for the survey and sale of lands on the Attoyac and Red Rivers; the minimum price of those on the first named being fixed at one dollar per acre, payable one-fourth down, and the residue in three equal annual instalments; whilst the lands lying on the latter stream were to be sold at various prices, according to quality, ranging from twelve and a half to fifty cents per acre. Major Cook was commissioned, on the twenty-ninth of July, to proceed to Pecan Point, and invite to the settlement of that section, by offering bounty lands to soldiers, and head-rights to actual settlers. These and many other regulations,‡ all salutary in their character, and well calculated to promote the objects intended, were adopted, and promised at the time much greater stability and more beneficial consequences than were realized. Whilst these arrangements were going on in the civil department, the

* This gentleman was well known as General Walker in Mississippi, and though now dead, is most favourably recollected by his numerous friends.

† This was the celebrated Judge Child of Mississippi, for many years recognised as the most learned jurist in the state, and who sat for several years upon the bench of the Supreme Court, where he continued to preside with eminent ability up to a short period before his death, which occurred about eight years since.

‡ A printing-office, the first establishment of the kind in Texas, was put in operation under the editorial conduct of Horatio Biglow.

disposition of the military force stood thus. David Long, the General's youngest brother, was stationed at the upper crossing of the Trinity with a large quantity of merchandise to barter with the Indians for mules and horses. Johnson was sent on a similar expedition; whilst Major Smith, who had brought into the country a company of forty men by way of Galveston, was stationed at the Cochattee village. On the twenty-second of September, Walker was ordered with twenty-three men to fortify on the Brazos, which he did, at the old Labahia crossing, meeting on his way five of Johnson's men, who uniting with him increased his force to twenty-eight. Matters being thus arranged, General Long makes preparations to go to Galveston for the purpose of establishing a small post at Bolivar Point, and also to obtain, if possible, some munitions of war from the celebrated lord of that island — John La Fitte. He had already opened a correspondence with this bold rover of the seas, who says in one of his letters, that having devoted the last eight years of his life in a struggle against Spanish cruelty and despotism, he could not do otherwise than wish well to the General in a similar undertaking; and then reminding him of the fate of those who had preceded him in the glorious cause of Texan Independence, admonishes him to be prudent as well as brave. Persuaded by this manifestation of friendly regard, that some assistance might be obtained from the pirate by a personal interview, the General resolved upon a visit; but before he departs we beg leave to bring up the history of another individual, whose adventures are no less romantic than his own, and who is, with all of his exalted qualities, his equal fully in every respect — in intellectual vigour as well as nobility of soul.

Indeed the history of Mrs. Long is so intimately connected with that of her husband, and is of itself so full of interest, that it cannot be omitted without material injury to the narrative. I doubt whether the reader will not find her story the more exciting of the two. Her situation at the time General Long left her at Natchez, was one of peculiar anxiety. In a few days after his departure, she became the mother of her second child. This materially increased the pang of separation; which soon became so intense and insupportable, that she resolved, when her infant as yet was not a fortnight old, to follow her husband and share his destiny, in despite of her feeble condition, and the most solemn entreaties of her friends. He was in a foreign country; in the midst of peril — with no home but the camp and no safety but his sword. To follow him under such circumstances, and in her situation, looked like self-immolation — a holy sacrifice of life at the shrine of affection—and to attempt such a journey, through a wilderness of savages in a distant land, with her two little children and no human assistance except a small negro girl, displays a resolution and fortitude unrivalled in romance, and which nothing but the tenderest and deepest feelings of the human heart could inspire. She started on the twenty-eighth of June. Mr. James Rowan, the friend of her husband and a wealthy merchant of the place, hearing that she was about to embark, came to the river bank to see her off and bid her farewell. He found her in tears. And well might she weep, for she was not only leaving the home of her happier days, but she was going, she knew not where, on a long journey in a strange land, with ruined health, almost destitute of means, and without a friendly hand to aid her on her way. These things pressed upon the heart; but the burthen was quickly lightened by the generous Rowan. It was impossible for this excellent man to see the dews of affliction in the eye of beauty without wiping them away. Unprepared as he was for such a trip, he nevertheless stepped into the boat, and with those elevated principles of benevolence and generosity which belong only to the virtuous and brave, he proffered to see her on her journey as far as her sister Calvert's, in Alexandria, where suitable arrangements could be made to con-

vey her with comfort and safety to her husband. In a few
minutes they were gliding down the river. The journey to
Alexandria was protracted and distressing. The weather
was bad; accommodations worse; and the boat finally
stopping on the route, a messenger had to be despatched to
Alexandria for means of conveyance. After much delay,
a courier made his appearance with a couple of horses.
Mrs. Long and her servant girl mounted one of the animals, and Mr. Rowan the other, with the little daughter
Ann, behind him, and the infant in his arms. They completed
the balance of the route, exhausted with fatigue and
drenched with rain. The boat with her trunks and other
effects arrived in a few days, bearing the unwelcome tidings
of the death of the young man who had been despatched
with the horses. He died of fatigue and exposure. The
trip from Natchez to Alexandria consumed nearly twenty
days. Mr. Rowan, after waiting a week at Mrs. Calvert's
for an opportunity of returning to Natchez, took his friendly
leave of the hospitable family — not however until he had
supplied Mrs. Long with what funds her journey might
seem to require, and placed in her hands a letter of credit
to draw on his house in the event of unforeseen contin-
gencies. Conduct like this is too noble and exalted to be
eulogized; it goes into the honest heart without the aid of
language, and requires no eloquence to make it attractive
and lovely.

For more than four weeks, Mrs. Long remained at her
sister's dangerously ill. The physicians believing that
mental anxiety, if not the cause of her declining health,
was at least a serious barrier to her recovery, advised her
to prosecute her journey without delay, which she could
do, they said, with benefit to herself by making short stages
and avoiding exposure. She accordingly set out in a close
carriage, leaving her infant to the care of Mrs. Calvert,
and made for Natchitoches, accompanied by a Mr. Randal
Jones and others, who were on their march to her hus-

band's standard. Tarrying a few days at Natchitoches, she proceeded thence to the Sabine, where she expected to be met by her husband. He had been there the day previous according to appointment, but could not wait her arrival, in consequence of intelligence received from Nacogdoches. At Mr. Gaines' she also remained a couple of days to resuscitate her strength, and then resumed her journey, still accompanied by her volunteer friends and several new recruits who joined them on the way. The first day's travel from Gaines' was to Mr. Early's, a distance of only seven miles, where she camped for the night. By daylight next morning she was again moving on the road, and that night reached the Attoyac between nine and ten o'clock, almost drowned in rain. The daughter of Mr. Alexander was kind in her attentions; and assisted in drying her clothes by the fire. In the morning the river was swimming; but all hands crossed it without accident; and though it was so late in the day as ten o'clock, she nevertheless reached Nacogdoches long before the setting of the sun, and experienced in the warm welcome of her husband an ample compensation for all her toils and sufferings past. She was now at the end of her protracted journey, blessed in the affections of a hero that she idolized; whose happiness was her study; whose glory was her delight; and whose misfortunes she was willing to share when she could not avert.

But the rainbow is not always the signal of serener hours. Though it often span the retiring clouds, it sometimes sits upon the brow of a gathering storm: and such proved the light that illumined the countenance of our happy heroine on meeting with her husband — it was but a rainbow joy upon a cloud of sorrow. She arrived upon the very eve of calamity. A few weeks only of perpetual excitement and alarm was spent with her husband, prior to his leaving for Galveston. The purposes of this trip have been already stated; and when their importance was explained to his

18 *

wife, she was of too sound an understanding to urge him against the calls of duty, however much she might feel inclined to exclaim, " Here we meet too soon to part." Leaving her in the family of a Mr. Amberson, and placing Major Cook (who had returned from Pecan Point,) in command at Nacogdoches, he departed for the Island, taking with him thirteen men. He had scarcely turned his back, however, before Cook relapsed into his old habits of dissipation and drunkenness; and the garrison fell into uproar and confusion. And now commenced the calamities of the whole expedition; and never was a longer train of misfortunes and disasters crowded into a briefer space. On arriving at the Cochattee village, the very first thing that saluted his ears was the unexpected tidings of the enemy's approach. The intelligence was derived from the Indians who represented the Spaniards as rapidly advancing, seven hundred strong. Orders were immediately despatched to Cook, Walker, and David Long, to repair forthwith to this village, a point most favourable for the concentration of his forces, and where he intended to give the invaders battle ; and then writing to his wife, directing her to retire to a Mr. Brown's as a place of safety, and wait the issue of the engagement, he hastened with all possible speed to Galveston Island ; but not receiving the desired and expected assistance from that quarter, he returns without delay to the village, where he is greeted with a letter from his lady, dated a day or two after his departure from Nacogdoches, apprising him of the approach of the enemy, and of the disorganized condition of that post. Exasperated at the conduct of Cook, he mounts his horse and dashes for Nacogdoches. On the way he meets his wife flying from the place, who tells him that it is useless to proceed — that all is lost — the garrison has dispersed and the families are evacuating the town as fast as possible. This information only made him the more restless to proceed. Leaving his lady in the family above mentioned (Mr. Brown's,) he put the rowels to his horse, and after riding all night, reached Nacogdoches just in time to assist some of the poorer families who had been left behind, and were struggling to escape.

The town was now entirely deserted; with no human being in it except himself. He commenced gathering the public arms and ammunition; and whilst he was busily engaged in concealing them in an old dry well, he heard his name articulated in a feeble voice that scarcely rose above a whisper. He seized his sword—but on turning to discover the person who had accosted him, he beheld a pale and emaciated being—the shadow of a human creature—whose cadaverous and wo-begone visage was the personification of famine and despair. The man was so worn down and altered by hunger and fatigue, that Long did not recognize his faithful Lieutenant. "My name," said the wretched being, "is Lightle." At the mention of Lightle, Long rushed to his support. "Fly," said the brave Lieutenant—"fly while you yet have a chance—the enemy is in close pursuit—be quick, and you may yet escape." "And leave you to perish?" said the generous commander; "I am a dead man," replied the other, "and can go no further."— "Yes, but you must," replied the compassionate General— "here is my horse—mount and I will follow." Lightle refused; but Long, with a gentle authority, forced him to comply by lifting him on the horse and urging the animal forward. On they journeyed the livelong night, through many a swamp and dismal forest. This brave and suffering Lieutenant was attached to Johnson's party; and from him Long now received an account of the fate of that gallant and unfortunate company. They had been surprised, defeated, and dispersed. Lightle himself had been taken prisoner, but making his escape, had fled to Nacogdoches in hopes of finding that place strongly garrisoned. He found it deserted. "And what of Walker and my brother David?" inquired the General. "Of them," said Lightle, "I know nothing." This news fell heavy on the heart of

Long; he read in it the ruin of his expedition. On arriving at Mr. Brown's where he had left his lady, and still expected to join her, he found the family had fled. Universal consternation prevailed, and the whole population were rushing like a terrified herd of buffaloe, to the Sabine. The enemy, who had entered Nacogdoches in an hour after Long and Lightle had left it, were pushing in pursuit of the flying populace. They were hard on their heels. There were two roads leading to the Sabine; the one by Lakey's and the other by Gaines' ferry. All who took the latter route, were overtaken and made prisoners. Fortunately for Mrs. Long she had followed the upper road. Her husband took the same, and after travelling all night, reached the river as the sun was rising. The day was spent in crossing the stream. He succeeded in getting all the families over, except that of Critchfield, who resided immediately on the bank of the river, and affecting no apprehensions of the enemy, declined crossing until morning. It was supposed by some that the old gentleman intended, in the event of the enemy's appearance, to join their ranks. If such were his feelings, his loyalty was very badly requited; for they showed him but little courtesy or kindness when he fell into their hands.

About eight o'clock that night, Captain Wormsley, at the request of Mrs. Long, went in search of some articles which she had left at Critchfield's; but no sooner had the boat touched the opposite bank, than a negro fellow who had accompanied him was seized by a party of soldiers. Wormsley sprang to his rescue, but finding himself suddenly surrounded, and likely to be taken by the insolent foe, he fired his pistols, and attempting to escape, was thrust through the body with a bayonet, and supposed at the moment to be mortally wounded. Himself, Bill, and Critchfield's family were all made prisoners. The noise and confusion in the encampment on the east side of the river were so great that the report of Wormsley's pistols had not been heard; and from his not returning as soon as was expected, it was concluded that he had determined to tarry the night with Critchfield; and nothing further was thought of his absence. The transactions of the night were not known until some time after. About day-break next morning, the report of a musket which was fired by the flames of Crutch-field's dwelling, gave the first intimation that the foe had been near. Thus came and departed a bloody and dangerous enemy, unobserved and unresisted, for the want of proper vigilance and discipline. The fault however was not with General Long; for on crossing the river his authority had ceased in the encampment, and the people, all being much fatigued, and feeling secure on the east side of the Sabine, were unwilling to encounter what they considered useless fatigue in standing guard. Mrs. Critchfield and her daughters were mounted on mules with their faces directed to the rear, whilst the old gentleman himself was fastened to the tail of one of the animals; and in this way they were marched off in triumph to Nacogdoches. From the interference of the military authorities at Fort Jessup, the families taken on the occasion were released, but it is believed that the men were all conducted to Monterey, where they remained for two years in captivity, and many never returned.

When the flames of Critchfield's house were first observed, General Long with a small party went in prompt pursuit of the retreating enemy; but not being able to overtake them, returned to the encampment, and moved with his lady and Mrs. Walker for the Red River. That night Mrs. Long received information of the death of her infant. This amiable and excellent lady seemed doomed to every variety of trials and vicissitudes. On reaching Natchitoches, she found her trunks and other effects in the custody of the sheriff. But no misfortunes—neither affliction, poverty, nor insult, could shake her high and lofty nature. She encountered every trial with dignity and fortitude, and never failed, in adversity as in prosperity, to extort admiration and respect by the strength of her principles and the magnanimity of her deportment. Taking an affectionate leave of her husband at Natchitoches, she proceeded in company with Mr. Alexander Pannell to her sister Calvert's, where she arrived some time in the early part of November, a little upwards of four months from the date of her departure from Natchez; whilst General Long himself returned to Texas with all possible despatch by the way of Culcasiu, and thence to Bolivar Point, the designated place of rendezvous in disaster. Here he collected the scattered fragments of his ruined forces, and learnt from them the sorrowful tidings of their discomfitures and sufferings : he was told that Johnson had been defeated on the Navasot. Ten of his men who were on a hunting excursion under Lieutenant Campbell, were surprised on the eleventh of October and made prisoners. Johnson himself and six of his men reached Walker's on the Brazos, on the fourteenth, with the enemy close at their heels. On the next day about nine o'clock, the post was attacked by the advanced guard of the invaders. They were easily repelled ; but about eleven o'clock, the main body of the enemy, three hundred and fifty strong, made their appearance, and after a brisk round or two, the Americans were forced to fly, leaving behind their entire baggage, arms, and provisions. They fled, destitute of everything; and fearing pursuit, left the highway and struck through the woods for the Cochattee village. The victorious army marched on with rapid pace to the Upper Crossing on the Trinity, where they met with a bold and desperate resistance from the gallant and intrepid David Long. Though valour was of no avail, he scorned to fly. His horse was seized at the beginning of the action by one of his own men—a recreant villain—who mounting the noble animal, dashed off and made his escape, leaving Long on foot with no weapon for defence except his sword, which he continued to use most heroically and effectually long after every one of his own band had deserted the field. Surrounded by the enemy, yet unsubdued, and undismayed, a musket was cocked at his temples and he was ordered to surrender. "Fire and be d———d," exclaimed the unconquerable youth—and in an instant he lay lifeless on the plain. He had purchased and herded nearly three hundred mules and horses, all of which, together with a large quantity of goods, fell into the hands of the enemy. The tidings of this defeat reaching Nacogdoches, Cook and his men broke for the Sabine, as if they were competing for the Stadium Crown. Walker and Johnson, who, after their overthrow on the Brazos, were aiming for the Cochattee village, being indifferent woodsmen, became bewildered and lost; and after suffering beyond description from famine and fatigue, at length arrived at the camp of Major Smith on the sixth of November, just in time to take another brush with the enemy; for the Royalists, on entering Nacogdoches, after despatching a detachment to the Sabine in chase of the flying families, marched with the main body of their force against Smith, who being apprised of their approach fell down about forty miles below the village, where he was however ferreted out by the invaders, and after a skirmish of some briskness, was doomed to the same disaster as his brother officers on the Brazos—he was forced to fly. And now it was at Point Bolivar that the fragments of this routed and ruined expedition were assembled, and such the doleful tale they had to tell their Commander-in-chief. But that Commander was a man whom no common misfortunes could subdue. His mind seemed to gain strength from calamity, as Antæus rebounded from each fall with redoubled vigour. Collecting his faithful followers around him, he exhorted them against despair, and invoked them to be steadfast in their purpose, and inflexible in their hate—telling them that though they had been routed, they were not conquered; and that if they would remain at their present post until he could repair to New Orleans and back again, he would return with a force which should ensure victory and vengeance. And so saying, he took an affectionate leave of all, and leaping into an open perogue, pushed from the shore, with no human being to accompany him, and coasted it to New Orleans, where he was met and well received by General Ripley, and other generous supporters of the cause.

Here the narrative of my distinguished friend is brought to a close, and seems never to have been completed by him; but I collect the following facts from his note-book, kindly placed in my possession. General Long returned to Galveston with a fresh supply of soldiers, attended by most of his former associates, having in his company likewise, the celebrated Col. *Milam*, whose singular adventures and heroic death at the capture of San Antonio, in 1835, have made him an object of peculiar sympathy and respect, as well to the votaries of romance as to the admirers of genuine valour. Providing vessels at Galveston for the transportation of his troops, Gen. Long proceeded to the mouth of San Antonio river, where he landed, and marched without delay to Goliad, or Labahia, of which he took easy possession. This post was occupied by the Patriot forces under his command until intelligence was received of the proclamation of the *Plan of Iguala*, by Iturbide, the complete success of the second revolution in Mexico, and the entire overthrow of Spanish authority. A short period only intervened before he was courteously invited by the new Government to visit the Capital of the Republic, that he might receive appropriate honours as one of the champions of Civil Liberty. Such an invitation could not well be declined, and he accordingly proceeded to the Capital with a suitable escort. But unfortunate was it for General Long that he did not act upon the principle of *timeo Danaos, et dona ferentes*; for he had not been in the city more than a few days, before he became an object of peculiar suspicion to Iturbide and his minions, who recognized in him a man whose Cato-like devotion to principle would never allow him to become a base auxiliary of this bastard Cæsar in those schemes of usurpation which his selfish cunning was then devising. Secret orders for his assassination are supposed to have been issued; and it is believed, upon satisfactory testimony, that General Long lost his life in the following manner: Being on a visit to some officer of the government one day, he had occasion to pass a small squad of the military on guard; and whilst drawing his passport from his pocket, he was shot by a soldier from an adjoining piazza, and instantly died. Thus perished by ignoble treachery, a Republican Chieftain, whose name deserves to be enrolled with that of a Brutus or Epaminondas of ancient times; whose enterprising valour and melancholy fate challenge a parallel with those of a Warren and Montgomery among modern Heroes. The indulgent reader will please pardon my concluding this chapter of " Fierce Loves and faithless Wars," in the appropriate words of the immortal bard, who sings:

> " O Love! O Glory! what are ye, who fly
> Around us ever, rarely to alight?
> There's not a meteor in the polar sky
> Of such transcendant and more fleeting flight.
> Chill, and chained to cold earth, we lift on high
> Our eyes in search of either lovely light;
> A thousand and a thousand colours they
> Assume, then leave us on our freezing way."

CHAPTER XI.

HISTORY OF THE FREDONIAN WAR.

Major Benjamin W. Edwards. Grant of lands by the Mexican government to Moses Austin: his death: confirmation of the grant to his
son, Gen. Stephen F. Austin, who establishes his colony on the
Brassos and Colorado rivers in Texas. Progress of Austin's Colony.
Grant of lands about Nacogdoches to Haden Edwards. Texas visited
by Major Benjamin W. Edwards in 1825.   His interview with Gen.
Austin at San Felipe de Austin.   He calls on his brother at Nacogdoches : finds him involved in serious difficulties.   Proceedings of
various kinds, resulting in the adoption of preliminary arrangements
for the prosecution of a War against the Mexican Government ; of
which arrangements a more particular account is reserved for a succeeding chapter.

DURING the summer of the year 1837, the good people
of Mississippi were suddenly called to mourn over the death
of a distinguished citizen, who had fallen a victim to disease,
whilst actively prosecuting an exciting canvass for the office
of Governor of the State.   Public meetings were held in
various places, composed of numerous citizens of all parties,
who declared, in energetic and affectionate language, the
uncommon admiration universally felt for the commanding
characteristics and endearing qualities known to have appertained to the illustrious deceased ; many gazettes put on
the habiliments of sorrow upon the melancholy occasion ; and
in the neighbourhood of his residence, the general sentiment
of the community demanded the pronunciation of a formal
eulogy upon the life and character of one so loved and esteemed by thousands.   The personage so lamented, and so
honoured, was the late *Benjamin W. Edwards ;* — a man
whose particularly modest and unobtrusive manners, and
whose well-known aversion for all the delusory arts so commonly put in practice for the acquisition of social consequence, make it next to impossible that the discerning and
intelligent community, in whose midst he had so long abided,

should have deliberately placed an estimate at all exorbitant upon his merits either as a citizen or politician. In giving to the world an account of " Texas and the Texans," I should hold it to be unpardonable to pass by without special notice, the efforts of Major Edwards and his high-minded associates, about fourteen years ago, to establish that Liberty and Independence in Texas which have been subsequently achieved by others, under more fortunate auspices. Indeed, an impartial review of the transactions alluded to, is due to the character of Major Edwards and others, on the score of justice ; since it is certain that· his magnificent Fredonian enterprise has long been grossly misunderstood by many very worthy persons, and has been denounced, at one period, by some, as a selfish and unprincipled project, altogether censurable ; whilst, by others, it has been freely ridiculed as a scheme which could receive respect nowhere save possibly in the region of the fabled Eutopia itself.

I am glad to have it in my power to present a true history of this affair, almost in the very words of my venerated friend, who, several years before the termination of his earthly labours, placed in my custody more than two hundred pages of manuscript prepared by himself, containing a spirited and well-written narrative of his Texan adventures. This manuscript was originally designed for publication ; but it was subsequently withheld from the press by the author, for reasons altogether substantial, one of which reflects much credit upon him as a man of generous sensibilities : he became, after the task of writing had been executed, and a season of cool reflection had intervened, somewhat apprehensive that, in the hasty composition of the work in question, drawn up as it was in a moment of strong *personal excitement*, and whilst the chagrin and irritation of disappointed hopes had not yet passed away, he might possibly have indulged in strictures upon the conduct of certain individuals towards himself and his brother, harsher and more *vindictive* than the principles of *strict justice* would entirely warrant, or a proper respect to the dignity of his own character would fully justify. He decided upon depositing what he had written in the hands of a friend, that, at a suitable time, such use might be made of it as that friend might deem right and proper. The individual thus delicately trusted will now perform the sacred duty which he owes to the honoured dead.

Those who have looked into the last edition of that charming little work entitled "The British Spy," have read in the preface attached to it, an interesting account of a gentleman who is described as the early *patron* and *friend* of *William Wirt.* That person was *Benjamin Edwards,* for many years a representative in the Legislature of Maryland from the county of Montgomery. The Benjamin Edwards there spoken of was uncle to the individual about to be described; from whom, indeed, he derived his Christian name.

Major Benjamin W. Edwards was born in the State of Kentucky, and reached the age of manhood whilst the last war between Great Britain and the United States was in active progress. With that hearty love of enterprise, and that generous ambition for honourable renown, which ever distinguished him above most men whom I have seen, he enlisted in the service of his country, and participated with great credit in most of the battles fought along the borders of the Northern lakes: in all of which, the prowess and patriotism of his native state were made conspicuously manifest. At the conclusion of the war, he married a lady of singular domestic worth, whose memory was tenderly cherished by him up to his latest moments, and engaged actively and successfully in agricultural pursuits. Some ten or twelve years of rural quiet and seclusion glided away; when, being deprived of his amiable consort by death, he removed to the Southern country, and, after itinerating for some time, resolved to fix his residence permanently in the state of Mississippi. The City of Jackson, at that time a small village, but then as now the capital of the state, received him as a citizen; and here, more for recreation and general improvement, than with a view to the performance of professional duties, he engaged in the study of the law. Long before he could pass through the *viginti annorum lucubrationes*, and, indeed, in a few months, he received a letter from his brother, Mr. Haden Edwards, then established as an Empressario, in the province of Texas, inviting him to visit that delightful region; which he did, in the Spring of 1825.

A statement of the condition of affairs in Texas at that period, will be here given, together with a concise account of some occurrences which had previously taken place. Early in the year 1821, Mr. Moses Austin, a native of Connecticut, but at that time a resident of Missouri, obtained a grant of land lying in the Province of Texas, from the Spanish authorities in Mexico, upon certain conditions, supposed to be sufficiently easy of performance; the principal one of which was, that he should procure the settlement of a limited number of Catholic families upon the lands granted, within a specified period of time. This grant was quite extensive, including a district of country nearly one hundred and fifty miles square, which was bounded on the east by the Brassos river, and on the south by the Gulf of Mexico. Austin, the original grantee, dying before he could avail himself of the advantages promised by his contract, the duty of performing its stipulations devolved upon his son, *Stephen Fuller Austin;* who afterwards became so distinguished in the Texan Revolution, and of whom much is to be said in connection with *the Fredonian War.* With a view to facilitating the execution of this interesting project, by means of which an opening was to be quietly effected for the introduction of liberal institutions, and an enlightened population, into the heart of the Spanish dominions in North America, — he contracted a financial connection with a certain Col. Joseph H. Hawkins of the City of New Orleans;

19 *

who agreed to supply all the money which he might need for the effectuation of his purposes, in consideration of being allowed to become interested in the prospective emoluments of the contract. The first body of colonists, consisting of only a small number of families, accompanied Col. Austin to Texas in the month of December, 1821. He was not able to remain long among them in person, deeming it necessary to proceed to the City of Mexico, for the purpose of procuring a confirmation of his father's grant to himself. He is represented to have encountered serious difficulties, and to have surmounted extraordinary perils, in the course of this trip to Mexico. The Camanches, who beset his route, once captured him and his whole party, and would probably have murdered them all, but for the seasonable discovery that they were *Americans* and *not Spaniards*, when they promptly set the prisoners at liberty, and even magnanimously declined plundering them either of horses, clothes, or money. Circumstances compelled this bold adventurer, in another stage of his journey, to travel for several days on foot, attended by a single companion, disguised in the tattered apparel of a *mendicant.* He at length arrived at his place of destination; but the second revolutionary struggle in Mexico being then in tumultuous progress, the confusion which prevailed in the administration of public affairs, rendered it wholly impracticable to effect anything immediately in furtherance of the object which had carried him thither.

About this period, likewise, arrived in Mexico, Colonel Haden Edwards, already mentioned as the brother of Major Benjamin W. Edwards, together with a Colonel Leftwich, and General Wilkinson; all of whom came in quest of grants of land in Texas. Austin, after considerable delay, and encountering many embarrassments of various kinds, succeeded in obtaining a confirmation, by the government *de facto,* of his father's grant, and prepared to set out on his return to Texas, where he knew he had been long anxiously expected by the colonists, and where he had reason to believe his personal presence to be altogether necessary. But just at this crisis, a sudden tempest of popular commotion shook the unsolid throne of Iturbide into ruin, and raised up obstacles in the way of Colonel Austin, even more serious than those which he had first succeeded in overcoming. Greatly disheartened, but yet not despairing of ultimate success, he resolved to await patiently the calming of the ocean which he beheld raging around him, and to hold himself ready to negotiate with any government which might chance to spring into existence. Whilst Col. Austin was thus detained, the Mexican Congress, *so called*, passed a law known under the title of the *National Constitutional Law of* 1824, by means of which, the several states in this ill-starred and tumultuous confederacy misnamed the Mexican *Republic*, were empowered to enter into arrangements, according to their own discretion, respectively, for the population of their vacant territories by colonists from abroad. The Province of Texas was thrown into temporary political connection with the neighbouring Province of Coahuila, under the denomination of the *State of Coahuila and Texas*, and was protected against the permanent continuance of this conjunctive arrangement by a *fundamental guarantee*, that so soon as the increase of her population should justify it, she should be disencumbered from the alliance with Coahuila, and be permitted to take her place among the Mexican sovereign States, on terms of perfect co-equality, in point of dignity and privileges, with the older members of the confederacy. This law threw Edwards and the other new applicants for unsettled territory, before the Legislature of Coahuila and Texas; by which body a law was passed, on the 24th of March, 1825, providing for the introduction of foreign settlers through the instrumentality of officers to be called *Empressarios ;* to each of whom, an allotment of unoccupied territory was to be made, on condition of his procuring its settlement by a stipulated number of families within a given period; for the

performance of which service, each Empressario was to
receive a compensation in lands proportioned to the number
of colonists then introduced by him.   Under this law,
Haden Edwards and several others succeeded, after some
delay, vexation, and expense, in obtaining the grants selected
by them ; and immediately commenced the active execution
of their contracts.   The grant of Edwards covered a large
surface of territory surrounding the town of Nacogdoches,
in which place he determined to fix his own residence.

In the meantime, Austin having brought his negotiations
with the Mexican government to a favourable issue, had
returned to his colony.   He found, that during his long
absence, the colonists had grown much dispirited, as was
but natural, and that some of them had actually abandoned
their new habitations and returned to the United States.
But when he communicated the glad tidings of success
which he brought with him, hope returned to every heart,
and joy sparkled in every countenance. Fresh emigrants
from the United States poured in rapidly, to enjoy the paradise which he had provided for them.

But the colonists were not permitted to realize all the
advantages of their felicitous location in the early stages of
their history ; on the contrary, they soon found, that they
had both dangers and inconveniences to encounter, calculated to call in requisition all the energies both of mind and
body which they possessed.   Most of these hardy pioneers
were in a state of extreme indigence at the period of their
emigration ; having no earthly property whatever, save a
slender stock of cattle and hogs ; and indeed not a few
of them were so entirely destitute, as to be compelled to
support themselves by the rifle, until they should be able
to rear a crop of corn from the rich soil which they occupied.   It is said, that at one time, there was such a want of
the absolute necessaries of life in the colony, that *the flesh
of wild horses** was used for some weeks, in order to avoid

---

* I have this fact from Colonel Gross, a gentleman of high standing,
and among the first settlers.

the pangs of famine; it is farther said, that this consumption of horse-flesh proved highly deleterious to those who experimented on it, and was supposed in some instances to have produced sudden death. The colonists were likewise not a little molested with disease arising from the rapid disafforesting of the wilderness and the consequent decay of vegetable matter. Even these were not the worst evils with which they were assailed; for the whole region round about was infested with savage Indians, of various tribes, who roamed over the country in every direction, and put to death all the colonists whom they chanced to surprise in an unprotected condition. But after the first year or two, the settlements became healthful in a very high degree; and the heroic colonists quickly learned to embody themselves and pursue their barbarous Indian foes to their own fastnesses, where they did not fail to take bloody vengeance for all the wrongs they had dared to inflict. The *Karankaways*, and other tribes along the coast, were in a short time effectually subdued; after the reduction of whom, the colonists had nothing to apprehend from this quarter, save from the outrages of the fierce Indians of the North—the Camanches, and other kindred tribes, hereafter to be noticed; who then, as now, from time to time, sallied out from their distant mountain homes, and on fleet and well-trained horses, took rapid excursions over the whole level country along the shore of the Gulf, and after committing numerous acts of devastation and bloodshed, escaped with the plunder which they had acquired beyond the reach of pursuit.

The number of emigrants from the United States, in a few years, became so large as to exhaust the first contract obtained by Austin, from the Mexican Government; when he made successful applications for additional grants of territory. He laid off the town of San Felipe de Austin, on the eastern bank of the Brassos, which he established as the capital of the colony, and his own place of residence. Other towns were gradually established likewise; within whose limits the colonists were able to enjoy greater security against the incursions of their savage assailants. Such was the condition of affairs when, as has been already mentioned, Texas was visited, in the year 1825, for the first time, by Major Benjamin W. Edwards. He proceeded to Nacogdoches, where he did not stop, as his brother was then absent, and extended his journey to Austin's Colony. Colonel Austin had been long known to him personally, and received him with marked politeness and cordiality, at San Felipe de Austin; at which place he sojourned for several months. It is not at all surprising that two such individuals as Austin and Edwards should at once have been mutually pleased with each other, and have contracted a cordial intimacy. Such, at least, was unquestionably the fact; for the correspondence which was kept up between them for a considerable period thereafter, and which I have this moment before me, is replete with the most striking indications of reciprocal esteem and kindness. Many conversations occurred during the sojourn of Edwards at San Felipe de Austin, between the two friends mentioned, in reference to the future prospects of the American population in Texas; and it is not strange that both of them should have come to the conclusion that nothing could be more unreasonable than the expectation that the colonists would always remain unmolested by the Mexican Government, and be permitted to enjoy the rights and privileges guarantied to them, without interruption. But the two friends concurred likewise in the opinion, that all prudential means should be used for the purpose of postponing collision with the Mexican authorities as long as possible; until the strength of the colonies should become sufficient at once to throw off the yoke of subjection, in the event of its becoming too galling and oppressive; and that, in the mean time, many grievances should be borne with patience, in anticipation of the grand objects which both had equally in view, viz:—*the firm establishment, in this favoured country, of the institutions of civil and religious freedom*, and the redemption of a region from foreign rule, which rightfully belonged to the people of the United States, and of which they had been notoriously bereaved by fraudful negotiation.

Major Edwards took his leave of Colonel Austin, and returned to the neighbourhood of Nacogdoches, on his way to the capital of Mississippi—which has been already mentioned as his place of residence. On passing through his brother's colony, he was gratified at finding that he had already arrived from the United States, and was proceeding actively in the performance of his functions as Empressario; his domicil being established in the town of Nacogdoches. There were, as yet, very few persons located within the boundaries of Edwards' Grant; though this particular part of Texas was far from being destitute of inhabitants; but these were to be found settled chiefly in a district of territory sixty miles in width, lying between the eastern extremity of the grant referred to, and the Sabine river.

It would seem, that the career of Haden Edwards as Empressario was from the beginning beset with most harassing difficulties. His good fortune in obtaining a cession of a body of land so extensive had excited the jealousy and ill-will of many of those who had been long residing in this section of Texas, who were not able to perceive what claims he had upon the respectful consideration of the Mexican Government superior to themselves; and they were, moreover, not a little apprehensive, that the Empressario might feel inclined to disturb them in the enjoyment of that territorial dominion which, heretofore, they had been exercising without interruption from any quarter. The Spanish population, in mass, conceived serious umbrage at an *American's* being permitted to come into their midst, armed with such extensive authority, and who was preparing to let in a flood of emigrants from the United States, of whom they had already a larger number than they could conveniently control. It is equally true, that there were several measures adopted by the Empressario in the enforcement of his authority, to say the least, not of a *politic* character; and it is evident, that in the commencement of his career, he neglected to employ those means of *conciliation* which could alone have secured a quiet acquiescence in his claim to exercise a superintending control over the interests of the colony. Two parties were quickly formed among the population; one of which rallied zealously to the support of the Empressario, whilst the other was ready to wage an uncompromising warfare against his authority.

I will here remark, that a dispassionate review of the history of the colony at this period, has satisfied my mind that there was much to regret, and not a little to disapprove, in the conduct of several of those who were prominently concerned in the contest which began to be fiercely waged in the bosom of the colony; and I am persuaded, that if the Empressario had enjoyed the benefit of his brother's sage counsels at this time, much of the bickering and strife which ensued would have been easily avoided. It appears, that the principal question then in agitation was one which arose out of conflicting claims to the office of Alcalde; a judicial functionary of much importance, and who would obviously have it in his power materially to facilitate or obstruct the plans of the Empressario. In a region so little under the dominion, as yet, of settled and known principles of *constitutional* law, it is not surprising that some disputation should have arisen as to the proper *source* of judicial authority. It is as little to be wondered at that the American population preferred the election of the Alcalde by the *body of the citizens;* and that the Mexican residents, with those in their interest, from force of habit, should feel partial to the form of *Executive appointment.* The colonists introduced by Edwards resolved to have an election at any rate; and chose a *Mr. Chaplin,* the son-in-law of the Empressario, to discharge the duties of Alcalde; who entered upon the exercise of judicial authority in the colony accordingly. In the mean while, the opposite faction had forwarded their application in behalf of another individual, one *Samuel Norris*, (who was understood to be entirely in the Mexican interest,) to the Political Chief at San Antonio, (Sancedo by name); who promptly yielded to their application, and transmitted a commission to Norris without delay. The election of Chaplin had placed in his hands all the official papers appertaining to the station of Alcalde; which, upon the appointment of Norris, as just mentioned, he refused to surrender to his custody, at least until his commission from the government should be sent to him (Chaplin) for examination. Upon which, the new Alcalde marched a body of armed men, chiefly Mexicans, about fifty in number, in front of the house of the Empressario, where Chaplin then was, threatening serious violence if the papers in controversy were not immediately yielded up. A parley ensued, which resulted in the exhibition of Norris's commission, and the surrender of the official papers by Chaplin.

From this period little social quiet was enjoyed in the colony; Norris proved arbitrary, venal, and oppressive, and the friends of the Empressario held him and his authority in absolute contempt. Various scenes ensued, tending to embitter the existing feud, and preclude all harmonious co-operation among men who should have felt themselves united by the ties of a common interest. The difficulties with which the Empressario had to contend were, about this period, greatly increased by an official communication transmitted by the Political Chief at San Antonio to the Alcalde — of a highly inflammatory tendency — containing language of strong denunciation agiainst Edwards, and reprobating his whole course of proceeding. The inhabitants of the surrounding country were formally convened to hear this document read; and many of them left the place of assemblage with sentiments of the fiercest unkindness towards the Empressario; whose life, indeed, was considered not secure from hostile assault. It was at this particular juncture, that Major

Edwards returned to the Colony after a short absence. His arrival was certainly fortunate ; for it is manifest that nothing but the interposition which he promptly exercised saved the vicinity of Nacogdoches from being completely drenched in colonial blood. The contending factions were mutually armed for contest ; and popular frenzy, on both sides was at its height. Major Edwards saw that no time was to be lost, and set to work at once as a *pacificator*, which, notwithstanding the indomitable fearlessness which distinguished him, was his favourite character. He approached the infuriated citizens as a friend and brother to them all, and poured forth a tide of dissuasive eloquence, of which those who have heard him speak, know him to have been a thorough master. The effervescence of his own and his brother's friends was at once seen to subside, under the charmful influence of pathetic rhetoric ; whilst remonstrances more energetic, mixed with the language of menace, so far as he deemed it prudent to resort to it, disarmed the enemies of the Empressario of their rage, and brought them into a promise of inaction, at least for the present. But the elements of combustion still slumbered in the bosom of the community, ready to blaze out again upon the first application of any new provocative to excitement.

A short interval of quiet which succeeded was not suffered to pass away unocccupied ; but Major Edwards and his brother at once availed themselves of the opportunity afforded of attempting the work of conciliation, which had been postponed so unfortunately to this late period. For this purpose, a memorial was addressed to the Political Chief, drawn up in temperate and respectful language, explaining the past, giving assurance for the future, and invoking his kindly offices for the restoration of quiet and good order in the Colony. Letters were at the same time despatched to leading men throughout Texas, with a view to correcting erroneous impressions supposed to have been conceived by them relative to the conduct of the Empressario, under the influence of false and distorted statements on the subject, which had been put in active circulation by his enemies. The Political Chief, who is represented to have been a beastly sot, and altogether hostile in his feelings towards the settlers from the United States as a class, instead of growing more temperate under the appliances tried on him, became, on the contrary, greatly more domineering and insulting, and replied to the decent communications addressed to him in language of most portentous threatening. Among the Spanish population, the bland and affectionate manners of Major Edwards, and the majestic dignity of aspect and demeanour, which he knew so well how to exhibit on suitable occasions, neutralized the enmity of many, and perhaps in some instances transformed active foes into ostensible friends. He is said especially to have won upon the sensibilities of Norris, the Alcalde, already so often alluded to, and to have extracted from him professions both of respect and kindness.

For several weeks, the affairs of the Colony seemed to wear a pacific and favourable aspect, and hopes began to be entertained, both by Major Edwards and his brother, that the clouds which had lately threatened a destructive tempest, would finally pass away without any more serious consequence than the transient gleaming of electricity along the firmament. But they were not permitted to entertain such hopes very long; for bulletin after bulletin was fulminated by the Political Chief against the Empressario, denouncing vengeance for crimes against the Mexican Government, known only to his own distempered fancy; and the Alcalde was both encouraged and commanded to re-commence and prosecute to the end a course of tyranny and violence towards the American colonists which it was evident must soon result either in the abandonment of their new homes, or an open resistance of oppression by arms.

The legislative *nullification* of the grant of the Empressario was now openly spoken of as an event which was likely soon to occur; and the consequent revocation of all

individual titles to land derived from him was greatly apprehended. Confusion and alarm spread rapidly through the
whole Colony, and the tide of emigration from the United
States was completely suspended.

About this time, the Colony of Edwards was visited by
*General Wavell,** an English gentleman of high accomplishments, who had just returned from a visit to the City of
Mexico, where he was reputed to have made arrangements
with the government for the introduction of several hundred
English colonists, and the establishment of them on the
Red River, in what was called the *Pecon* settlement. Gen.
Wavell spent nine weeks in Nacogdoches, formed an intimacy with Major Edwards and his brother, and professed
to sympathize with them deeply in regard to the difficulties
with which he saw them contending. When he was about
to depart with the avowed intention of revisiting Mexico, the
opportunity was embraced of transmitting a memorial to the
National Congress, in which all the grievances under which
the colonists were then groaning were distinctly pourtrayed,
and the interposition of the government earnestly invoked
for their speedy removal. But no reply was deigned to
this communication, though drawn up in the most respectful
terms ; and it now became manifest, that the colonists were
fully committed to the tender mercy of the Political Chief
and his unprincipled subordinates.

The official tyranny of the Alcalde at length grew altogether insupportable. The Spanish, or, rather, the Mexican
inhabitants of the Colony, encouraged by the rumour which
prevailed that the grant of the Empressario would be shortly
revoked, boldly set up claims before the Alcalde to most of
the valuable lands then in the occupancy of the American
settlers ; and such was the daring profligacy of this officer,
that these claims, which appear to have had no earthly foun-

---

* This is the gentleman whose published description of Texas is to
be found in Ward's Mexico, and of whom more will be said in this
work after a while.

dation, save the cupidity of those who preferred them, received ready sanction and enforcement at his hands.   Many of the colonists who displayed some little reluctance to giving up their lands, their title to which had remained for years undisputed, and upon which they had expended much labour as well as money, were rudely expelled from their habitations by the application of military force; for it seems that in the person of this Alcalde were concentrated both Executive and Judicial power, neither of which was subject to any limitation either, save such as might chance to arise from his own caprice, or be dictated by those maxims of selfish and semi-barbarous policy, in conformity with which he delighted to regulate his whole conduct as a public functionary.   Nacogdoches now became a scene of wild uproar and confusion; acts of lawless and cruel violence marked the history of every day, and indeed of every hour; bands of *Regulators,* as they were called, pervaded the whole country, under the ostensible sanction of the Alcalde, and ready to execute any mandate to which he might give utterance.   These self-constituted assertors of order were kept in vigorous action by the prospect of recompense to be derived from the spoliation and robberies which they were allowed to commit upon the persons and property of all who were even suspected of disrelishing the course of the Alcalde and his base allies.   Private families were forcibly driven from their habitations, to make way for the minions of the Alcalde, who sighed for the comforts which the honest assiduity of the colonists had assembled about their domicils, and which they were too lazy and luxurious to acquire, except by violence exercised upon their peaceful owners.   Respectable colonists were dragged from their beds at midnight, by an armed mob, and hurried before the Alcalde, in order to undergo a secret inquisition relative to acts that they had never so much as even thought of committing.   Without being confronted with their accusers; without having the benefit of adducing a particle of vindicatory testimony, or being even permitted to cross-examine the wit-

20 *

nesses suborned to appear against them, they were subjected, in some instances, to a heavy pecuniary fine; in others, to the forfeiture of property; and, in many cases, were thrown into prison, there to remain until it should please his high mightiness, the Alcalde, to permit them once more to breathe the air of heaven. Even the passing traveller was not free from molestation and outrage, but was compelled to pay *tribute* for the privilege of transit through the country, under the penalty of forfeiting whatever of merchandise or other property might be found in his possession.

Meanwhile, a rumour began to prevail that various Indian tribes, some of whom were not distant from Nacogdoches more than fifty miles, were preparing to make an attack upon the settlement, for the avengement of wrongs supposed by them to have been received from the Mexican government. No response had yet been made by that government to the memorials and letters transmitted by the Empressario; and there was no reason to hope for the least relief from that quarter. The Political Chief at San Antonio was still inexorable. Every attempt to communicate with the American settlers in Austin's Colony had been hitherto unsuccessful, and there is no doubt that the true condition of things about Nacogdoches was never made known at San Felipe de Austin at all. A more alarming crisis than that which had now arisen could not well be imagined, and it must be acknowledged that it demanded astonishing powers, both of soul and mind, to stand up calmly and fearlessly amidst such multiplied difficulties and dangers. Few would have been able to remain firm where there was so much to alarm and paralyze, without being tempted to seek guidance from despair rather than reason,—without resorting to measures of violence ere all pacific expedients had been thoroughly exhausted. But, happily for his own fame, if not beneficially for his individual fortunes, faculties commensurate with the perilous conjuncture now developed, were found united in *him* who is about to become the *Leader* in the Fredonian war.

Before I enter upon an examination of the incidents of that war, there are several occurrences which claim a passing notice, without a knowledge of which it is possible that the subsequent conduct of the Fredonian heroes might fail to be properly appreciated.

A *private* quarrel chanced to arise between the Alcalde, Norris, and two brothers of the name of *Dust*, which was very near terminating in the chastisement of this officer by one of the brothers.   This transaction irritated Norris, who seemed to imagine the whole majesty of the Mexican government to be concentrated in his sacred person ; and without hesitation he issued orders to his favourite band of Regulators, who chiefly belonged to the Ayoush Bayou settlement, as it was called, directing them to march forthwith to Nacogdoches and take the individuals who had given him offence into their custody, as preliminary to the exemplary punishment which he had determined on inflicting. The command of the Alcalde was received whilst the inhabitants of the Ayoush Bayou were convened on a musterground, where Major Edwards happened also accidentally to be.   The case, as was natural, was no sooner made known to the crowd assembled, than great excitement began to display itself.   The Regulators were preparing to set out in obedience to the summons of the Alcalde, when Edwards, being familiarly acquainted with the transaction between the Dusts and the Alcalde, and knowing that any attempt to apprehend the brothers would infallibly rouse the whole American population at Nacogdoches, and probably bring on a bloody conflict of arms, determined to interfere as a peacemaker, and endeavour to prevent the march of the Regulators as required.   With this view, he proceeded to their midst, and harangued them, in that bold and energetic manner for which he was so remarkable, for twenty-five minutes ; judiciously blending the language of remonstrance with that of menace — both persuading against, and denouncing the contemplated movement.   His speech was completely successful : these fierce and lawless warriors, to a man, resolved to abandon their ignoble purpose ; not one of them was now willing to become the vile minister of official vengeance ; and the disappointed Alcalde was compelled, however reluctantly, to relinquish the pursuit of his destined victims.

Another incident took place about the same time, which should not be here omitted. This section of the Province of Texas had been, for many years, divided into several distinct districts ; in each of which, a separate Alcalde had been uniformly appointed. Norris, the Alcalde of Nacogdoches, and as such, having it in his power to interfere more harassingly than any of his brother Alcaldes, with the designs of the Empressario, having tasted of dominion once, became eager to *monopolize* all authority, civil and military, throughout the Colony ; and accordingly, pretending to have received orders from the Political Chief* at San Antonio, directing him to proceed, he suddenly announced the *abolition* of all the Alcalde districts save his own, and the *consolidation* of all judicial power in the Colony in his own person ; thus openly aiming, by this enormous extension of his official authority, to become the exclusive and despotic administrator of Justice, civil and criminal, throughout the whole circumjacent region, — or rather striving, by this movement, to constitute himself an absolute *Dictator*, whose mandates, enforced, as they were sure to be, by a band of faithful Janissaries, would command as full and ready obedience from the whole population of the Colony as ever greeted the edicts of a Dey of Algiers. The first step taken by him, in execution of this scheme of dominion, was the issuance of a mandatory letter to the Alcalde of the Ayoush Bayou settlement, prohibiting henceforth the exercise of judicial authority by that functionary, and directing him, without delay, to transmit his official papers to himself, at the

---

* An officer corresponding with what, in the United States, is called *Governor.*

Town of Nacogdoches.   The Alcalde who received this order was greatly surprised thereby, and was not inclined to submit peaceably to what he was bound to consider a naked and unauthorized attempt at usurpation ; and therefore at once announced his inclinations in the premises.   The citizens who dwelt in his vicinage, and who were quite numerous, alarmed at what they regarded as an invasion of their own municipal rights, resolved to stand by their Alcalde in the position which he had assumed.   Upon which, Norris, incensed in the highest degree, directed a body of troops to march into the mutinous district, to seize by violence upon the official papers withheld, and to summon the rebellious Alcalde to his august presence, to answer charges thereafter to be preferred against him.   All these operations were performed according to his orders, and roused the people of the Ayoush Bayou Settlement to a state of violent rage ; and they would certainly have marched at once to Nacogdoches, and avenged themselves upon Norris and his myrmidons, but for the seasonable exertions of Major Edwards, who visited them in the midst of their highest excitement, and urged upon them the exercise of forbearance and moderation, at least until the Political Chief could be appealed to, and the views of the Government touching the outrage they had suffered should be clearly ascertained.

A few days after the occurrence just related, another affair arose at Nacogdoches greatly more shocking than anything yet mentioned—though of inferior dignity, as involving only the rights of a single individual.   A young gentleman, from the State of Mississippi, by the name of *Bassett*, arrived at Nacogdoches.   He is described as having been genteel and modest in his manners, and he brought with him testimonials of character and good conduct in the United States, which at once introduced him to the confidence and friendship of the American population around Nacogdoches.   About a week after his arrival, he deposited in the office of the Alcalde all his important papers for safe-keeping ; a short time subsequent to doing which, he had the misfortune, in some way or other, to incur the displeasure of Norris; upon which he sent a polite message to him, requesting the re-delivery of the papers placed in his custody. To this application a rude refusal was returned, which induced Bassett to visit the Alcalde in person, in order to remonstrate against the uncivil treatment he had received. He had no sooner reached the presence of the Alcalde, than he was arrested by 10 or 12 armed ruffians in waiting for the purpose, dragged before the tribunal of this modern Appius Claudius, and, without the preferment of any accusation of misconduct, or being heard to say a word in vindication of himself, was sentenced to *immediate death.* The Americans in the vicinage, hearing of this diabolical outrage, promptly flew to arms for the rescue of their countryman; and the prisoner would soon have been signally avenged upon the tyrant, and the country have been relieved from farther oppression at his hands, but for his becoming alarmed, and commuting the sentence of *death* which he had pronounced, to that of *banishment* from the Province. This modification of the sentence induced the Americans to lay aside their arms, and Bassett was placed in the charge of two or three Mexicans, who were directed to hurry him to the Sabine; *private* instructions being at the same time delivered to these caitiffs that when they should have carried him thus far, they should *cut his throat from ear to ear.* The Americans, suspecting some device of this kind, deputed two or three of their number to follow upon the heels of these villains, in order to intercept any act of violence which might be attempted; and, in the sequel, nothing prevented the tragical catastrophe contemplated, but the presence of these Americans, who threatened instant *retaliation* if the prisoner should receive the slightest injury.

Such was the precise posture of affairs in Edwards' Colony, when an extraordinary personage appeared upon the scene of action; of whom some account will be given in the next chapter, as he stands closely associated with the *Fredonian War*, which a few weeks after broke out, and, next to Major Edwards himself, may be recognized as the most conspicuous actor in the attempted Revolution; the particulars of whose history will be presently detailed.

CHAPTER XII.

Attempt of Fields the Cherokee Chief to obtain a grant of lands from the Mexican government. Dishonest conduct of that government towards him. Some account of John Dunn Hunter. League offensive and defensive formed between the Fredonians and twenty-three Indian tribes. Fredonian Declaration of Independence. Various exertions to maintain the war about to be commenced against the Mexican government. Fredonians seize upon Nacogdoches; defeat an attack made upon them by Norris the Alcalde. Circular addressed to the settlers in Austin's Colony, to the neighbourhood of Pecon Point, and to the citizens of the United States. Conduct of Col. Austin at this period: motives for it. The Fredonians threatened with an immediate attack by the Mexican government, which is postponed by causes not known.

About the period that the City of Mexico was visited, as has been narrated, by Haden Edwards and others, for the purpose of negotiating for grants of vacant territory, appeared at the same place, the celebrated Cherokee Chief, Richard Fields, who went thither upon a similar errand. Fields seems to have been what is called a *half-breed*, but was most affectionately devoted to the welfare of the tribe of Indians with which he claimed connection, and is understood to have been particularly solicitous to promote their advancement in civilization. He petitioned the Mexican Government for a cession of that district of country lying contiguous to the United States, along the Red river, and North of the great road from Natchitoches, which crosses the Sabine river and penetrates Texas in the direction of Nacogdoches. What were the precise boundaries specified in his application, is not to be conveniently ascertained ; but he desired to obtain a body of lands of sufficient extent to accommodate not only that portion of the Cherokee tribe who were desirous of settling in Texas, but several other tribes also, who had agreed to unite in the formation of a Confederacy with them. After remaining in Mexico several months, Fields is said to have received a verbal promise that his application would be favourably treated, and resting satisfied with this, returned to his tribe,—announced to them the supposed success of his efforts, and prepared for the immediate occupation of the country ; a sufficient title to which was considered as having been obtained. He proceeded to establish a village fifty miles north of Nacogdoches. The Mexican Government had, in truth, never designed to make the proposed grant ; but, in order to get rid of further importunities from Fields, and to conciliate the Cherokee Chief, had been willing to amuse him with vague and deceitful promises ; all of which, at a convenient moment, were intended to be dispensed with. In the year 1825, Fields was quietly established at the village mentioned, and the tribes in his care were rejoicing under his paternal government, and were doubtless making rapid progress in agricultural pursuits. About this period arrived in the Cherokee village an individual whose romantic history has attracted at one time much attention and sympathy on both sides of the Atlantic : the famous *John Dunn Hunter*. It is supposed that most of those who may chance to honour these pages with a perusal, will have heard, at least, if they shall not have read much of this extraordinary person ; since he was, many years ago, the writer of his own strange life and adventures, and, at one time, was an object of such uncommon curiosity, both in England and the United States, that all his movements were minutely observed upon in the gazettes of either country ; and his most trivial remarks were deemed worthy of elaborate scrutiny and solemn criticism. To many, it will be unnecessary to state, that Hunter

professed to have been reared, from early infancy, among
the Nottoway tribe of Indians, and to have known nothing
of the usages of civilized men until about the age of sixteen ; when he was rescued from his savage custodiants, and,
through the liberality of several distinguished individuals in
the United States, was maintained at an eminent institution
of learning until he had become in a high degree remarkable for his proficiency both in classical lore and in the
stricter sciences. The point is still left in doubt, whether
Hunter was altogether of *white* extraction, or had some
inconsiderable proportion of Aboriginal blood flowing through
his veins; but it is certain, that his leading characteristic
was an affectionate fondness, ever displayed by him, for the
untutored children of the forest ; and the leading object of
all his exertions was the promotion of civilization and knowledge among their scattered and decaying tribes. It is known
that Hunter received much attention and respect anterior to
his visit to England, from Mr. Jefferson, and many other
distinguished individuals in the United States, and was by
them zealously encouraged to persevere in those philanthropic designs which he had so much at heart ; it is equally
certain, that he was everywhere received, especially in the
renowned " Island of the sage and free," not only with tokens of respect, but even with eclat, up to the moment when
he became suspected, upon grounds which do not seem to
have been at all sufficient, of being a mere *impostor*—prac-
tising upon the credulity of the public by the assertion of
pretensions to regard and sympathy not entirely warranted
by his true history. The following sketch of this singular
person, extracted from the columns of an old newspaper,
will serve to introduce Hunter to the reader in such a point
of view as will prove at least interesting. The name of the
writer of it is not known.

" I had casually seen him in New-York in 1821 : and in
London in January 1824. At breakfast with an American
gentleman, among other persons I met J. D. Hunter and

Robert Owen.   The visionary character of the latter was less developed then, than now, and I had never heard a suspicion of the genuineness of Hunter's pretences.   I was glad to meet them therefore; and now that one has turned out an enthusiast and the other an impostor, I cannot with many other discerning persons, pretend to have "*foreseen*" either the one transformation or the other.

Hunter at this time, and I believe always while in London, had cheap lodgings, where Washington Irving had lived, at Mrs. H.'s in Warwick street, in the neighbourhood of Charing Cross.   He, with the equally famous John Neal, and one other person, constituted, I believe, all Mrs. H.'s boarders.   In this obscure place, Hunter received the visits of many of the first gentlemen in London.   His card-rack was crowded with notes and cards, from persons of the highest distinction.   I saw one or two very sentimental notes of condolence from the Duke of Sussex to Hunter, while the latter was confined to his room by a dislocated shoulder; which, by the way, was attended to in behalf of the Duke, by his surgeon, Dr. Petingale.

During the winter of 1823—4, Hunter was the *Lion* of the fashionable world in London.   He was freely admitted at Almack's, and was pressed with multitudes of invitations to routs, balls and parties, from ladies of the highest rank and fashion.   Such was the strife for his society, that he had often several engagements in the same evening, and happy was the lady whose party was distinguished by his presence.   On these occasions the ladies were eager to converse with him, and esteemed it a felicitous moment in which they could fancy that they were filling his eyes and thoughts. Such was the delusion, that Hunter, though small, ill-made, and ill-mannered, appeared in their eyes the most interesting man, the most charming *creature*, they had ever seen.

It is remarkable that Hunter never seemed flattered by these attentions.   His dress was plain; his manners, though coarse, were always grave; he seldom smiled, and even when surrounded with beautiful women, whose eyes yielded a tribute that might have turned the head of a giddy fellow, he seemed to be unconscious of their notice and indifferent to it.

Nor were the females the only persons who paid their court to him. There was a large number of scientific and literary men whose interest he strongly excited. Among these were Mr. Sabine, Secretary of the Horticultural Society, Captain Parry, who was then in London, and many others. With these gentlemen, and in society like theirs, Hunter was in the habit of dining frequently, and so eagerly was his company sought, that it was with difficulty he could satisfy the numerous claims upon his time. I may add here too, that he seemed not to be in any degree flattered or elated by all this; he seldom spoke of the notice taken of him, and never within my observation, unless in an incidental way.

In the summer of 1824, in June, I was in Edinburgh. Hunter had been there some time before. He had excited a deep interest there too, partly of a personal nature, and partly on account of a project for civilizing the Indians, which he held up as the object to which he intended to devote his future life. His plan was to form a settlement of Indians on the Wabash, and by partially adopting Indian manners at first, to introduce civilization by slow and invisible progress. This he represented as the only way in which the savage could be drawn from his woods, and persuaded to lay aside the spirit-stirring pursuits, which the associations of youth and the inherent love of hazard and adventure, rendered dear to him.

I was here frequently inquired of, about Hunter, and my opinion was often asked as to the probable success of the scheme. Among the individuals who expressed an interest on the subject, were Sir Walter Scott, and his accomplished daughter, Mrs. L——.

I might add many other similar evidences of the extraordinary interest which Hunter excited in England. I will only say that he was a particular favourite with Mr. Coke, and received many tokens of his regard. The newspapers frequently spoke of him in terms of the liveliest interest, and no less than three editions of his travels were sold during his stay in England. Besides, he had considerable presents made to him, among which was a splendid watch from the Duke of Sussex. He received also, I think, from Mr. Coke, a valuable set of mathematical instruments. Other presents, I believe, were offered to assist him in his enterprise for civilizing the Indians, which he declined.

Hunter left England for America in the summer of 1824. His departure was noticed in most of the papers, and drew forth expressions of the liveliest interest in his welfare, happiness and prosperity.

I should add, that I have never heard that he took any advantage whatever of the confidence he obtained, and of the rich opportunities which he had to profit by it, in England; with the exception only of receiving the presents of Mr. Coke and the Duke of Sussex. On the contrary, he refused presents and the use of money, and returned as he went, excepting, perhaps, a little sum which he must have received as the avails of his book. If his story had been true, his conduct, at least as far as I observed it, or heard it reported, was dignified and irreproachable.

Nor is this all: Hunter uniformly spoke in terms of praise of everybody of whom he had occasion to speak; he always expressed great attachment to America, and espoused its cause, sometimes with indiscretion. He seemed to be fond of the society of Americans, and to some of them did kind offices. He persuaded Mr. Coke and the Duke of Sussex to sit to an American portrait-painter, who had just arrived in England, and who, by the way, is one of the first artists of the day, and thus introduced him to distinction in London."

I am saved from the necessity of adding any thing to what has been already said relative to the character of this remarkable man, by the affectionate diligence of a gentleman, who, after the untimely death of Hunter, published a vindicatory article relative to him, in one of the leading newspapers of the United States; from which the following interesting extracts are drawn. The author of the article alluded to is *H. B. Mayo*, Esq., well known, a few years since, as a high-spirited and useful editor of a political journal in the State of Mississippi, and whose name will again appear several times, in the progress of this chapter, in connection with prominent scenes of the Fredonian war : "I first saw Hunter in Nacogdoches, in the early part of last summer. His narrative, the reputation it had given him, and the charge which had so suddenly blighted his fresh fame, were all known to me, and little did I expect to meet him in the wilds of Texas. His countenance and demeanour, before I knew who he was, drew my attention; and though no physiognomist, nor pretending to any unusual tact in penetrating the character through the external appearance, I was aware, notwithstanding the plainness of his dress, and the simplicity of his manners, that I was in the society of a highly intelligent man and a gentleman.   *   *   *

   *   *   *   *   *   *   *   *

Hunter was in person about the middle size, stoutly made, and apparently of much strength. His countenance, though far from handsome, was very expressive. The strong lines of a marked character were there, indicating the powerful feelings and the glowing enthusiasm that belonged to the man. His manners were, in general, quiet, grave and gentlemanly; but they would burst out into singular vivacity, when his feelings were raised, and then, at times, his high excitement would render him masterless of himself, and, while it made him eloquent in gesticulation, frequently deprived him of all command over words. Any discussion relative to the situation and character of the Indians would rouse the level calm of his ordinary manner into a storm that agitated his entire soul. Grave, deliberate, and intelli-

21*

gent on every other subject, the moment that chord was touched, his enthusiasm and ardour overpowered the sluggishness of calculating investigation, and his imagination burned with the distant prospect of the civilization and happiness of the persecuted Indians—the long-cherished object of his philanthropic ambition.

Can it be that this man was an impostor? Apparently with all the artlessness and simplicity of a child, glowing with generous and chivalric feeling, manifesting always a fastidious delicacy of sentiment and of honour, can it be that the odious name of an impostor can be justly imputed to him? I for one will not yet believe it. The accusation has been reiterated from one extremity of the country to the other, and the reputation of this interesting individual blotted for ever, upon evidence the most uncertain. Some Indian trader, it seems, has been among one of the tribes, with whom Hunter relates he had lived, and one or two Indians of the tribe, being interrogated, had no recollection of such a person. If I am rightly informed, this is the only foundation upon which rests this damning charge, and the world, more willing at all times to hear accusations than defence, has, without investigation, blindly and implicitly branded with odium the man it once delighted to honour, as if to revenge itself of its former kindness. Yet it is most certain that Hunter had been and lived long among the Indians, and that he was familiarly intimate with their character and customs. I went with him last summer to the Cherokee village, and while there, was informed, by some of that tribe, of a Nottoway Chief who well knew Hunter in his early life, when he lived with that or some neighbouring tribe, and whose account, as far as I learned it, and as my memory now serves, corroborates his own narrative.

I shall ever deeply regret that a false delicacy withheld me from ever mentioning to Hunter the subject of this odious accusation, for I am convinced that he died profoundly ignorant that any stain rested upon his reputation. He could then, if innocent, have had the opportunity to restore his name to its former purity. He had been, from before the time when he was first stigmatised as an impostor, travelling through Mexico, or living among the Indians. He once mentioned to me that he had not seen a newspaper of the United States, since he had left them. He could not, therefore, have known that such an imputation had an existence.

The object for which Hunter had exiled himself from the enjoyments and the blandishment of a world he was fitted to instruct and adorn, and for which he devoted laborious days, travelled over the desolate waste of the interior of Mexico, encountered danger and endured every privation, was the civilization of the hunted, expatriated Indian—the original and Heaven-invested proprietor of our soil. He lived with the wild natives of the forest in their own rude way, partook of their own rude fare, and mixed in their simple sports and hazardous enterprises, that he might gradually and imperceptibly introduce one useful improvement after another, and at length wean them from their savage and uncivilized habits. This was the object for which he lived and died.

Would it be more than common justice to such a man to suspend at least our judgment respecting his character, for a time, with the view that some more light may be reflected upon this dark mystery, which may enable us finally to condemn with conviction, or to consecrate the memory of a martyr to Philanthropy?"

The arrival of Hunter at the Cherokee village has been already noticed. It would indeed have been somewhat strange, had a man of his discernment failed at once to perceive the flimsy and precarious nature of the tenure by which his Aboriginal friends claimed the territory then in their possession; it would have been yet more surprising had he concealed from them their true condition in reference to that territory. In fact, he promptly unfolded to them all the uncertainty which hung over their prospects, and besought them to grant him a commission to negotiate

with the Mexican Government immediately, for a more stable
and definite title.   His friendly zeal was still farther manifested by a voluntary assumption of the task of visiting the
City of Mexico in person, upon this momentous business.
But his mission proving fruitless, he returned to the Cherokee village, full of grief and indignation at the cruel treachery which ˉhe conceived to have been practised towards
Fields, and, through him, upon the Cherokees, and other
Indian tribes in alliance with them.   These sentiments he
announced in full Council, and depictured in strong and
glowing language, the gloomy alternative, now plainly presented to the Indians, of abandoning their present abodes and
returning within the limits of the United States—or preparing to defend themselves against the whole power of the
Mexican Government by force of arms.   The fierce multitude of savage warriors who listened to him, were not long
in determining in favour of energetic measures, and they
unanimously declared for the immediate commencement of
hostilities upon the neighbouring Colonists in Edwards'
grant—considering them as a part of the population of
the Mexican Republic.   They believed themselves capable
of overrunning the country about Nacogdoches with little
or no difficulty ; and many of them were quite eager for
the *spoils* which they expected to gather in their contemplated course of conquest.   At this crisis, the attitude of
Hunter became one of great and painful responsibility : if
he ventured tȯ dissuade his tawny associates from this terrible project before their ardour had a little moderated, it
was obvious that he must, in a great degree, forfeit their
confidence, if he did not draw down their vengeance upon
himself; if he coincided in the plan of attack suggested,
he must soon witness scenes of devastation and bloodshed
which would fill his soul with horror, and render him for
ever miserable.   Under such circumstances, he adopted a
middle course, acquiescing in the proposition of war, but
urging the expediency of suspending hostile movements for

a week or two, until he could have an opportunity of visiting Nacogdoches, and ascertaining the exact condition of the colony. Having succeeded in staying the fierce operations of war for a short period, he repaired, according to his engagement, to Nacogdoches, and after remaining a day or two there, without much social commerce with the colonists, he at length determined to have an interview with the Empressario and his brother, and to lay before them a proposition for the formation of *a league, offensive and defensive,* against the Mexican government,—towards which government he discovered the colonists entertained sentiments of unkindness little inferior to the raging malignity that he had lately seen displayed among those warriors of nature who had so fiercely responded to his inflammatory eloquence.

Accordingly, he approached the brothers. He found them affable, frank, and even kindly, both in demeanour and in language. After establishing some acquaintance with them, listening to the pathetic story of their wrongs, and hearing enumerated the long and melancholy list of grievances under which the American colonists had so severely suffered, he ventured by degrees to unfold the object of his visit. He painted to his new acquaintances the exposed condition of the colonists, and the certainty of their being shortly attacked by an uncontrollable host of savage warriors, who were then arranging for the dreadful onslaught; he expatiated upon the fact, which was but too manifest, that they could expect no succour from the Mexican government, which would not if it could, and could not if it would, interpose for their rescue, and urged them, in terms replete with affection and reason, to unite with the Indian tribes under the control of himself and Fields, in a war against the common enemy. At this period, the inhabitants of the colony had risen up against the tyrannical Alcalde, Norris, deposed him, and dismissed him into exile; having found it utterly impracticable any longer to endure his atrocities. Another Alcalde had been elected, and they were expecting every day to hear that the Political

Chief would adopt measures for restoring this tyrannical functionary, and punishing those who had dared to rebel against his authority. Intelligence was received that their apprehensions on this score were not without foundation,—that the Political Chief was already in motion, at the head of one hundred and fifty men, and was marching in the direction of the colony, threatening confiscation and death to all who did not submit themselves to his mercy. News at the same time reached them that the grant of the Empressario was actually *annulled* by the Congress of Coahuila and Texas, and that all the derivative titles of the colonists would be regarded as of no validity. Under such circumstances, a meeting of the leading settlers about Nacogdoches was finally convened, and the preliminaries of a compact of alliance with the Indian tribes were soon arranged; of which a more particular account will be presently given. It should be here stated, that a strong motive for this alliance was derived from the fact, ascertained now for the first time, that the Mexican government had been, for several weeks, actively engaged, through the medium of emissaries then among the tribes, to incite them to an attack upon the colonists; and it was seriously to be feared, that the least delay in warding off this danger might be of fatal effect. As soon as this friendly understanding was brought about, Hunter returned to the Cherokee village, for the purpose both of obtaining sanction there of what he had done, and of detaching, as soon as he might find it practicable to do so, a body of Indian warriors to Nacogdoches, to unite with the colonists in the measures of defence now become necessary. On the 13th of December, Major Edwards and his brother set out, with one or two chosen friends, for that part of the colony which it was conjectured would be likely to experience the first hostile attack from the Mexican invading force, in order to apprise the settlers of the perils to which they stood exposed, and to rouse among them the spirit of heroic resistance. This was not difficult to effect, for no sooner was the actual state of affairs in the colony made known to the settlers, than they everywhere flew to arms, and evinced a readiness to do all that might become the descendants of a glorious ancestry, forced to battle in defence of their altars and firesides.

Major Edwards remained only two days at this place, when, putting himself at the head of only fifteen men, he returned in the direction of Nacogdoches; but before he could arrive at that post, on reaching a river called the Toyac, he learned that the enemy was expected at Nacogdoches that very night. Alarmed on account of the Americans in that vicinage, he resolved to push on with the small force accompanying him, in order to repel the invaders or perish in the attempt. He delayed only long enough to prepare a suitable *Flag*, to be raised over the heads of his valiant soldiers, upon which their names were inscribed, and a solemn pledge that they would stand by each other and the cause of Independence, as long as life should last; and galloped into Nacogdoches on the morning of the 16th of December, amidst the rejoicing of the colonists and to the terror of all the adherents of the government. The report which he had encountered at the Toyac proved to be in part only well-founded: Col. Beene, an officer in the employment of the Mexican government, had advanced at the head of about thirty-five soldiers, within a few miles of Nacogdoches; but, upon hearing of the hostile preparations which were going on in the Colony, and of the probability existing that he would be compelled to make good his position by dint of hard fighting, he retreated precipitately to the Trinity river; where he awaited the arrival of the main body of the Mexicans, expected shortly to come up. Had he pursued his original design of marching into Nacogdoches, he would have been infallibly strengthened at that point by some seventy-five or one hundred Mexicans, who only waited an opportunity of co-operating with the government in suppressing the rising insurrection; in which event he would have been able to defend the Town successfully against the little company of Americans who now dashed into it — and who ran triumphantly along the streets, proclaiming *Freedom* and *Independence* in the ears of all whom they met, and waving the *Fredonian Standard** over the house-tops of all who were known to be resolved upon breaking the chains of vassalage to the semi-barbarous government by whose minions they had been so cruelly oppresssed.

Being fully satisfied of the propriety and even *necessity* of all that had been done, and sustained by a confident hope that the whole American population in Texas would in due time sanction and sustain the bold and efficient measures which had been adopted for the present safety and eventual happiness of them all; the Spartan handfull who had valorously rescued this important post from the dominion of Mexico, took possession of a large stone house near the centre of the Town. Here they experienced an immediate increase of strength, by the accession of a considerable number of Americans belonging to the settlement: and here they hung out the banner of Liberty, and commenced fortifying themselves against sudden attack. In a day or two their ranks were swelled by nearly two hundred colonists residing in remote neighbourhoods, who becoming apprised of what was going forward, had rushed to the scene of action, ready to hazard their lives, their fortunes, and their sacred honour, in behalf of the cause of Freedom.

In a few days more it was ascertained that there was no reason to apprehend the immediate approach of a Mexican force; and inasmuch as only a small number of soldiers would suffice to keep in check the Mexicans of the neighbourhood, it was deemed expedient by Major Edwards, after organizing what was called the " Committee of Inde-

---

* This very standard was often unfurled afterwards in the Town of Clinton when meetings were held in behalf of Texas, and waved in the view of hundreds when the last honours were done to Major Edwards, which have been already alluded to.

pendence," to dismiss the greater part of the colonists who had so promptly volunteered to serve under his command. The small number who were retained for the defence of Nacogdoches, being placed under the direction of Col. Martin Parmer, an active and enterprising officer, were expected to exercise a constant vigilance in reference to all hostile movements, and to give prompt notice to the colonists of any occurrence which might make their co-operation necessary.

On the 20th of December, four days subsequent to the erection of the flag of Independence, Hunter returned to Nacogdoches, accompanied by Fields, and various Indian Chiefs besides, prepared to enter into *council* with a view to settling definitely the terms of alliance with the colonists heretofore alluded to. An assemblage was accordingly convened, composed of the delegates in attendance from the Indian tribes, and individuals authorized to act as representatives of the colonists, which assumed the title of "The General Council of Independence." By this body a scheme of alliance was matured, which, through the agency of Commissioners appointed for the purpose, took the form of the compact which follows:

"Whereas the Government of the Mexican United States, have by repeated insults, treachery and oppression, reduced the White and Red emigrants from the United States of North America, now living in the Province of Texas, within the Territory of the said Government, into which they have been deluded by promises solemnly made, and most basely broken, to the dreadful alternative of either submitting their free-born necks to the yoke of an imbecile, faithless, and despotic government, miscalled a Republic; or of taking up arms in defence of their unalienable rights and asserting their Independence; They — viz:—The White emigrants now assembled in the town of Nacogdoches, around the Independent Standard, on the one part, and the Red emigrants who have espoused the same Holy Cause, on the other, in order to prosecute more speedily and effectually the War of

Independence, they have mutually undertaken, to a successful issue, and to bind themselves by the ligaments of reciprocal interests and obligations, have resolved to form a Treaty of Union, League and Confederation.

For the illustrious object, BENJAMIN W. EDWARDS and HARMAN B. MAYO, Agents of the Committee of Independence, and RICHARD FIELDS and JOHN D. HUNTER, the Agents of the Red people, being respectively furnished with due powers, have agreed to the following Articles.

1. The above named contracting parties, bind themselves to a solemn Union, League and Confederation, in Peace and War, to establish and defend their mutual independence of the Mexican United States.

2. The contracting parties guaranty, mutually, to the extent of their power, the integrity of their respective Territories, as now agreed upon and described, viz : The Territory apportioned to the Red people, shall begin at the Sandy Spring, where Bradley's road takes off from the road leading from Nacogdoches to the Plantation of Joseph Dust, from thence West, by the Compass, without regard to variation, to the Rio Grande, thence to the head of the Rio Grande, thence with the mountains to the head of Big Red River, thence north to the boundary of the United States of North America, thence with the same line to the mouth of Sulphur Fork, thence in a right line to the beginning.

The Territory apportioned to the White people, shall comprehend all the residue of the Province of Texas, and of such other portions of the Mexican United States, as the contracting parties, by their mutual efforts and resources, may render Independent, provided the same shall not extend further west than the Rio Grande.

3. The contracting parties mutually guaranty the rights of Empressarios to their premium lands only, and the rights of all other individuals, acquired under the Mexican Government, and relating or appertaining to the above described Territories, provided the said Empressarios and individuals

do not forfeit the same by an opposition to the Independence of the said Territories, or by withdrawing their aid and support to its accomplishment.

4. It is distinctly understood by the contracting parties, that the Territory apportioned to the Red people, is intended as well for the benefit of the Tribes now settled within the Territory apportioned to the White people, as for those living in the former Territory, and that it is incumbent upon the contracting parties for the Red people to offer the said tribes a participation in the same.

5. It is also mutually agreed by the contracting parties, that every individual, Red and White, who has made improvement within either of the respective Allied Territories and lives upon the same, shall have a fee simple of a section of land including his improvement, as well as the protection of the government under which he may reside.

6. The contracting parties mutually agree, that all roads, navigable streams, and all other channels of conveyance within each Territory, shall be open and free to the use of the inhabitants of the other.

7. The contracting parties mutually stipulate that they will direct all their resources to the prosecution of the Heaven-inspired cause which has given birth to this solemn Union, League and Confederation, firmly relying upon their united efforts, and the strong arm of Heaven, for success.

In faith whereof the Agents of the respective contracting parties hereunto affix their names. Done in the Town of Nacogdoches, this twenty-first day of December, in the year of our Lord one thousand eight hundred and twenty-six.

[Signed.] B. W. EDWARDS,
H. B. MAYO,
RICHARD FIELDS,
JOHN D. HUNTER.

We, the Committee of Independence, and the Committee of Red People, do ratify the above Treaty, and do pledge

ourselves to maintain it in good faith. Done on the day and
date above mentioned.

[Signed.]   MARTIN PARMER, President.

Richard Fields,   *Haden Edwards,*
John D. Hunter,   *W. B. Legon,*
Ne-ko-lake,   *Jno. Sprow,*
John Bags,   *B. P. Thompson,*
Cuk-to-keh,   *Jos. A. Huber,*
                         B. W. Edwards,
                         H. B. Mayo.

The Treaty of Alliance being executed, the Commissioners
on the part of the colonists laid the same forthwith before
the colonists, and obtained their sanction to it without difficulty or delay. Hunter and Fields, with the other Indian
Chiefs who had assisted in framing the Treaty, returned as
soon as possible to the Cherokee village, for the purpose of
procuring the correlative ratification of the various Indian
tribes whom they represented; but were not able to effect
this object, either so speedily or so completely as the Colonial Commissioners, in consequence of several unfavourable
circumstances about to be mentioned. The hunting season
was now considerably advanced, but had not yet expired;
and many of the Indian warriors, of no little influence,
were absent on distant expeditions, and their return might
possibly be postponed for some weeks to come. It was yet
more unfortunate that the Kickapoos, one of the strongest
and most warlike of the associated tribes, were found averse
to any friendly arrangement with the colonists: they cherished sentiments of deadly hostility towards the whole white
population, on account of injuries, either real or imaginary,
alleged to have been experienced by them during the last
war between Great Britain and the United States. Much
precious time was lost in endeavouring to procure their
acquiescence in the change of policy which had taken place;
but to the last their hostile feelings remained unconquered.
It was deemed politic that Fields should remain for a week

or two at the Cherokee village, whilst Hunter should set out for the colony at the head of thirty chosen warriors; in conformity with which arrangement, the latter arrived at Nacogdoches about a week subsequent to his last departure from that place. When he reached the fortress, a scene was displayed to view which proved, in the sequel, of most detrimental operation. The commanding officer being necessarily absent for a few hours, and it being impossible to establish strict discipline in a camp of volunteers—*Bacchus*, that mischief-loving god, who in all ages has been the arch promoter of disorder, had caused an angry quarrel to break out among the Fredonians; which was waged so tempestuously for some time that the fitting rites of hospitality remained wholly unaccorded to the warlike guests in waiting, and who stood in mute wonderment at what they were inclined to recognize as signs of serious and permanent dissension among the colonists. When the ferment was allayed, which in truth was the case upon the return of the officer in command, it was found that nearly half of the Cherokee warriors had disappeared, and were then on their way back to the village; upon arriving at which, it may be conjectured, they made a report of what they had witnessed calculated greatly to impede the operations of Fields, and to sustain the Kickapoos in the stand they had taken against co-operating with the colonists in the struggle for Independence.

Hunter remained at Nacogdoches, with eighteen or twenty of his warriors, and in a few days enjoyed an opportunity of signalizing his fidelity to the cause to which he had pledged himself. The occasion thus arose: The Mexican forces, expected long before to have marched within the limits of the Colony, were still lying inactive in the vicinage of San Felipe de Austin. In the mean time, Norris, the deposed Alcalde, whose life had been generously spared, grew impatient for revenge, and embodied a considerable Mexican force, for an attack upon the colonists. Alarms

22 *

of intended assault grew frequent, and produced much excitement at Nacogdoches; but as full confidence of victory nerved the bosoms of the Fredonians, no call was made upon the distant settlers for aid against the foe. Several skirmishing encounters occurred between the Fredonians and the Mexicans under Norris, which all resulted unfavourably to the latter. Finally, on the fourth day of January, the Mexicans under Norris, with ten or twelve Americans, who were members of his immediate family, learning that not more than fifteen of the Fredonians were at that moment in Nacogdoches, (a considerable number having just been *furloughed* for a short period,) were daring enough to march into the heart of the Town, with the avowed design of hanging up all the Fredonians whom they might be able to apprehend, and plunder the whole American population. The number of the assailants was, indeed, quite sufficient for the execution of these purposes, had they been as valiant as they were enterprising; for they mustered at least eighty men in all. They advanced on horseback, with a drum beating, and the National Standard of the Mexican Republic unfurled. When they had reached a point only two hundred yards distant from the Fredonian fortress, they leaped quickly from horseback to earth, and formed, in a regular line, in the rear of a long row of houses there situated. The Fredonians, enraged at the sight of the enemy, and glorying in the opportunity afforded them of doing battle in the cause of Freedom, scorned to take shelter behind their fortifications, as they could conveniently have done; and, leaving a portion of their small force to guard the stone house which they occupied, they sallied forth to the number of eleven men only, and took a stand in front of the Liberty pole which had been there planted. Being joined, at the instant, by Hunter and eight of his Cherokee warriors, they impetuously rushed upon the enemy with fierce shouts, and, in three minutes, put the Alcalde and his myrmidons to rapid flight. The Fredonians had one of their number only wounded slightly in this encounter; whilst the Mexicans left one man dead upon the ground of conflict, and ten or twelve others wounded in such a manner as to be incapacitated for joining in the retreat. Twenty or thirty of their mules and horses were likewise captured; and even "the spirit-stirring drum," under the inspiration of which they had so pompously challenged the strife of arms, was found too unwieldy to be borne off in such a hasty flight as they resorted to, and fell into the hands of the Cherokee warriors; who seized upon it with eagerness, and reserved it as a special trophy of victory, rejoicing not less over its acquisition than would the Romans of old have done over the earning of the *Spolia opima.* The retreat of the Mexicans was continued for a full half mile, to the edge of a thicket, where they halted, and sought covert for a moment; into the recesses of which thicket, the Fredonians and their Aboriginal companions in arms did not judge it expedient to pursue them, and returned to the fortress; where they had the satisfaction of finding themselves reinforced by thirty or forty of the neighbouring colonists, who, hearing of what was going on, had hastened to secure a part of the glory of the day. Thus strengthened, the pursuit was immediately renewed; but on advancing to the thicket where the enemy were supposed to be still ensconced, it was quickly ascertained that they had not tarried long at a point so proximate to danger, but had dispersed in every direction, so as now to be entirely beyond the reach of their conquerors. The Fredonians, therefore, again returned to camp, where abundant rejoicing was indulged over the event of this first battle with the enemies of Freedom.

It must not be imagined, that Major Edwards was at this time in a state of inactivity; on the contrary, he had been constantly occupied, from the moment when the league with the Indians was effected, up to the encounter which has been described, as Chief of the " General Committee of Independence," in concerting all necessary arrangements for sustaining the Fredonian cause against the army which had for weeks been threatening to enter the confines of the colony. For this purpose, not relying confidently upon any material aid from his Indian allies, he resolved if possible to rouse up the whole American population in Texas, and to use all suitable means for awakening sympathy in the United States; being certain, as he well might be, that if he succeeded in attaining these two objects, the release of Texas from Mexican rule would be inevitable. With these views, he addressed the settlers in Austin's Colony as follows:

"Nacogdoches, January 16, 1827.

To the Inhabitants of Austin's Colony.

FELLOW-CITIZENS:

AN important crisis is at hand—the clouds of Fate are fast gathering over our heads, full of portentous import—the rude clarion of War already reverberates through our forests; whilst the majestic Flag of Liberty is joyously waving over this once hopeless country. Yes, fellow-citizens, that glorious Flag which conducted our Fathers to Freedom, has been reared by descendants who burn with a generous ambition to equal their immortal deeds; and under its shadow and protection, we invite you to unite with us in brotherly confidence, and in bloody battle, if our common enemies shall force this issue upon us. You have been much more fortunate than we have been, in being permitted to enjoy the benefits of self-government, without the continual intrusion of tyrannical monsters appointed to harass and to persecute in the name of the miscalled Mexican Republic. Your laws were merely social, and such as were compatible with your own feelings; and dictated by the genius of that constitution which gave you political birth. But here the true spirit of this perfidious government has operated in its natural channel. Here have we seen exemplified the melancholy fact, that an American freeman, so soon as he enters the confines of the Mexican Empire, becomes a slave. Here have we seen tyranny and oppression in its rankest shape, not surpassed by monarchy itself, even in the darkest period of colonial bondage. Not only the petty tyrants here, but the *Governor* himself has sanctioned those oppressions, and has decreed the expulsion, and even the sacrifice of your fellow-citizens for asking justice. Yes, fellow-citizens, the documents found in the Alcalde's office at this place develope facts, that speak awful warning to us all. They prove, too, that a brutal soldiery were, ere this time, to be let loose upon this devoted country ; and that our best citizens were selected as victims of destruction. In a little time you too would have felt the rod, the galling yoke, that bore us down. Your chains were already forged, and so *soon* as the laws and genius of this government, administered by its own officers, had operated upon you, you would have awoke from your fatal delusion, and like ourselves, have sprung to arms for the protection of your rights and liberty. And yet, fellow-citizens, we are told, we shall meet you in the ranks of our oppressors, and that the flag of liberty, which now waves on high, is to be assailed by Americans; and that the first bloody conflict must be " Greek against Greek." Forbid it Heaven!!! O no, this can never be! The world will never witness such a horrid sight! What! Americans marching in the ranks of tyrants, to prostrate the standard of Liberty, raised for the protection of their oppressed and suffering brothers? The graves of our forefathers would burst open, and send forth the spirits of the dead! The angel of Liberty, hovering over such a scene, would shriek with horror and flee from earth to Heaven! Fellow-citizens, I know you better. I have already pledged my honour upon your patriotism and your bravery. I am now willing to stake my life upon it, and to lay my bosom bare to the bayonets of you, my fellow-citizens and friends, in such a case. I am not ignorant that attempts have been made to invoke your hostility against us, and that even *official documents* have been read to you, impugning the motives and misre-

presenting the designs of those who have rallied around the
standard of Liberty.   But, my friends, those imputations are
false as hell, and only worthy of those who know not how
to appreciate the holy feelings of freemen, and whose great
ambition is to be the pliant tools of power.

We have undertaken this cause in defence of our violated
rights, and are actuated by such feelings as prompted our
forefathers to draw their swords in *seventy-six.*   Our oppressions have been far greater than *they* ever bore; and we
should be unworthy of those departed patriots and of our
birthright, had we any longer bowed our free-born necks to
such abject tyranny.   You have been told, fellow-citizens,
that we are *robbers,* and that your lives and property are in
danger from us.   You cannot believe it.   We have saved
you, fellow-citizens, from impending ruin.   A few months
will develope to you *facts,* that will draw forth ejaculations
of gratitude towards those who are now shamefully traduced,
because they are too proud to be slaves.   We have made a
solemn treaty with Colonel Richard Fields and Dr. John D.
Hunter, as the representatives of twenty-three nations of
Indians, who are now in alliance with the Camanche Nation.   In that treaty your rights, your *lands* are guarantied,
unless you take up arms against us.   Fellow-citizens, most
of you know me, and will do my motives justice.   I have
been honoured with the chief command of our forces: I will
pledge my life, my honour for the security of your rights,
and the safety and protection of your wives and children.
You have nothing to fear from us, or from our allies.   You
have every thing to hope from our success.   We have not
taken up arms against you, my friends; but to protect you
and ourselves.   If we meet in bloody conflict, we at least
will not be the aggressors.

Fellow-citizens, we must succeed.   We will be freemen,
or we will perish with the Flag.   Be firm, be faithful to your
brothers, who are now *struggling* for *their rights,* and the
conflict will be short.   We have rejected the overtures of

peace, because we know this perfidious government too well to be betrayed a second time. Liberty and Independence we will have, or we will perish in the cause. Like Americans we will live—like Americans we will die. I have pledged myself, you will do the same.

Your friend and fellow-citizen,

B. W. EDWARDS."

Numerous copies of this address were transmitted, in the form of printed circulars, to Austin's Colony, and it was sanguinely hoped by the Fredonian leaders that its distribution might prove efficiently useful to their cause, in the dispersion of unfounded prejudice believed to be cherished among the American settlers there, and in the engenderment of a cordial sympathy among them; which, if not sufficiently potential in its influence to draw them into active co-operation in the impending contest, might at least secure their *neutrality.* Whether or not this skilfully devised document was, in fact, ever freely circulated in Austin's Colony, I am not prepared to assert; but that the conciliatory effects, desired to be accomplished by its agency, were never realized, is a melancholy truth whose fearful unfoldment was destined in a few weeks to deprive the boldest among the Fredonian revolters of all hope of a successful termination of their struggle for Independence, and to postpone for eight years more, the disruption of Texas from the Mexican Republic. The causes of this disappointment may be concisely stated as follows : Col. Austin * was a man of singularly cautious and politic mind—as free, however, from all alloy of *selfishness*, in the ordinary sense of the term, as it is possible for any human being to be. He had been for years quietly, but industriously, occupied in carrying into effect his scheme of colonization, and had so far succeeded beyond his own original anticipations. Possessed

* He was then known as *Colonel*, afterwards *General* Austin, during the Revolution.

of much more *discretion* than falls to the lot of ordinary mortals, and endued with a *political tact* which few men so pure-hearted have ever evinced, he had been able to maintain at all times the most friendly and harmonious relations with the Mexican Republic, — and was, indeed, a decided favourite with several individuals of eminent influence in the councils of this anomalous nation.   The bounds of his father's Grant had been greatly extended for his accommodation ; and, as is plainly declared in the address of Major Edwards, just noticed, the colonists located under his paternal guardianship were allowed the enjoyment of all those social and political privileges which, among men born and educated under the shadow of free institutions, are indispensable to happiness.   His colonizing operations were still in active progress; and he knew that several years must yet elapse before his labours as an Empressario could be fully consummated.   William Penn himself could never have been more solicitous of cultivating peace and amity with all men than was Col. Austin, at this period of his extraordinary career.   It has been already said that he calculated, as early as Major Edwards's first interview with him, upon the ultimate separation of Texas from Mexico. He never doubted for an instant, that the hour would sooner or later arrive, when the Anglo-American race in Texas would find it necessary to dissolve all political connection with a people so inferior to themselves in every moral attribute, as he knew the Mexicans to be.   But he was unwilling to plunge into a war with a nation numbering eight millions of inhabitants, demi-savages though he held them to be, until the American population in Texas had grown strong enough to achieve their deliverance, without being forced to a copious expenditure of blood, or even incurring any serious hazard of being either shot or hung up as traitors.   Entertaining such views, it is not at all astonishing that he heard of the revolt in Edwards' colony with deep regret.   Occupied, as he constantly was, with the harassing affairs of his own colony, it was impossible that he could become fully apprised of all the oppressions practised upon his brother Americans, in the vicinage of Nacogdoches. He knew nothing of the infernal efforts of the Mexican Government to inspirit to dire hostility against the innocent and unoffending settlers from the United States, the whole mass of Indian population scattered over that portion of the Province; and he was, therefore, not at all prepared to estimate the *domineering necessity* to which the Fredonians had been constrained to yield. He heard, therefore, of the incipient revolutionary movements about Nacogdoches as misstated to him, with deep chagrin. He endeavoured to interfere as a Pacificator between the contending parties, but without success. When he received intelligence of the *Declaration of Independence* by the Fredonians, and of the offensive and defensive league which they had formed with untutored and uncontrollable savages, (as he considered the Cherokees and their allies to be,) his mind was filled with apprehension, and his soul with undissembled horror. He saw, or imagined that he saw, all his beloved plans of social happiness in danger of immediate frustration; his tortured and excited fancy prefigured the sudden ruin of his own promising colony, and the cruel dispersion of thousands, over whose happiness he had so long presided with all the solicitude of parental affection. He saw the wild Indians, whose thirst for blood no humanizing counsels would be able to assuage, whose rabid eagerness for plunder no *fresh-acquired* authority of a mere leader of insurrectionists, could be expected to hold in check—turned loose among the white settlements, with arms in their hands, which either accident, caprice, or treachery, might in a moment cause to be levelled against the bosoms of those for whom they at present professed amity. A dreadful and perplexing alternative was now submitted to this extraordinary man; *War with Mexico*, and, in the feeble and unprepared condition of his colony, *certain destruction ;*—or *War with the Fredonians* and their Indian confederates, which, though his heart shuddered over the prospect of battling with brother Americans, would, in all probability, be terminated without any serious loss of life, whilst he might be able, by his personal presence in the Mexican invading army, to prevent those scenes of barbarous cruelty that would otherwise inevitably accompany the triumph of their arms.   After much hesitation, his resolution was taken, and was declared in the following address to the settlers of his colony.

" San Felipe de Austin, Jan. 22, 1827.

To the inhabitants of the Colony :

The persons who were sent on from this Colony, by the Political Chief and Military Commandant, to offer peace to the Nacogdoches madmen, have returned—returned, without having effected any thing.   The Olive Branch of peace that was magnanimously held out to them has been insultingly refused ; and, that party have denounced massacre and desolation on this colony.   They are trying to excite all the Northern Indians to murder and plunder; and, it appears as though they have no other object than to ruin this country.   They are no longer Americans, for they have forfeited all title to that high name by their unnatural and bloody alliance with Indians :—they openly threaten us with Indian massacre, and the plunder of our property.

Ought we to hesitate at such a moment? shall we hesitate to take up arms against them because they were our countrymen ? No, they are our countrymen no longer, they have by a solemn treaty united and identified themselves with Indians ; and pledged their faith to carry on a war of murder and plunder against the principal inhabitants of Texas. They are worse than the natives of the forest with whom they are allied ; and, it is our duty as men, as Americans, and as adopted Mexicans, to prove to those infatuated criminals, and to the world, that we have not forgotten the land of our birth, nor the principles of honour and patriotism, we inherited from our fathers ; and that we are not to be dictated to and drawn into crime and anarchy by a hand-full of desperate renegades. The Civil and Military Chief of Texas, accompanied by a chosen band of national troops, march with us, who in union with the brave and patriotic militia of this colony, will be fully able to crush in its infancy, this mad, unjust and unnatural rebellion.

To arms fellow-countrymen! to arms in the cause of liberty, of virtue and justice! to arms in defence of your property, your families, and your honour! to arms in defence of your adopted government; and hurl back the thunder upon the heads of those base and degraded apostates from the names of Americans, who have dared to invite you by a threatening invitation to join their mad and criminal schemes. Every man able to bear arms is now wanted. Temporary inconvenience and loss, must and ought to yield to necessity and duty. You will receive the pay allowed by law to national troops of the same class, and the commander will see that it is punctually discharged, as soon as possible.

The people of this colony, after a full understanding of the pretended cause of complaint on the part of the rebels, as well as of the mild and magnanimous course of the Governor, in offering them a full and unreserved amnesty, and an impartial and public investigation of their alleged grievances, have unanimously and voluntarily pledged themselves in writing to the Government, to oppose the factionists by force of arms. You are bound in honour to redeem this sacred pledge. To arms then, my friends and fellow-citizens, and hasten to the standard of our country; hasten to the protection of your property, and your families, and all that you hold dear and sacred upon earth. The approbation of every honest and honourable man of your native country; of your adopted government; of a just and omnipotent God; and, the consciousness that you will have done your duty, and saved yourselves, will be your reward.

The first hundred men who were called out will march

on the 26th inst. I now call on you to turn out *en masse*, and join us on the road to Nacogdoches, as soon as possible.

The necessary orders for mustering and other purposes, will be issued to the commanding officers.

Union and Mexico.

S. F. AUSTIN."

It would be unjust to Col. Austin, and not a little injurious to Major Edwards, to suppose that the conduct of the former at this crisis was dictated by feelings of *personal* unkindness towards the latter, or that he did not continue to cherish towards the Fredonian Chieftain sentiments of the most elevated esteem. It has been already mentioned that they were intimate friends, and as such maintained an affectionate and confidential epistolary intercourse. The extracts which follow, taken at random from the budget of Col. Austin's letters to Major Edwards, now in my possession, will serve to explain the relations existing between them up to the period when the Fredonians resolved upon war with Mexico.

In the month of September, 1825, Col. Austin wrote a very long letter to Major Edwards, chiefly on Colonial affairs, and concluded the same as follows : " My friend, I have had a laborious and perplexing time of it, but I look forward to better days, and I shall persevere to the last. I have the consolation to reflect that I have performed my duty to the settlers and to the government, so far as my situation would permit. I should be happy to get a letter from you, *a long letter*, and such a letter as one *friend* should write to another — that is to say, a blunt, frank, and candid one. I have felt the want of a candid and intelligent friend to advise with, one who was *disinterested*." In a postscript to the same letter he adds : " I should like to hear your ideas as to the Waco war, and as to the best way to avoid difficulty with the Indians."

A very long letter, written in August 1826, was commenced by Col. Austin thus :

"Dear Sir,—I received your letter by Mr. Pettus, and embrace the opportunity, by Mr. John A. Williams to answer it. I am happy that you have not so far misconstrued the true intent and meaning of my letters to your brother as to believe (as it appears he has), that they proceeded from unfriendly feelings. I assure you I never entertained any such feelings towards him; and as respects yourself, *any person who has insinuated that I ever, in any manner, expressed or manifested other than friendship and respect for your character, has uttered a gross falsehood.*"

It appears that Major Edwards, some time in the summer of 1826, wrote to Col. Austin, requesting counsel as to the best course to be pursued by his brother and himself in order to remove the prejudices entertained towards them by the Mexican authorities, and if possible to avoid an appeal to arms for redress. The letter of Col. Austin, in reply, contains the following paragraph: "This is a truly disagreeable and unfortunate subject, mortifying to you in the extreme, and I hope you will credit me, when I assure you, that I sympathize with you fully on account of the unpleasantness of your situation. The affair will be highly injurious to the future prospects of emigration, and of general detriment to the whole country. The subject has caused me great unhappiness, but I had determined not to interfere with it in any way—*it is a dangerous one to touch, and particularly to write about.* You wish me to advise you. I scarcely know what course will be best. The uncertainty as to the precise nature of the charges against you, renders it difficult, nay impossible to make a regular defence. I think, however, I would write directly to the Governor of the State. Give him a full statement of facts and a very minute history of the acts of your principal enemies, and their opponents, and their manner of doing business in every particular, both in regard to your brother as well as all others. State the general situation of the country, the confusion and difficulties which exist, and the causes of them,

23 *

&c., in order that the government may have the whole subject fully before them, and be enabled to judge of the motives that have influenced those who have been most clamorous against you.   Write in *English*, and make an apology for doing so, as that it is impossible to procure translators, &c.   I advise the utmost caution and prudence on your part and that of all your friends as to your *expressions*, for every word you utter will probably be *watched and reported if considered exceptionable.*"

This was the last letter received by Major Edwards from Col. Austin, and it was concluded as follows : " I am just recovering from fever, and have only been able to attend to business for a few days past.   Wishing you *health* and *prosperity*,

I remain your Friend,

S. F. AUSTIN."

Let us withdraw our attention for a moment from the hostile movements going on in Austin's Colony, and recur again to the neighbourhood of Nacogdoches, where Major Edwards was diligently occupied in concerting suitable arrangements for strengthening the ranks of the Fredonians, and enabling them to meet the perils by which they stood surrounded. Various messengers were despatched by him to different parts of the province, besides Austin's Colony, with a view of inviting the American colonists everywhere to enlist in the war against Mexico.   It would seem, that but little advantage arose from these embassies in general, owing to different causes of obstruction ; and in one instance particularly, much evil instead of benefit was experienced.   Two or three days before the Fredonian flag had been erected, a man by the name of *Huber*, reached Nacogdoches.   Huber represented himself to have been born in the United States, to have been in the service of Mexico for several years past, as a surgeon in the army, and to have resigned his station in resentment of certain indignities inflicted upon him.   In speaking of Mexico, he used language of the fiercest invective, and announced his ardent desire to wash out the injuries which he complained of having received in the blood of the whole Mexican race. His vehement denunciations of the Mexican Government, and his thundering clamour for vengeance, induced most of the Fredonians to suppose him worthy of confidence; but Major Edwards, from the first, regarded him as a base impostor, was disgusted both with his appearance and manners, and looked upon him either as a madman or hypocrite, or both, so far as an imagination grievously distempered can be supposed capable of holding alliance with a soul full of treachery and mischief. In spite of the earnest remonstrances of Major Edwards, this man was deputed to Pecon Point, where, according to his own declarations, he had a numerous personal acquaintance, and many friends whom he could control, and whence he engaged to bring to Nacogdoches, in a few days, a splendid body of recruits to the cause of Independence. When he left Nacogdoches, instead of proceeding to Pecon Point, he pushed on rapidly to the town of Natchitoches, and immediately commenced flooding the whole circumjacent country, through the medium of a newspaper there published, with the most distorted accounts of the Fredonian movements, and presented such a statement of the condition of affairs about Nacogdoches, as, uncontradicted, was well fitted to discourage enterprising citizens of the United States who might have otherwise felt inclined to lend assistance to their persecuted fellow-countrymen, from embarking at all in a project which they saw now depictured as not only hopeless of accomplishment, but as being in a high degree disreputable to all concerned in it. The publications of Huber were drawn up, it must be confessed, in language both glowing and plausible, and finding simultaneous insertion in various gazettes, produced an impression highly unfavourable to the Fredonian cause in the United States; and in this way doubtless prevented material aid both in men and money from be-

ing received by the Fredonians—succours upon which they
had all along sanguinely calculated.   No one acquainted
with the sound and investigating mind of Major Edwards,
would suppose it possible that he had entered upon this conflict of arms with the whole power of the Mexican Republic
without relying mainly upon the assistance which he expected to derive from the United States; the population of
which, as has been seen, had for many years been ready to
second any favourable scheme set on foot for the purpose
of re-conquering by physical means the fair territory which
had been lost to them by a want of diplomatic address, and
opening the way for the diffusion of institutions truly free to
the southernmost boundaries of this vast continent.   The
history of popular feeling on this subject among his countrymen was perfectly well known to Major Edwards; nor did
he even doubt, that if he could once take a firm and solid
stand in the heart of Texas against the forces deputed to act
against him on the part of the government of Mexico, and
succeed in giving satisfactory evidence of his own capacity
for command, thousands on thousands of the valorous descendants of those heroes who immortalized themselves in
the battles of the Revolution, would flock to his Fredonian
standard, and bear it triumphantly onward, far, far beyond
the walls of Mexico.   With such views and sentiments, he
had draughted and despatched the following address " to the
citizens of the United States of North America," which was
published in several leading newspapers, at the period, but
unhappily not soon enough to be of any service to the Fredonian cause.

To the citizens of the United States of North America.
         FELLOW-COUNTRYMEN :
   If it be permitted to the bounded intellect of man to fathom
the beneficent desires of an Almighty Providence, and from
what is passing, and what has passed, to conjecture what to-
morrow will bring forth, we shall be compelled to believe

that a political millennium is approaching, when the thrones
of despotism shall be prostrated, the fetters of mankind un-
bound, and slaves, by a resurrection as miraculous as that
which shall raise our moulded dust into eternal life, be exalted to freemen.   The history of the last century is but a
history of the struggles of liberty.   Inspired by the energies
of her spirit, our common ancestors threw off the yoke of a
powerful nation.   The beautiful regions of France, where
despotism had grown into portentous magnitude, witnessed
her succeeding struggle.   Her efforts were gigantic, and the
contest was dreadful, but the hold of tyranny was too strong
on that devoted country.   Yet even defeat was victory.
Truth was struck out by the collision, and men discovered
their rights.   The foundation of society and the principles
of government were elucidated, and from that moment, the
voice of fredom has been heard, where before her name was
unknown.   Her holy spirit has been silently and secretly
undermining the thrones of tyrants.   But America is her
favourite soil.   By a mighty effort she has severed the des-
tinies of Spain and Spanish America, and this whole continent, which from its discovery has groaned under European
despotism, is now, with the exception of the Islands of West
India, and the inhospitable region of Canada, a chain of Independent nations.   Still the work of freedom even here is
not complete.   People who from their birth have inhaled only
the atmosphere of slavery—whose first impressions and feelings have been formed in its mould, and confirmed by the
powerful influence of habit, cannot be regenerated in a moment.   Reason should teach us this, but freemen overlook
even such palpable considerations in their enthusiasm at the
name of Liberty.

Such, fellow-countrymen, has been the case with the emigrants from the United States of North America, to the province of Texas, in the Republic of Mexico.   They fondly
believed that they were merely exchanging one free land for
another.   They knew that this country had separated her-

self from the monarchy of European Spain; that she formed a government which she termed republican, and had adopted a constitution similar to that which they had ever venerated; but, alas! experience has taught them, that if the theory is republican, the practice is weak, treacherous and despotic.

Invited under promises of land, they have not yet obtained a title to an acre. Seduced by professions of friendship, they have been received with an eye of jealousy and suspicion. Living in a remote corner of the Republic, they have been left by the government to the despotic will of an Alcalde, who has ruled over them with a tyranny more intolerable than that of a feudal lord over his vassals. The man who dared to complain, was instantly branded with the displeasure of the government, and banished from the country. The servile adherents of the Alcalde, received his protection —were licensed to give loose to their private resentments, and to set justice at defiance. The government has sanctioned those acts of unendurable oppression, and without investigation, without giving its victim the privilege of being heard in his own defence, confirmed whatever punishment the malignity of the Alcalde may have dictated.

Having from their infancy been taught by that sacred instrument which declared the independence of their native country, "That to secure the unalienable rights of life, liberty, and the pursuit of happiness, governments are instituted among men, deriving their just powers from the consent of the governed; that whensoever any form of government becomes destructive of those ends, it is the right of the people to alter or abolish it, and to institute a new government, laying its foundation on such principles, and organizing its powers in such form, as to them shall seem most likely to effect their safety and happiness;" and being by better experience convinced that the present government will afford them no protection, and that they have nothing to expect in the future, but, as they have felt in the past, a continued invasion of their unalienable rights, they have accordingly resolved, after a deliberate examination of their situation, to declare themselves independent of the Mexican United States.

In pursuance of this resolution, the Committee of correspondence, appointed by the General Committee of Independence, have addressed Circulars to the various Districts of this Province, inviting them to send Delegates to a Congress to be assembled on the first Monday in February next, in the town of Nacogdoches.

They are aware, fellow countrymen, of the difficulty and the dangers that surround them. But, remembering the courage, the fortitude, the perseverance of their fathers while defending the rights of their persecuted country, and asserting her Independence, and feeling in themselves the same unconquerable spirit of freedom which animated *their* hearts and nerved *their* arms in the hour of peril and dismay, they are resolved to imitate such an illustrious example, and to perish rather than submit!

They do not doubt, fellow countrymen, that your sympathies are with them. They do not doubt that the sympathies of every lover of liberty, in every part of the world, are with them. The thought inspires them. Their greatest ambition is, to show themselves worthy of their descent and of their cause. They trust that they are now finishing the work of freedom in this fine country. Her severance from her parent land was indeed a gigantic step towards its accomplishment, but many, many years, were required to render it complete. If an approving Heaven shall give wisdom to their councils, and success to their arms, the world will behold in a few years another Republic, small indeed in extent, but blessed with every advantage of nature, and under the fostering care of Consitutional freedom, enriched with an enlightened population, and adorned with the beauties of science, of literature, and the arts.

We need not enlarge upon the advantages which this

country affords to enterprise and industry. The most salubrious climate, the richest soil, adapted to the cultivation of every valuable product of nature, and intersected by navigable streams, are the prominent features of this favoured land. Fellow countrymen, we invite you to enjoy it. You shall partake of every advantage equally with ourselves. Such a country was designed only for freemen. *You* are freemen, you are our countrymen, our brothers. It is such a population we desire.

H. B. MAYO,
B. W. EDWARDS,
Committee of Correspondence."

CHAPTER XIII.

Major Edwards declared Commander-in-Chief of the Fredonians. Pursuit of Norris, the Alcalde. Approach of the Mexican army. Alarm and confusion of the Colonists. Death of Hunter. Abandonment of Nacogdoches by the Fredonians and termination of the war. Correspondence between Major Edwards and the Mexican commander. Character of Major Edwards.

THE victory won by the Fredonians, on the fourth of January, 1827, over a body of Mexicans greatly superior to them in number, has been already recounted. On the morning subsequent to this occurrence, Major Edwards, having now been declared *Commander in Chief* of all the forces raised, or to be raised, for the prosecution of the war of Independence, placed himself at the head of sixteen chosen soldiers, and set out in quest of the fugitive enemy. It was very soon ascertained that the Alcalde, Norris, who had commanded the Mexicans in the recent encounter, had gone in the direction of his own residence, attended by several of those who had accompanied him in his attack upon Nacogdoches. Thither were they followed by the Fredonian commander, and arriving at the domicil of the Alcalde about sunset of the same day, two of his comrades were there surprised; who gave information that the Alcalde had not tarried at the place more than a few minutes, but, being apprehensive of pursuit, and greatly dreading the vengeance of the Fredonians, had immediately mounted a fresh horse and fled with all possible speed in the direction of the Sabine river; designing to seek refuge within the limits of the United States. The individuals imparting this intelligence being found in arms, and confessing that they had been concerned in the assault upon the Fredonians on the fourth instant, were declared *prisoners of war*, and would have been retained as such, but for the earnest protestations which they made of having been entirely deluded by the Alcalde, and the pledge which they voluntarily gave never to bear arms again adversely to the Champions of Independence; whereupon they were both set at liberty, and Major Edwards and his trusty Fredonians returned to Nacogdoches.

So far, the tide of fortune had flowed most propitiously to the interests of the Fredonians; but about this period it became understood at Nacogdoches, that the colonists on the Brassos, instead of uniting with them in the war against Mexico, were then on their march, under the command of Col. Austin, in the direction of Nacogdoches, prepared to do battle on the side of the government. This intelligence was of a nature calculated greatly to paralyze the energies and chill the ardour of the Fredonians, who, however devoted they were to the cause in which they were enlisted, and however eager to be avenged upon their Mexican oppressors, naturally felt a strong repugnance to shedding the blood of men of the same race, and complexion, and language, with themselves, who had never heretofore done them the least injury, and among whom they recognized many old and dearly-loved friends. This unwillingness to conflict with the settlers in Austin's Colony was much strengthened too by the conviction generally entertained among the Fredonians, that their brother-colonists were acting under gross misapprehension in regard to themselves and their objects, and had been persuaded to march against them under a belief that this movement was necessary to their own defence against the tomahawks and scalping-knives of Indians whom the Fredonians were about to bring down in fury and desolation upon their settlements.

Hunter and Fields were still at Nacogdoches, but the quota of warriors whom they had agreed to furnish had not yet come on; and it began now to be apprehended that the Mexican emissaries sent some time before among the tribes, in order to tempt them from their fidelity to the Fredonians, had to a great extent succeeded, and that the arms of their own pledged allies would be thus turned against them. Attempts were secretly made, likewise, to detach Hunter and Fields from their association with the Fredonians, through the medium of several individuals in the Mexican interest in the vicinage of Nacogdoches; but to the last these chiefs proved honourably faithful to their engagements. As much cannot be said of all the Indian chiefs then sojourning at Nacogdoches; for Bowles, a man who has subsequently become somewhat famous among the Cherokees, and who met a deserved death at the hands of the Texans eighteen months since, began about this period to exhibit symptoms of recreancy, and in a short time openly renounced the stipulations of the Treaty of Alliance. The Cushattees, a tribe of Indians residing along the borders of the Trinity river, at this time also entered into a Treaty with the Mexican government, by which they bound themselves to unite with the troops expected from Austin's Colony, when they should come on, for the destruction of the Fredonians; and Col. Beene, the Mexican officer already spoken of as having fallen back to the Trinity river, whilst Major Edwards was in the act of marching to Nacogdoches for the first time in hostile array, had been ever since industriously occupied in embodying all the smaller Indian tribes in that region and preparing them to take part in this terrible enterprise.

The month of February was now on the wing, and the day had almost arrived when the assemblage of Congressional delegates from different parts of the Province, had been expected to take place; from the action of whom the Fredonians had anticipated a signal advancement of their cause; but the aspect of affairs, as described, was such as to forbid the hope that this body could at present be convened.

Under such unfavourable circumstances, the soul of the Fredonian Commander-in-Chief remained wholly unmoved; his hope of final success was yet as confident as ever. Nor was he inactive at this perilous and perplexing crisis; on the contrary, his efforts were more than redoubled. In a few days, he had fifty regular soldiers, all of whom were enlisted for the whole war, ready at a moment's warning for any movement which he might order, either offensive or defensive, and a much larger number of militia, as they were called, stood pledged, whenever summoned for the purpose, to aid him in any emergency which might arise. Hunter and Fields were again despatched to the Cherokee village for such recruits as they could muster, and promised to return in time to unite in the defence of Nacogdoches. Neither of them, in fact, ever did return; but it is only just to them to say that they were in no respect to blame on this point. "Fields and Hunter," (says an accomplished Fredonian, Mr. Mayo, who has been already mentioned as the friend and vindicator of Hunter), "strained every nerve to rouse the faithless Indians to the performance of their reiterated promises, and their solemn obligation by treaty; but in vain. The emissaries of the Mexican government had been among them, and the renewed promise that the land they contended for would be granted, with other and great advantages, seduced them from their faith, and thus rendered the revolution hopeless.   Hunter, finding every effort fruitless, for the few who had not been bought over were unwilling to act with so small a force, left them, saying he would go alone and share the fate of his American friends in Nacogdoches.   His opposition to their treachery excited their deadly hostility.   He proceeded to join the Americans accompanied by two Indians.   He stopped at a creek near the Anadagua village, to let his horse drink, and while thus unguarded in his security, one of his savage companions shot him with a rifle in the shoulder.   His horse started, and he fell into the creek.   The monster raised another fatal weapon, and while the unfortunate Hunter implored him not to fire, for it was hard, he said, to die by the hands of his friends,—sent this extraordinary spirit to appear before an unerring tribunal."

A longer delay occurring before the arrival of the Mexican forces than had been expected, about twenty of the Fredonian regulars, stationed at Nacogdoches, were permitted to visit their families for the last time before the main battle for Liberty and Independence should be fought, under orders to return as soon as possible to camp.   During their absence, a scout, who had been sent out to watch for the approach of the enemy, returned, announcing the arrival within the limits of the Colony of a strong body of Mexican troops, backed by most of the settlers in Austin's Colony. Major Edwards immediately despatched an express to the American settlement below Nacogdoches, demanding fifty or one hundred men as soon as they could possibly march to his aid ; and he did not doubt that this call would, in accordance with previous arrangements, be promptly obeyed. A messenger was at the same time sent to Hunter and Fields, who had not yet been heard from since their last departure from Nacogdoches, requesting them to come with all convenient speed to the aid of their American brothers in arms.   Several days elapsed, during which no news was received either from the Cherokee village or from the

American settlement. Nor had the twenty Fredonians yet returned to camp. Their absence at such a moment was a most perplexing circumstance, and to their commander wholly unaccountable. In the mean time the Mexicans in the vicinage of Nacogdoches, who had been for some months absolutely quiet, taking courage from the near approach of the troops from San Felipe de Austin, began to disclose symptoms of renewed hostility, and evidently watched for a favourable opportunity of commencing offensive operations. A second messenger was despatched to the Ayoush Bayou Settlement, to hasten the auxiliary movements of the colonists, and to urge them, without farther delay, to rally under their chosen commander, who only awaited their presence to march forth and bid defiance to their common enemy. This last messenger returned with the astounding intelligence that the settlers having become completely panic-stricken at the near approach of the enemy, and at the disastrous condition of affairs generally, had already submitted, without a struggle, to the Mexican commander; upon a promise of the full pardon of past offences, and being permitted, in addition, to retain possession of their lands. It was likewise now rumoured that the twenty Fredonian regulars, mentioned as absent on furlough, had been captured by the enemy, and were then held in close custody as prisoners of war.

In this sad and fearful conjuncture, Major Edwards resolved to subject his remaining soldiers to a sort of *experimentum crucis*—a test so rigid as might enable him with certainty to determine how far they were to be relied on for the execution of such measures of desperation as were alone reserved to men standing, as it were, upon the very edge of a precipice, with certain death before them, and whose utmost good fortune would be restricted to the privilege of selling their lives to the enemy as dearly as possible. For this purpose, he convened the thirty Fredonians left, around the Flag of Independence, which waved mournfully in the

24 *

breeze.　Before he disclosed all the unfavourable intelligence which had been communicated to him, he delivered to them a short and spirited address ; towards the close of which he pointed to the Banner which they had sworn to defend, and upon whose folds their names were enregistered, and touchingly reminded them of their own victories under it.　He alluded to the glorious achievements of their ancestors, and painted to their view the undying renown which had been acquired by the champions of Freedom in other ages.　He presented *death* to them in all its ignominious forms—as the probable consequence of awaiting the coming of the enemy ; and then announcing to them, that if a single Fredonian thought proper to withdraw from the standard, he would be permitted to do so, without punishment, and without reproach, he demanded of them, in a voice of thunder, whether they were for *Liberty or Slavery?*　His own enthusiastic language thus declares their valiant response : " Not an eye winked ; not a heart quailed ; not a pulse fluttered in its vibrations, whilst the soldiers of Liberty, with one voice, acclaimed their determination to stand by the Flag of Independence, or to perish in its defence."

This resolution being adopted, Major Edwards proceeded to strengthen the fortress then occupied by the Fredonians, so as to enable them to hold out as long as possible, when the enemy should arrive ; and then directed his soldiers to lie down upon their arms and endeavour to snatch a few moments of repose.　During the night, news arrived confirmatory of all the ill-tidings previously received, and the additional fact was now made known to the Fredonian leader, that the Cherokees were advancing in great force, breathing revenge and murder along their course, and were by that time united with the Mexican army, for the overwhelment of their late confiding allies.　The whole multitude of the enemy was supposed to be distant not more than ten or twelve miles, and might be expected to advance upon the Fredonians in an hour or two, when this little band of warriors would be surrounded by at least seven hundred armed soldiers, ready to subject them to instantaneous destruction. Certain death, without the possibility of inflicting serious injury upon the enemy, would obviously result from adhering to the resolve of the night before.

At this crisis, it was seasonably suggested by some one, that a portion of the Fredonians were already in the hands of the Mexicans as prisoners, and would infallibly endure much indignity, and perhaps pass through a course of protracted suffering, in the event of their not being rescued ; if their fellow-soldiers waited to be slain in their present position, all possibility of the escape of these prisoners would be thus cut off : were not the Fredonians who yet were masters of themselves bound to use all proper exertions to redeem their unfortunate companions in arms ? Was it not at least possible to do so, by retreating, whilst retreat was yet practicable, and making a generous effort in the United States to resuscitate their exhausted ranks with a hundred or two more bold and resolute Americans, who might be easily persuaded to unite with the yet unvanquished Fredonians, either in rescuing their captive friends alive, or in avenging them bloodily in case they should find them to have been previously sacrificed ? This striking view of the subject was welcomed on all sides ; and the valiant Fredonians now resolved, under a *sense of duty*, to do what the promptings of *self-love* would in vain have recommended to them for approval : they unanimously declared their willingness to abandon Nacogdoches immediately, since the place was evidently no longer tenable. Upon which, Major Edwards ordered the subaltern officers to get the soldiers in readiness to take up the line of march in an hour, and in the meanwhile occupied himself in securing all the public documents deemed worthy of preservation. At the precise instant designated, the Fredonians bade farewell to Nacogdoches, of which they had reigned undisputed masters for nearly six months, and with their beloved banner still displayed in advance, marched out of the Town in perfect order.

For three days they were seen slowly and sorrowfully traversing the country, in the direction of the Sabine River. On the fourth, which was the 31st of January, 1827, they trod upon the soil of their native country. Then descending the river which now flows between two sister Republics, in boats procured for the purpose, they reached a point, then, as now, known as " the Old Sabine Crossing ;" where they encountered about twenty of the colonists from Ayoush Bayou Settlement, who had fled upon the advance of the Mexican army. From these persons they learned, that the Mexican commander, Colonel Ahumada, attended by the whole force which he had brought with him for the destruction of the Fredonians, had entered Nacogdoches on the day that their arrival had been expected, had taken quiet possession of the whole country, and that the captive Fredonians were to be brought on to Head-quarters, in a few days, for capital punishment. It may be easily imagined that the sensibilities of the Fredonian leader were greatly shocked at this melancholy intelligence, and that he was not at all inclined to remain inactive whilst persons so dear to him were involved in so much danger. He had little confidence in Mexican clemency, but he knew that the timidity of that degraded race might be appealed to with some prospect of success. He accordingly addressed to the officer mentioned an earnest but dignified communication, in which he vehemently protested against the maltreatment of the prisoners, and threatened signal retribution if their lives should be assailed. He then pushed on without delay into the American settlements, in order to enable himself, as far as possible, to make good his menaces, in the event of their being disregarded by the enemy. But before his preparations for vengeance were completed, he received an answer to his letter, conveying positive assurances that the Fredonian prisoners should be forthwith set at liberty, and that a general amnesty should be granted to all who had borne arms in this unhappy struggle against the Mexican government. It is well ascertained, that the liberality practised in this instance, so much at variance with the well-known rules which prevail in Mexican warfare, is exclusively attributable to the interposition of Colonel Austin and other generous-spirited Americans holding authority in the Mexican army, who would certainly not have submitted patiently to the infliction of such barbarities upon their unhappy countrymen, as among Mexicans are regarded as nothing more than the legitimate consequences of civil strife.

After the arrival of Major Edwards at Natchitoches, the following interesting correspondence ensued between himself and the Mexican commander at Nacogdoches, with which the history of the Fredonian war will be terminated.

"Natchitoches, March 25th, 1827.

COLONEL MATEA AHUMADA:

Dear Sir,—You will be surprised at receiving a communication from one with whom you have no personal acquaintance. Your surprise will not be diminished when you recognise in the man whose signature is affixed to this address your enemy, and the very man who was honoured with the chief command of that little band of patriots, who rose in arms in opposition to your government in defence of their violated rights, and for the preservation of their lives and property.

The chances of war are at present in your favour. The treachery of my own countrymen, and more especially of the very men who called loudly for redress and opposition to your government, has given you an advantage that your own strength could never have acquired. I have been compelled to yield to fate, and have been driven to the necessity of selecting an asylum in my native country.

Sir, I have now no policy or motive in renewing the war in Texas. I have no disposition to force the inhabitants of that country to be free, and have as little inclination to risk my life again for a set of creatures, who, after having loudly complained of their grievances, and claimed my protection, would have yielded me up a sacrifice to the authorities of your government, to propitiate its vengeance against themselves. There was but one motive that could have prompted me to renew the struggle, and which would have given to it a sanguinary character at which my soul revolts. You, sir, have saved me of that necessity, and have prevented the effusion of human blood. The liberation of our prisoners has sheathed my sword. Yes, sir, you have gained a conquest over me that I never expected. What the arms of your country could never have done, your magnanimity has achieved. Your noble and generous conduct towards our much abused and unfortunate prisoners, which should put their treacherous and unfeeling countrymen to eternal shame, has partly subdued a soul which the power, yea, the racks of the Mexican empire could never conquer. Sir, had such conduct been pursued by the Political Chief, and the governor of your State, I should never have raised arms against it. I should still have been, as I once was, its warmest advocate and friend. But the rights of a *brother* outraged and trampled under foot in violation of the constitution of his adopted country, which emphatically declares that there shall be no forfeiture or confiscation of property;—the repeated wrongs and outrages upon my fellow-citizens around me, which for nine long, long months, were represented to the government in vain; and at last an outrage upon my own feelings and my rights, being ordered into banishment for no other crime than that of appealing to the government in the most respectful terms for an investigation, at least, into the conduct of my much persecuted brother, were the considerations which caused my sword to spring from its scabbard in opposition to the authorities of your country.

These are the considerations which made me your country's enemy,—though still an enemy to that government, (for

I never can forget my wrongs,) yet I trust I shall ever feel superior to blind prejudice and enmity against such of its distinguished citizens as merit confidence.

I am aware of the vindictive hostility of your government towards me. That feeling may likewise be nourished in your bosom, and perhaps your reason and duty approve such a sentiment.

But, sir, whatever may be your feelings towards me, or your views of my character, I shall always have the firmness and magnanimity to do my duty, and do justice even to an enemy.

Your kind, your friendly and generous deportment towards my friends and fellow-soldiers, while prisoners of yours, entitles you and the officers under your command to the expression of my thanks, and has insured to you and them a distinction in our hearts, that will ever separate you from the rest of your countrymen who have oppressed us.

As a foe to your country, I view you still as a national enemy ; but as a man and a philanthropist, you have powerful claims upon my heart.

He in whose bosom throbs a SOUL, (and how few there are who possess it,) no matter what clime or country claims him, shares all a brother's confidence and friendship. It is the influence of those feelings which prompts me to make this communication. The free and candid manner in which I have spoken of my wrongs and justification as an enemy, was due to myself, and in behalf of my fellow soldiers, is due to you and your brother officers.

With sentiments of respect,

Yours, &c.,

B. W. EDWARDS."

"Nacogdoches, 31st March, 1827.

Citizen B. W. Edwards :

DEAR SIR,

By Major A. Heard, I received yesterday your communication of the 25th of this month : in answer to which, I think it necessary to let you know with the frankness that characterizes a freeman, my opinion, on the contents of the said communication. The fortune of war, which is now in my favour, does not proceed from the perfidy of some of your countrymen who proclaimed opposition to my government; but from that justice which accompanies my system— had not the troops under my command been sufficient to overpower those of the party you have espoused, then it would be inferred that my comrades in arms, and myself in the fulfilment of our duty, would have remained dead on the field of battle; but my country being abundant in every sort of resources, would never have abandoned the entire preservation of its territory, and particularly when a few men contended for it.

The inhabitants of this country are free, in the full signification of the word. If you would, with impartiality, peruse the Mexican Constitution, you would discover this truth. If the local authorities of this settlement have infringed the laws, the legal resource was to make a representation to the State Government, directed to the Political Chief of that Department, and, in case he should not have answered, for reasons to you and to me unknown, then it would have been proper that those who were aggrieved should make their representations against the government itself, if necessary, and forward them to Saltillo, manifesting the encroachments on the Constitution, and the injustice done to them. The liberty of the Press exists in its plenitude. The government of the State is not absolute; the Legislature has its limits. The Federal Executive power is bound by the Laws. The orbit of the Legislature is traced; every thing is distinguished briefly in the General Constitution of Mexico; and, if you did not apply to any of those authorities, and make manifest your grievances, can you say with justice, that the government of my country is unjust? You think probably that the authorities are exempt from responsibility, and that the liberal institutions that rule us are mere theories; if you think so, you injure my nation very much, and are deceived. If I had (setting my duty aside,) ill-treated those prisoners I had, who belonged to your party, you would say that my government was barbarous and inhuman, and even should I have done so, you would be wrong in so thinking, for the government is not guilty of the faults of its subalterns unless it should know and not punish them. I say, therefore, that if any of the authorities have acted thus with you or your brother, those wrongs cannot be attributed to the government, as it was not aware of it.

Perhaps your representations have not reached the authorities: if notwithstanding an infraction of the law has been made, there are tribunals before which those complaints are brought. The conduct which my companions in arms and myself have observed towards the prisoners of the party under your command, and on which you have pronounced an eulogy, is conformable to that system by which we are governed, and also to the orders I have from his Excellency, the Commander-in-Chief, under whose authority I act, and from whom I receive instructions for the Military operations on this frontier. Amongst other things, he tells me officially, (and these are his words,) ' *The love of humanity inspires me with the most ardent wish that every thing may terminate in a friendly manner.*' This is an unequivocal proof of the philanthropy of my government, and for this reason I do not believe I deserve so much praise for having treated kindly the prisoners I had in my possession, as in this instance I executed the orders I had, and the duties of humanity that do not permit an outrage on a man who surrenders himself. I believe if the war had been in your favour, you would have acted in the same manner with any individual of my party; and if you had not, you would have stained the character of a Republican. I, also, consider you as an enemy, because you are so to my dear country; my feelings and my duty require it: but I cannot help saying that I esteem you as a man, and particularly as a Republican. The officers under my command are grateful for your kind remembrance, and beg to reciprocate your good wishes. I remain, with the most cordial expressions,

Yours, &c.

AHUMADA."

I do not feel willing to bring this chapter to a close without inducting the reader into a somewhat more familiar acquaintanceship with the remarkable and interesting person of whose short career as a Revolutionary chieftain so much more has probably been said than all will deem worthy of record. Few men have lived who were better fitted, both by nature and education, to participate prominently and efficiently in any grand movement in behalf of liberal principles — more capable of calling the energies of the often-times listless and apathetic multitude, into potent and majestic action — and of controlling the fierce *democracy*, when unduly excited, within the limits of discretion and order, than was Major *Benjamin W. Edwards*. Endowed with uncommon strength and solidity of mind, he was simple and practical in his views, both of men and things, above most of his contemporaries. His sensibilities were naturally quick and excitable ; yet were they ever under the control of enlightened reason and refined benevolence. His acquaintance with books was quite extensive ; and his knowledge of the conflicts of party in the United States was hardly surpassed by those among his countrymen who have occupied positions more favourable than any attained by him for the rendition of signal service to mankind. He possessed a discernment of individual character, both acute and profound, and evinced an astonishing perception of the secret springs of social conduct. His conversation was at the same time instructive and entertaining, and there was a radiant and winning complaisance about his manners of which all who approached him were at once sensible. As a public speaker, he was

dignified and imposing, in a very high degree, and never
failed to find the way both to the understandings and hearts
of his auditors : he indeed possessed a grace and readiness
in giving expression to his manly views in spoken language,
which might have attracted the envy of a majority of *professed orators.* At several periods during his residence in
Mississippi, he took part in public transactions of most momentous interest ; and never did he show himself unequal to
any social emergency, however appalling and paralyzing it
might be to inferior spirits. His personal courage was as
unquestionable as his love of social quiet, and " to the daunt-
less temper of his mind he had a wisdom which did guide
his valour to act in safety." It would be difficult to imagine
a happier mixture than he presented of firmness, blended
with benignity, enthusiasm tempered by discretion, indignant
abhorrence of crime, set off and embellished by the most
amiable allowance for human frailty. If he left an enemy
behind him, certain it is that he has yet to avow himself;
and no instance is believed to have occurred in which a decided friendship once formed for him, by an intelligent and
virtuous man, was afterwards either wholly relinquished, or,
as is but too common in this inconstant world, was even
permitted to subside into cold indifference.

Whilst the late Revolution in Texas was in progress,
Major Edwards constantly evinced an intense sympathy for
those who were valiantly struggling there for Liberty and
Independence. He presided at various public meetings called
in Mississippi for the purpose of raising men and money in
behalf of Texas, and his eloquence was freely poured out in
aid of those whom he recognized as fighting in support of
the old Fredonian cause. He had accepted a commission
in the Texan army, and was actually embodying a regiment
of which he was to take command, when news was received
of the victory at San Jacinto. It being now evident that his
services would not be needed, he declined the assumption of
an attitude which might expose him to the suspicion of aspi-

ring to divide the glory which had been fairly won by others, and permitted his friends to bring him forward for political advancement in the State of Mississippi ; always intending, though, sooner or later, to join the van-guard of Liberty in Texas.

———

CHAPTER XIV.

Prosperous condition of Austin's Colony after the suppression of the Fredonian insurrection.   Conduct of Colonel Austin as Empressario. His difficulties and trials.   Letter to Major Edwards.   View of Mexico in 1824, and for some years afterwards.   Political conflicts there : Presidency of Victoria ; that of Guerero ; downfall of Guerero and elevation of Bustamente ; prostration of Bustamente in consequence of his attempt to crush the State authorities and to establish a consolidated system of government.   Elevation of Santa Anna, who proves unfaithful to his declared principles : his conflict with, and triumph over Congress and most of the State governments. Massacre of Zacatecas.

THE suppression of the Fredonian revolt, and the annulment of the grant of Edwards, could not have failed to operate as a serious check to the settlement of the country about Nacogdoches by emigrants from the United States ; nor does it seem that this district of Texas evinced any very striking increase of population up to the commencement of the Revolutionary struggle in the autumn of 1835.   Far different was the scene which expanded before the eyes of Colonel Austin ; his colony continued to advance rapidly in numbers, in wealth, and all those moral institutions which distinguish a high order of civilization ; and he at the same time commanded for himself the respect of the Mexican authorities, and secured the good-will of the settlers, by the most disinterested and scrupulous fidelity in the performance of his duties as Empressario.   On several occasions, he had enjoyed an opportunity of signalizing his regard for the safety and welfare of the Colony, by turning out in person,

at the head of a few valorous Texans, against the neighbouring savages, and had earned the gratitude of the settlers
by the constant watchfulness which he caused to be exercised
towards these subtle and ferocious enemies,* as well as by

---

* I am indebted for the following description of the Indian tribes in-
habiting Texas, and of several of the conflicts above referred to, to the
manuscript kindly placed in my hands, as already stated, by my friend
General Lamar.

" The general characteristics of the Indians found in Texas are much
the same with those appertaining to the rest of the Aboriginal race in
differents parts of North America. The same love of plunder, the
same subtlety and address in pursuing their prey and evading pursuit,
mark the tawny rover of the wilderness here as elsewhere; yet there
are some peculiar traits belonging to the Aborigines of Texas, as well
as some singular usages prevailing among them, quite worthy to be
noted. In their warfare, they are neither so cruel nor so vindictive as
their brethren farther North; neither are they reputed to be altogether
so brave. Their expeditions are chiefly undertaken for purposes of
plunder; but if, at such times, they encounter persons in an unprotected condition, nothing is more certain than that they will put them
to death. They are never known to attack a fortified place, and have
been seldom known to attempt an entrance into a dwelling-house when
only protected by its inmates. A huntsman has been able to keep a
half-dozen of them at bay with his rifle, until he could find an opportunity of escaping. They commonly approach the white settlements with
a great deal of caution and address, carefully concealing themselves, for
several days, if necessary, waiting for the desired opportunity. If,
whilst thus lurking in ambush, a white person should chance to come
in reach of the weapons of death which they constantly bear about
with them, woe be to that luckless wight! When they judge the circumstances favourable to their designs, they advance stealthily to the
farm-house or settlement which they desire to spoil, collect all the
horses in view, and carry them off. If they happen to encounter feeble resistance, they are sure either to kill those venturing to oppose
them, or, as is not uncommon, bear them off as prisoners. Their retreat from one of these scenes is very rapid; for, mounting their horses,
they ride night and day until they know themselves to be completely
beyond the reach of pursuit. They are not apt to torture their prisoners
like the Northern Indians; but make servants of them, and retain
them thus until their friends, or some humane trader, shall ransom
them. The Osages, of Arkansas, who sometimes make incursions
into Texas, are accustomed to leave some article of their own at places
where they have committed pillage, such as the skin of a buffalo, or
that of a bear, a fine pair of moccasins, or sometimes a few strings of

25 *

the promptitude with which their oft-repeated incursions had been either seasonably checked or worthily avenged.

It must be acknowledged that for some years neither he

---

meat. They do this, they say, in order that *good luck* may still attend upon them, seeing that they have thus acknowledged the gifts of fortune.

"Each tribe has a distinct language, but it is very much limited in number of words, and, as would be supposed, is otherwise imperfect. They have all a method of conversing by means of *signs*, the same signs being common to many different tribes: two individuals, belonging to independent tribes, have been known to converse thus by signs for hours together, without the articulation of a word by either, and, apparently, with a reciprocal comprehension of what has been said on either side. Their arms are mostly the bow and arrow, and the lance; some of them have rifles, which they are quite expert in using. Their bows are generally made of cedar or *bois d'arc*, and the height of a man is the length of his bow. Their arrows are made of some light kind of wood, surmounted with a steel-head, which is ground very sharp. A good marksman among them will hit the size of a hat-crown at the distance of fifty yards with certainty; and their arrows are hurled from the bow with such force as to transpierce the body of a man with ease. In close fighting the bow and arrow, as used by them, is a more formidable weapon than the rifle, on account of the astonishing rapidity with which they shoot and re-shoot them. The Northern Indians employ the bow and arrow exclusively in hunting the buffalo, and not unfrequently bring down the stoutest of the herd with the first arrow which they lanch at him. They are all supplied with horses, and are exceedingly expert in managing them. Their best horses are those which they have stolen from the Americans or Mexicans. The prairies and bottoms which constitute their hunting grounds are full of game, and they rarely experience a scarcity of food. In general they are more friendly to the Americans than the Mexicans, whom they hold in great contempt and plunder without mercy.

"The *Karankaways* were formerly quite a warlike tribe, and lived on the sea coast. They were not stationary anywhere, but wandered about from one point of the coast to another, and subsisted chiefly by fishing and hunting. They were tall and athletic. The Spaniards entertained much dread of this tribe, and spoke of them always in most exaggerated terms, representing them as ferocious even to *cannibalism;* but no evidence of their appetite for human flesh has ever come to the knowledge of the colonists.

"The *Karankaways* were the most troublesome tribe to the early settlers of Texas, whose numbers at first were not sufficient to hold them in awe. They committed much mischief anterior to the year

nor his colonists had any ground of complaint in reference to the action of the Mexican Government towards them; they were left pretty much to the guidance of their own

---

1824; when the colonists, having grown more numerous, resolved to subdue, or at least chastise, this audacious tribe. Some emigrants who had arrived at the mouth of the Brassos, where the town of Velasco is now situated, and who attempted to make their way into the interior, were never more heard of. Several white men, about the same time, were found killed on the prairie. These murders could be attributed only to the Karankaways. Finding it necessary to do something to repress their violence, Colonel Austin ordered Captain Randall Jones, in the month of September, to take a company of twenty-three men, to pass down the Brassos river, and scour the whole coast as far as Matagorda Bay; and should he perceive any hostile indications on the part of the Indians, or should he encounter any evidence of their having been connected with, or concerned in, the recent murders, he was instructed to attack and drive them off. Captain Jones procured a small sloop, and taking his men on board, went down to Bailey's, where they stopped and laid in provisions for their voyage, and then proceeded to the mouth of the river, according to directions. There they found it necessary to repair their vessel, which began to leak considerably, previous to going out to sea. They drew the vessel to land, calked her seams, and, for want of pitch, used sea-wax in filling up the crevices, which they found to answer the purpose remarkably well. Whilst at this place, they were visited by several Karankaways, who observing their strength, presented tokens of decided amity. But, ascertaining that a party of about thirty of the Karankaway tribe were then encamped upon a bayou, on the Western side of the river, distant only seven miles, and that ten or twelve of their party had gone up to Bailey's to purchase ammunition, the colonists accompanying Captain Jones felt much solicitude about their families, whom they had left in that vicinage, and in a very exposed condition. Captain Jones immediately despatched two of his company with orders to raise an additional force, who found, when they arrived at Bailey's, eight or ten of the colonists collected, watching closely the movements of the Karankaways, whose visit had excited 'their suspicions. The utmost vigilance was exercised during the night, which was just coming on, and in the morning, about day-light, the symptoms of an intended attack upon the whites became so evident, that the colonists rushed in upon them, killed several, and drove the rest off.

" In the mean while, Captain Jones had embarked the remainder of his company, and had passed up the river as rapidly as possible, so as to participate in any conflict which might occur. His men rowed all night, but did not succeed in reaching the Indian encampment on the

good sense, and the lofty regard which they felt and constantly manifested for the principles of an elevated, enlarged, and unpuritanical morality; and being thus unmolested,

---

bayou until day-light had begun to streak the horizon. It being now too late for an attack, the colonists concealed themselves as well as they could until evening, and then sent out two spies to ascertain the position of the savages. These did not return until after midnight, when they reported that they had found the Indians on the West side of the bayou, about two miles and a half from the river, and, as they supposed, at some distance from the bayou. Not being able, upon this report, to form an accurate judgment of the precise position of the enemy, Captain Jones determined to delay operations for yet another day, and in the mean time to seek concealment as before. This chanced to be the very day that the party were routed at Bailey's. About sunset Captain Jones and his companions distinctly heard the howling and war-whoops of the savages who had been roused by the arrival of their defeated comrades, who brought with them their dead and wounded. Captain Jones now marched his men half a mile above the Indian encampment, and proceeded then to fall down in the direction of the foe. When he arrived within about sixty yards of the encampment, he directed his men to halt for the appearance of day-light. When it became light enough to enable the soldiers to discern the sights upon their rifles, they discovered the Indian camps to be pitched immediately upon the margin of the bayou, where it widened out into a small lake, and to be built among tall reeds and flag-grass, that extended some distance from the water. Captain Jones then, forming his men, marched briskly to the attack. Upon the first fire of the musketry, the Indians retreated to the long grass, and discharged a volley of balls and arrows at the colonists; who finding themselves wholly unable to maintain their position, and having already one of their number killed, and several others wounded, were ordered by Captain Jones to retreat up the bayou, to cross it, and return to the boat. This movement was accordingly executed, the Indians pursuing them until they had succeeded in crossing the bayou. Captain Jones, at this moment, perceived one of the Indians rising up out of the grass, and saw him aim at himself with an arrow; but he was too quick for his adversary; for he shot him dead whilst in the act of contracting his bow. After this occurrence, the party retreated to the boat without farther difficulty. This encounter took place at what is now called *Jones's creek*. The Karankaways, as was afterwards ascertained, had fifteen killed and several wounded. Of the colonists, a son of Mr. Bailey was killed, and two others mortally wounded, by name *Singer* and *Spencer*. Captain Jones and his company proceeded to Bailey's, where being reinforced, they returned to the scene of action. Finding that the

they were able, without foreign assistance, to secure the prevalence of justice, order, and social happiness. The number of immigrants from the United States increased every

---

Indians had retreated immediately after the battle, they pursued their trail as far as the Bernard, when not being able to discern it any farther, they returned. During the next winter, a party of Surveyors discovered some Karankaways on the Bernard, gave the alarm to the colonists, and they were quickly driven off.

" About the same period of colonial history, the citizens of Bay Prairie, discovering that some depredations had been committed by savages in their vicinage, collected together, had one or two encounters with the Karankaways, and destroyed a good many of them. Though the Indians retreated, they still manifested hostile intentions; whereupon Colonel Austin called out a party of the colonists, and pursued them along the road they had taken as far as the creek five miles East of Labahia, where he was met by a deputation from the Karankaways soliciting peace; which application, being seconded by the Priest, Alcalde, and principal citizens of Labahia, was acceded to, on condition that the Karankaways should never again come to the East of the San Antonio river. This compact was faithfully kept by the Karankaways; nor did they ever again commit depredations of any kind upon the colonists; the war just terminated had broken up the strength of their tribe, and exhausted their inclination to conflict with the whites.

" The *Cokes* are said by some to be a branch of the Karankaways; but they are a more diminutive race, of a more uncouth and irregular formation of body, unwarlike, beggarly, and thievish, in their habits. They were found near the mouth of the Brassos, by the first colonists, and were few in number, and of wandering propensities. They were continually to be seen roaming about the bays, rivers, and along the coast, subsisting chiefly by fishing. A party of the Cokes, in 1823, being robbed of their horses, by the Alabamas and Cushattes, pursued the spoilers, and overtaking them whilst crossing the Brassos, recaptured their horses and killed several of the pillaging party. The surviving Alabamas and Cushattes, returning home and recruiting their numbers, came back, and surprising a party of nine Cokes, at a point a little below the present town of Richmond, fell upon them and killed every one. The remnant of the tribe afterwards joined the Karankaways, were with them when routed and driven off, and have never been since known as a distinct tribe.

" The *Towkaways* are a small tribe, or rather remnant of a tribe, living near the mouths of the Guadaloupe and San Antonio rivers. They have no reputation as warriors, and are inferior to all the other tribes of Texas in size, strength, and courage. This too is a wandering tribe.

year, and the period was evidently not far distant when Texas would be authorized to claim a separate recognition of herself as a sovereign member of the Mexican Confederacy.

"The *Lepans* are but few in number, though they were once a powerful tribe. They are remarkable for strength, activity, and courage, and are of fine physical conformation. They inhabit, or rather roam over, the same district of territory which is the rambling ground of the Tonkaways.

"The *Camanches* are to be met with in the North-Western part of Texas, between the Brassos river on the East, and the Rio Grande on the West. Most of the general remarks already made relative to the Northern Indian tribes, are strictly applicable to them. They are migratory in their habits, and follow the numerous herds of buffalo which roam over the immense prairies that abound in the region where they dwell. They seldom hunt any other game, though the deer are found in vast numbers in the same district of country. The Camanches are a robust and almost Herculean race, being generally six feet at least in height, and frequently weighing, notwithstanding their active habits, from two to three hundred pounds. They have a large number of fine horses among them, most of which they have stolen from the Mexicans, and hold in high estimation; and they are perfectly skilled in all the arts of horsemanship. As warriors, they are about equal to the Mexican cavalry; but regard themselves as altogether superior to them. The men are exceedingly vain of their persons, and are frequently seen walking about their camps surveying themselves in a mirror, with evident delight, and whilst the mirror is held in one hand, the other is busily employed in retouching their bodies and faces with fresh paint, where the previous tints are discovered to be slightly faded. They neither cultivate the ground, nor raise stock of any kind; and many of them are wholly unacquainted with the use of *bread* or *ardent spirit*. They are very friendly to the white traders who go among them, escorting them into their villages, and assigning them quarters near the chiefs to secure them from robbery. The Mexican race is cordially hated and despised by the Camanches, and their marauding parties are constantly in motion towards the Rio Grande, where they take away large droves of horses and mules, and sometimes Mexicans, as prisoners, whom they invariably convert into servants.

"The *Cherokees* are quite a numerous tribe, from the United States, and inhabit that portion of Texas lying around the sources of the Sabine, Angelina, and Neches rivers, and between the latter and Red river. They are superior to all the other Indians in Texas in valour, as well as in the progress they have made in the arts of civilized life.

"The *Cushattes* and *Alabamas* are two tribes found along the waters

It must not be supposed by any means, that the career of Col. Austin, as an Empressario, had been entirely free from difficulty and vexation, or that he had been even so fortunate as always to be accompanied and sustained by the unanimous approbation of the colonists. On the contrary, several instances occurred in which very respectable and intelligent individuals among the settlers, evinced strong and decided symptoms of discontent at particular official acts of the Empressario; and once or twice popular excitement rose so high, (doubtless under a misconception of the reasons which influenced his conduct,) as to call into requisition, for the suppression of social discord and the preclusion of perilous collisions, all the discretion and energy

---

of Trinity. They have two or three villages, and are somewhat advanced in agricultural pursuits. They have a considerable stock of hogs, horses, and other cattle, and raise annual crops of corn, potatoes, and other vegetables; after the gathering of which, in Autumn, they sally forth upon hunting excursions. They are said to be branches of the Creeks, and came originally from the Coosa and Talapoosa rivers in Alabama. They have been always friendly to the American colonists in Texas.

"The *Wacos* and *Tawoconies* are two tribes supposed to be branches of the Camanches, whom they resemble in size, strength and bravery. They are found high up on the head waters of the Brassos. They are supposed to have in each tribe about one hundred warriors.

"The *Caddoes* reside within the limits of the United States, but are frequently to be seen over the Texas border, in the neighbourhood of Red river. They are not numerous.

"There are several other mere remnants of tribes in Texas, now quite insignificant, and indeed almost extinct, of whom but little is known: These are the *Kickapoos*, found between the Sabine and Red rivers; the *Kaiches* or *Keeches*, between the Neches and Angelina, North-West of Nacogdoches; the *Shawnees*, also North-West of Nacogdoches; the *Redais*, or Spring Creeks, few in number, and very friendly; the *Wichataws*, who live far North, on the Brassos; the *Ironies*, or *Iondes*, dwelling on the waters of the Angelina; the *Nacogdoches*, from whom the town of Nacogdoches takes its name, of whom only a family or two remain; the *Delawares*, established about the Sulphur fork of Red river; and lastly, the *Souwiash*, who have a small village at the Red fork of Brassos river, who are doubtless a branch of the Camanches."

of which he was master. Let it be said though, to the honour of Colonel Austin and his colonists, that no dissension ever sprung up among them which eventuated in the effusion of blood in civil strife, or which left in the bosoms of the most excited, permanent sentiments of ill-will or discontent; and it is confidently believed, that at the period of the death of this extraordinary personage, three years since, there was not a man, woman, or child, in all Texas, to whom his whole history as a public functionary was familiarly known, who was not inclined to do hearty homage to the extraordinary wisdom and unsurpassed virtues of this efficient and truly philanthropic champion of free institutions.

The following extract from a letter written by Colonel Austin, in the year 1825, to Major Edwards, the Fredonian chieftain, of whom so much has been already said, will be read at the present moment with some interest, as presenting the view which Colonel Austin himself was disposed to take of the responsibility with which he stood environed, and as serving to throw some additional light upon several leading traits in his character. It seems that Major Edwards had invited his attention to a claim brought forward by the heirs of a certain individual by the name of *Harrison*, to lands in Austin's Colony, to which the decedent was supposed to have been entitled at the period of his demise. To the application of Major Edwards in behalf of the heirs, Austin thus replies: " In regard to Mr. Harrison, I will state to you frankly the difficulties which present themselves to my mind, to the proposition of investing his heirs with a title to land in this colony, requesting that you will point out any course which will probably obviate the same. The authority under which titles to land in this colony have been granted, emanated originally from the Emperor Iturbide, under his Decree of the 18th of February, 1823. After he was dethroned, this Decree was presented by me to the sovereign Constitutional Congress, was by them passed over to the Supreme Executive Council, by an order bearing date the 11th of April, of the same year, and the Supreme Executive Council, by virtue of said order, and anterior Decree, confirmed the aforesaid Imperial grant to me, by their Decree bearing date the 14th of April, 1823.

The law of Colonization, under which this Colony has been settled, requires positively that the lands awarded to settlers should be *bona-fide cultivated*, within two years from the date of the deed made to each settler, respectively. Now, Harrison died before the date of the confirmatory grant afore-mentioned. The question which now arises, is : Whether a grant to B. Harrison, in his own name, would be good, he being defunct at a period previous to the coming into existence of the authority, on which such grant must rest ? Would a grant to his heirs, who are not now in the country, and never have been, be valid ? The chief impediment in the transaction seems to be, that the heirs could not be described in the deed, as deriving their authority *through* the decedent, but would have to receive title in their own names, without mentioning him at all. Possibly a conveyance to some one in the Colony, *in trust* for the heirs of Harrison, might be so contrived as to stand the test of legal scrutiny. If so, I should be glad to have the business so arranged. On my return from Mexico, all the embarrassing circumstances stated, suggested themselves to my mind, and I confess I have not been able to see my way through them. I laid the subject, some time since, before the commissioner, and he was of opinion that nothing could be done. In consequence of this declaration of the commissioner, no land was reserved for Harrison ; and now a new obstruction has arisen in the case, in consequence of engagements which have been entered into, in favour of the *whole hundred families*, excluding him, all of whom must be provided for, in the event of their coming on. I engaged to give Harrison *six hundred and forty acres*, which was the quantity at first assigned to each settler ; the government having, posterior to his death, increased the amount to what is now allowed.   I consider Harrison as worthy of land as any person who ever came to the country, or ever will ; and I now am willing to give his heirs a tract of land, of the size mentioned, out of my own private property, if no other plan can be devised for securing it to them ; and you will oblige me by stating to his father, that it was not my fault that a league of land was not saved for B. Harrison's heirs.

The claims to lands in this colony are rather novel, and not a little complicated in their character ; in consequence of which they appear not to be in general well understood out of its limits ; and I am doubtless oftentimes censured by very good persons, who would be far from blaming me did they know all the facts.   My whole task has been a difficult and harassing one ; and the government has greatly added to my troubles, by not compelling the commissioner to remain here until the whole business of adjusting and establishing the titles of the settlers shall be finally disposed of.   He is now a member of the Legislature, and is at the present moment at the seat of government, which you know is Saltillo.   Thus the whole burthen and responsibility of acting upon the claims to lands is thrown upon my shoulders ; whilst I am able to procure aid from no quarter, and I have been cast upon the slender resources of my own judgment.   I have not been furnished either with any code of written laws, nor enjoyed the benefit of detailed instructions.   My authority as Empressario is truly very ample, far too much so, in truth ; for I am invested with sweeping discretionary powers as to the reception of settlers, the government of the colony, and the distribution of lands,——the exercise of which powers must inevitably subject me to censure, proceed as I may.   The authority which I exercise is still subordinate to that held by individuals who are totally ignorant of the wants and disposition of the people of whose interests I have been constituted guardian ; so that, in very many instances, I have been constrained by imperious circumstances to disobey the monitions of my own judgment.   That I have committed errors,

I readily admit; I should have been more than mortal if I had been able to avoid their committal always, in the situation which I occupied. I have sometimes been compelled to war against my own sympathies, in individual cases, from regard to the general welfare of the colony. Whether it was wrong or right to do so, my motives, I feel certain, have been upright. Some of these cases have been laid hold of in the abstract, and I have been much denounced by men who knew nothing of the difficulties which surrounded me. The chief source of my troubles is that most of the settlers are wholly unacquainted with the language, laws, prejudices, disposition and habits of the Mexican government and people. We have no interpreters here, save my secretary and myself, and, consequently, the colonists have no means of ascertaining the orders of the government except through me. This circumstance renders my position truly unpleasant; for you know that it belongs to the American character to suspect and denounce a public officer upon very slight pretexts, and oftentimes without his deserving it. I have had a mixed multitude to deal with—collected from all quarters, strangers to me, save from the testimonials of good character which they are expected to bring with them — strangers to each other, to the language, laws, and customs of this country. They come here, with all the feelings and ideas of Americans, unwilling to make allowance for the peculiar state of things existing, and expecting to find all in system, and harmony, and organization, as in the country they have left. They seem not at all to have reflected that this government is yet in its infancy, and that time, and many other things which might be named, are necessary to bring the social elements into a state of order, and harmonize the details of public business. They demand the exhibition of a *written law* in application to every measure which is adopted, and a few of them are animated with all the turbulent feelings of *frontier men.*

Added to all this, when the emigrants arrive here *Ava-*

rice, the most fiendish of all passions, is excited to the highest degree, and leads the van-guard of all the attacks made upon me; Jealousy and Envy hover on the flanks, and Malice lurks in the rear, to operate as occasion may require. Could I have met all the objections to my official conduct with a *written code of Laws* — and have presented for their inspection a *positive statute*, defining the amount of the land which each settler was to receive, I should have had but little comparative trouble. But they saw at once that my authority was *discretionary*, and that a great augmentation of their grants was at least possible; and thus the Colonization law and the authority given to me by it, have presented me as a public mark to be shot at by all the discontented. In some instances, if a settler gets a league of land, instead of thanking me for it, he becomes dissatisfied because he cannot obtain a larger quantity, and is disposed to accuse me of treating him with *injustice*. In this state of things, such as approach me and offer their advice, being *interested* advisers, if there be a weak part about me they are sure to attack it. Some precedents, too, have been established by the Power which controls my official action, in opposition to my own wish and judgment, and these precedents have involved me in endless difficulties. For instance, in the case of G * * * *, the Political Chief, whose orders I was bound to obey, designated *ten leagues* as the smallest quantity which he ought to receive. This produced great dissatisfaction; many others at once considering themselves as fairly entitled to ten leagues as G * * * *; and because they did not receive as much, I was complained of. It was my duty to the settlers to retain, if practicable, the good will and confidence of the officers of government, upon whom I was so immediately dependent for my fate, with which that of the Colony also was necessarily interlinked, and must so remain until the whole colonizing process shall have terminated. I have suffered also from causes personal to myelf: My temper is naturally hasty and impetuous; the welfare of the settlement required that I should control it effectually; for one in my situation, falling suddenly into a fit of passion might do hurt to the interests of hundreds. My disposition is by nature, also, open, unsuspecting, confiding, and accommodating almost to a fault: I have been, therefore, subject in a peculiar manner to imposition. Experience has enlightened me as to this latter deficiency, I fear almost too late; for I am apprehensive of having fallen somewhat into the opposite extreme.

It is said by Philosophers, that he who knows himself is a wise man; he who controls himself and amends his faults is certainly much more so. In striving to amend mine, I am apprehensive that I have not entirely succeeded; for at this time I am, perhaps, too easily inclined to suspicion, and exhibit too much tameness under injuries and insults. If I have run into errors in these respects, at least my intentions have been good; and the colony of which I have had charge has, I hope, not received detriment. Under all circumstances, I have no self-reprehension to indulge on the score of excessive forbearance; for amongst a certain class of Americans with whom I have had to deal, *independence* means resistance and obstinacy, right or wrong; this is particularly the case with most *frontier men ;* and a violent course with men of this cast would have kindled a flame that might have consumed the colony. For it was with the greatest difficulty, and after more than 18 months' solicitation, that I obtained the consent of the Mexican government to progress with the settlement, and the principal objection expressed to my doing so, was, that the Americans were considered in Mexico a turbulent and disorderly people, difficult to govern, and predisposed to resist authority. This impression as to the American character, it was not easy to remove; and the least commotion among the settlers, in the infancy of the colony, would have revived that impression anew, and probably have proved fatal to all our hopes."

*   *   *   *   *   *

26 *

Whilst the American settlers in Texas were prospering in the extraordinary manner described, and the abundant resources of this charming region were in a course of rapid developement, the Capital of the Mexican Republic was the theatre of operations which threatened, if not seasonably counteracted, to dash the cup of happiness from the lips of the colonists, and to extinguish those hopes of future freedom which they had all along so fondly cherished.   In order to enable the reader to comprehend the precise nature of the dangers alluded to, it will be necessary to take a rapid view of the leading governmental measures which had been adopted since the year 1824, and, after a while, to examine also somewhat more closely than we have heretofore done, certain singular provisions in the heterogeneous Constitution of the Mexican Republic.

It was in the month of January, 1825, that the first session of the Mexican Congress assembled under the new Constitution, was held.   The proceedings of that body appear to have been marked with less tumult and disorder than were to have been expected, from the character of the population and their antecedent history.   A few even have gone so far as to assert, assuredly upon very slight grounds, that the legislative enactments which then originated evince some indications both of disinterested patriotism as well as of political sagacity.   During the two years of comparative quiet which succeeded, no event occurred, a notice of which would be at all profitable.   In 1827, the Message of President Victoria announced the continued prevalence of peace and good order, and presented quite a glowing, and most certainly an overdrawn picture of the happy internal condition of the Republic.   In a month or two after the appearance of that document, a law, both unconstitutional and impolitic, as well as outrageously unjust and oppressive, received the sanction both of Congress and the Executive, providing for the immediate expulsion of all the natives of old Spain who were then residing within the limits of the Mexican Republic.

A more tyrannical and barbarous law could not well have been devised; and its enforcement proved in the end deeply injurious to the Republic, in a way not anticipated, by depriving the national councils of nearly all those whose accomplishments were such as to enable them to aid efficiently in keeping the machine of government in order, giving equality and dignity to its movements, and preventing that erratic and exorbitant action which has been ever since so observable.

Considerable domestic dissension signalized the year 1828, and municipal repose, so far as it existed at all, was compelled to owe its enforcement mainly to the bloody and dangerous interposition of *military tribunals.* When the official term of President Victoria was about expiring, a fierce contest arose for the succession, between General Guerero and one Gomez Pedraza. The latter of these individuals received the majority of popular votes; but the friends of Guerero, Santa Anna and others, alleging that *fraud* alone had prevented the election of their favourite candidate, prepared to sustain his claims by the instrumentality of military force; and so intimidated the House of Representatives of the Mexican Congress, as to induce that body to make a declaration in favour of Guerero, who was installed as President accordingly. Guerero had hardly taken possession of the station to which he had been thus raised, as it were, upon the bucklers of the soldiery, when the fleet of Spain was announced to be hovering upon the Mexican coast, prepared to make another attempt to re-conquer the fair dominions which had thrown off her yoke; and so excessive was the alarm of Congress on this occasion, that it was judged politic to invest a usurping Executive with dictatorial powers, in order to enable him to meet the much *dreaded*, but certainly not at all dreadful, crisis. The English people, when they beheld the boasted Armada of Philip majestically riding the seas, did not evince half the solicitude that was aroused throughout Mexico, by this wretched band of timid adventurers, who

came, and *saw*, and *retreated*, before the unvalorous squad
of mock-heroes who went forth to do battle against them.
And now Guerero, who had been so fortunate as to acquire
great political power, more by the *management* of his friends
than because he was an object of popular confidence, could
not lay down the extraordinary authority which accident and
an unreasoning panic had placed in his hands, ere he had
done something else to shed splendour upon his administration ; and, with a view to the enhancement of his own glory,
he resolved to become the magnificent *Liberator* of all the
sons and daughters of Africa then devoted to servitude in
Mexico ; and, accordingly, issued his Dictatorial edict for a
sweeping emancipation of this whole class, and the induction
of each and every one of them at once into all the rights and
privileges appertaining to citizenship.   Could he, by some
process not yet ascertained, have re-organized the intellectual
faculties of these unhappy creatures, and have imbued their
minds with knowledge, and their souls with liberal and elevated sentiments, perhaps this measure would not have been
so highly censurable ; though the act clearly involved a gross
breach of faith, and was likewise palpably derogatory to the
existing Constitution of Mexico.   But the evil which resulted
from this act of amalgamation, under the circumstances, was
beyond estimation ; since the general population of Mexico,
exclusive of the negroes, was immersed in a state of ignorance and degradation almost unknown in modern times,
save amongst acknowledged savages ; since, in addition, the
most intelligent class of citizens, consisting of native Spaniards, had been already driven from the country; and, finally,
since it cannot be pretended that the vast multitude, now called
to the exercise of political rights in Mexico, and made a portion of the very base-work of the system of representative
government, could possibly have received into their untutored
minds any notions except such as belong to the condition of
abject bondage.   Thomas Jefferson, whose opinions on such
a subject are worth much, and whose enthusiasm in behalf

of free principles is above question, it has been seen, thought, in 1817, that the whole body of Spanish colonists in America, before their moral capabilities had been diminished by the course just noticed, were incapable of entering at once upon the work of *self-government.** The same political sage thought, in 1815, and so expressed himself, in a letter to the Marquis De La Fayette, that even in France "a full measure of liberty was not to be expected ;" and adds: "nor am I confident they are prepared to preserve it. More than a generation will be requisite, under the administration of reasonable laws, favouring the progress of knowledge in the general mass of the people, and their habituation to an independent security of person and property, before they will be capable of estimating the value of freedom, and the necessity of a sacred adherence to the principles on which it rests for its preservation. Instead of that liberty which takes root and growth in the progress of *reason,* if recovered by mere *force* or *accident,* it becomes, with an *unprepared* people, a tyranny still, of the many, the few, or the one."

The wildest and least calculating Fanaticism could scarce-

* Mr. Jefferson says: "I wish I could give better hopes of our Southern brethren. The achievement of their Independence of Spain is no longer a question. But it is a very serious one, what will then become of them ? Ignorance and bigotry, like other insanities, are incapable of self-government. They will fall under military despotisms, and become the murderous tools of the ambition of their respective Buonapartes ; and whether this will be for their greater happiness the rule of one only has taught you to judge. No one, I hope, can doubt my wish to see them and all mankind exercising self-government, and capable of exercising it. But the question is, not what we wish, but what is practicable ? As their sincere friend and brother then, I do believe the best thing that can be done for them, would be for themselves to come to an accord with Spain, under the guarantee of France, Russia, Holland, and the United States, allowing to Spain a nominal Supremacy, with authority only to keep the peace among them, leaving them otherwise all the powers of self-government, until their experience in them, their emancipation from their priests, and advancement in information, shall prepare them for complete independence."—*Jefferson's Correspondence,* 4th Vol. p. 304.

ly be mad enough to anticipate beneficial effects from the high-handed act of Guerero which we have been considering; and the most heated advocates of the abstract principle of *universal equality* might well have recoiled before the consequences that almost immediately flowed from it. From this moment the state of things grew rapidly worse and worse in Mexico; the rude and indecent violations of the organic law, never understood and never respected, which had so often taken place, had thrown the Constitution of 1824 into absolute contempt; the precedent of *military violence triumphant over civic authority*, which had now grown into usage, had diffused a spirit of factious lawlessness throughout this ill-fated country; and it was at this time apparent to all discerning men, that what had been heretofore known as the Mexican *Republic*, would soon become nothing less than a cruel and tyrannical Despotism. Guerero was not permitted long to enjoy his irregularly acquired power: a man much less worthy of respect than himself, and whose subsequent career has been distinguished by almost every enormity which could well find display in the conduct of an ambitious, unprincipled, and vain-glorious military chieftain—*Bustamente* by name, (who was then occupying the station of Vice President), secretly and suddenly got together a considerable military force, and demanded of Guerero his immediate abdication of the Presidential office. This demand was promptly obeyed by Guerero, who doubtless expected to save his life at least by this unhesitating surrender of Executive authority. But this turned out in the sequel to be but an idle calculation; for Bustamente, immediately mounting the vacant car of power, and laying hold of the reins of government with a firm hand, commanded the arrest of the *quondam* Dictator, and had him soon afterwards put to death without the least ceremony. Bustamente had been expected by some to recall Pedraza, the President elect, and to yield up to him the administration of public affairs. But he did not permit his real intentions, which were in fact exclusively *selfish*, to remain long concealed; for not only did he not reinstate Pedraza, but audaciously laid claim to the Presidential authority for himself, upon the ground of *conquest* alone, and proceeded as quickly as he could to entrench himself in the possession and exercise of absolute power.

For a short period, his pretensions as a Despot remained wholly undisputed; there was nothing which he commanded to be done, that was not immediately executed, from one end of Mexico to the other; a corrupt and servile Congress became a mere machine in his hands, and gave sanction to his magisterial edicts with as much promptitude as ever did the trembling Roman Senate to those of the Tyrant of Capreœ. But the reign of this vile usurper was fated to be as brief as it was inglorious; for Santa Anna, another *Captain of Sedition*, as unscrupulous as Bustamente himself, and of much greater subtlety and address, advanced against him at the head of an army of disciplined ragamuffins, and compelled the dethroner and murderer of Guerero himself to descend from his blood-erected throne and hide his contemptible person in a far distant land. After which, Santa Anna passed adroitly through the *forms* of a popular election, and, no competitor of course daring to oppose him, became President by the unanimous choice of an enslaved populace. This was early in the year 1833. Santa Anna had not been in the occupancy of the Presidency more than one short month, ere he proved in the plainest manner the slight estimation in which he held that mockery of a popular election, to which he nominally owed his elevation to power, by notoriously attempting to obtain at the hands of his soldiery, a proclamation of himself as Dictator. Failing, from accidental circumstances, in this device, he remained for a brief season in a state of grim and ominous quietude, and suffered Congress to proceed, without interruption, in the work of general legislation; resolving to seize upon supreme power so soon as that body should adjourn. Nor did he, upon the withdrawal of Congress, lose time in executing his design; but, uniting himself with the clergy, as Bustamente had done before him—a body of men who had been uniformly inimical to Republican institutions,—he demanded of the General Council, (who, in conjunction with the President, have, in the recess of Congress, according to the Mexican Constitution, full powers of legislation,) an instantaneous repeal of all laws objected to by the Priesthood; and the Council, not at once testifying obedience, he dissolved it by his own decree, and constrained its members to disperse, by menaces of military violence. Then, distributing armed soldiers about the country to overawe the people, he managed without difficulty to procure the election of his own creatures to a new Congress; upon the convocation of which, he moved with singular vigour and despatch towards the consummation of his accursed designs.

In his message to this human *menagerie*, in January, 1835, the Veiled Prophet of Khorassan tore away the mask beneath which his Satanic features had been till then partially concealed, and unblushingly denouncing the Mexican people as unworthy of a free government, demanded the immediate adoption of such measures as he deemed necessary for the establishment of that Despotism which he had determined to erect. The Bishops of each Diocese, always willing to lend a helping hand to the ruin of Liberty, at this period, undertook to procure *pronunciamentos*, declarations of popular sentiment in Town meetings, favourable to the wishes of their arch ally; and were altogether as good as their word, nothing being more easy than for these juggling fiends to frame any declarations they pleased, and afterwards persuade an ignorant and superstitious rabble to yield their assent to them. Upon the reception of these *pronunciamentos*, Congress proceeded to abolish the Constitution of 1824, and with it, of course, all *state authority*, throughout the Republic, and concentrated all civil authority, of whatever kind or description, in the hands of the National Rulers: knowing that so long as *state sovereignty* existed, even in name, a rallying point for freedom would yet remain, and the fabric of monarchy, however cemented with human blood, or protected by a hired soldiery, would never be entirely secure. Nor was there sufficient virtue in the general population of Mexico to raise any serious obstruction to the execution of this unprincipled scheme. In *Zacatecas* and *Texas* alone were any men to be found bold enough to take a decided stand against the monster of *Centralism,* and to brave the avenging sword of a heartless and until then *unconquered* usurper. Zacatecas * was fated to fall a victim

---

* " Zacatecas, where in some of the darkest periods of the Revolution, Liberty had found a last refuge, again served as a rallying point for the few faithful votaries now remaining among the degenerate Mexicans. An army of five thousand men, composed principally of the militia of the State, were assembled near the City of Zacatecas, prepared to resist the authority of the Tyrant. Mexico had drawn its best troops from Zacatecas. In the long contest with the mother country, no part of Mexico had made equal sacrifices in aid of the common cause. The blow which robbed them of that Liberty which was so dear to them, and which they had so well merited by their liberal outpourings of blood and treasure, must have been keenly felt from whatever hand it may have come, and doubly so from the hand of the present usurper, who was principally indebted to them for the means of success against Bustamente, and consequently for his elevation to the Presidency. Their wrongs were therefore aggravated by the sting of ingratitude. Santa Anna well knew the character of the people he had to encounter, and the spirit which would animate them on the present occasion; he therefore prepared to accomplish by the basest treachery, what he feared to attempt in a fair contest. Several officers of the army, pretending to be unwilling to aid the President in destroying that Constitution which they had sworn to support, resigned their commissions, and repaired to Zacatecas, and there affected to join the people in supporting the authority of the State. They offered their services to command the militia in the approaching contest, which were accepted; and this devoted band of five thousand men was placed under their command. Santa Anna was now apprised of the success of his *stratagem,* and advanced with a superior force, while his progress was concealed from the Zacatecans by their treacherous officers until they were surrounded and attacked; and thus more than half their number were literally cut to pieces before they had an opportunity to make the least resistance; a few rallied to arms and made a desperate attempt to check the advance of the invaders, but they were driven before them

to a diabolical plot which in cold-blooded cruelty and con-summate treachery has no rival in modern annals; and in Texas, among the Anglo-American race, shall we shortly find the only people in a Republic numbering eight millions, resolved to do battle in behalf of *state sovereignty* and civil and religious freedom.

---

into the City of Zacatecas, where the victors for several days indulged themselves in excesses too shocking for recital. Foreigners, as well as natives, who had taken no part in public affairs, and who were quietly pursuing their avocations without intermeddling in any manner with the political concerns of the country, were butchered without ceremony, and their property given up to the pillage of the soldiery, or confiscated to the use of the officers. When the tyrant had sufficiently glutted his vengeance, the inhabitants who had escaped the sword, sub-mitted unconditionally to his power."—*History of Mexico, by John M. Niles, member of U. S. Senate.*

END OF THE FIRST VOLUME.

CPSIA information can be obtained
at www.ICGtesting.com
Printed in the USA
BVHW090933270819
556819BV00014B/2981/P